D1497987

Our Hearts Invented a Place

# Our Hearts Invented a Place

Can Kibbutzim Survive in Today's Israel?

Jo-Ann Mort & Gary Brenner

CORNELL UNIVERSITY PRESS
ITHACA & LONDON

First published 2003 by Cornell University Press

Printed in the United States of America

Library of Congress Cataloging-in-Publication Data

Mort, Jo-Ann, 1956–
  Our hearts invented a place : can kibbutzim survive in today's Israel? / Jo-Ann Mort and Gary Brenner.
     p.  cm.
Includes bibliographical references and index.
  ISBN 0-8014-3930-2 (cloth : alk. paper)
  1. Kibbutzim—Social conditions—20th century.   2. Hatsor Ashdod (Israel)   3. Gesher ha-Ziv (Israel)   4. Gan Shemu'el (Israel)   I. Brenner, Gary, 1950–   II. Title.
  HX742.2.A3M68   2003
  307.77'6—dc21

                                                          2003009189

Cloth printing          10 9 8 7 6 5 4 3 2 1

*Our hearts invented a place,*
*yes, a place in the world*
*where we would know life without end.*

*Abba Kovner, "My Little Sister"*

# CONTENTS

Preface ix

1 Setting the Stage: Kibbutzim on a Continuum 1

2 From One Century to the Next 16

3 The Crisis and the Search for Solutions 34

4 Gesher Haziv: A Kibbutz Privatizes 51

5 Hatzor: A Third Way? 84

6 Gan Shmuel: The Classic Kibbutz in a Time of Change 124

7 End of Kibbutz or a New Beginning 165

Notes 183

Glossary 195

Index 205

# PREFACE

There are many ways to tell the story of contemporary Israel. There is the still unresolved war between Israel and the Palestinians, which overshadows all other aspects of life in Israel. There are the stormy battles between the secular and religious Jews; the social and economic inequities borne by Israel's Arab citizens who represent nearly 20 percent of the population; and there are the social and cultural struggles between Ashkenazi Jews who hail from Eastern Europe and the Sephardic or Mizrachi Jews from North Africa and other Arab countries. There are tensions that came with the huge immigration of Russians in the 1990s and with the earlier immigration of Ethiopian Jews. There is the tension of the increasing economic stratification between the haves and the have-nots, as a once-egalitarian society becomes less so. There is the tension of growing from a near-scarcity society to one with an extremely successful high-tech sector and a standard of living comparable to that of Western Europe.

Israel has changed profoundly from its early pioneering days that culminated in an independent state in 1948. The multitude of overlapping issues—war and peace, economic disparity, social and cultural differences—present an extraordinary challenge to any writer. We decided to focus on one aspect of Israel that is central to the country's history. The story of the kibbutzim is a way to tell the story of contemporary Israel, because the creation and the fate of the kibbutzim are intimately linked to the tenor of Israel's development as a state, to where it is today and where it may be headed.

Both of us come to this book with a fierce commitment to social democracy and to a just and peaceful society in Israel, having spent our lives in a variety of Jewish and secular radical causes. The Israeli kibbutz is one of the grand social experiments of our lifetime. To many Americans, even those fairly familiar with contemporary Israel, the kibbutz is something frozen in time. Whether as university students in the classroom or as volunteers in the 1960s and 1970s who arrived in time for harvests in the cotton fields or citrus orchards, or as the general educated public, our readers may know something about the communal child rearing and dining rooms that are part of the only example of pure voluntary communism in the twentieth century. But that romantic kibbutz vision has undergone dramatic changes in the past few decades. Gradually, as Israel has changed so has the kibbutz, taking on many different guises to the point where today one can argue about the very definition of a kibbutz.

We are not anthropologists, sociologists, political scientists, or economists. We write this book as a journalistic treatise, telling a story that one of us lives day in and day out and the other has observed through the years as a frequent visitor to Israel. The concentrated research was done in 2000 and 2001 and the early part of 2002 to try to capture a snapshot of the vast—and rapid—changes taking place on the kibbutzim today. The kibbutzim of the future, like the country in which they are situated, are a work in progress.

Although there are many ways to write about the kibbutz, we have chosen to concentrate on what has come to be known in Israel as the *shinui* (the change) in the economic, social, and legal structure of the kibbutz. The economic changes go to the heart of kibbutz life, while also reflecting other social and cultural changes. Kibbutzim today are moving away from the traditional communal ownership structure toward what in Israel is called privatization, although even the starkest privatization schemes still look very collective or solidaristic in the eyes of most Americans and would be familiar as a social democratic model to Europeans and others.

While we have witnessed and researched the changes on many kibbutzim, we concentrate on three in particular because they represent three very different—but representative—models of change. Kibbutz

Gan Shmuel is the more classic kibbutz model; Hatzor is what we will call the third-way model; and Gesher Haziv is the most privatized of the three kibbutzim. However, as we conducted our research, we realized that, to our surprise, these three kibbutzim are on more of a continuum than we imagined, and probably more than many of those who live on them would imagine. Only the decades will tell how it will all sort out.

We used several other parameters in selecting the kibbutzim. We looked for geographic diversity. We also wanted to choose kibbutzim from the two main kibbutz movements, although during our research these two large kibbutz movements, the United Kibbutz Movement or Takam (affiliated with the Labor Party) and the Kibbutz Artzi Federation or KAF (now affiliated with the Meretz Party) merged into one movement called, aptly enough, the Kibbutz Movement. This merger is the result of earlier mergers and in itself represents a change in the ideological atmosphere in Israel, mostly by putting to rest the old ideological differences within the left, which more often than not related to political outlook and had nothing to do with the specifics of kibbutz life. There are also a handful of kibbutzim associated with the National Religious Party and one with the ultra-Orthodox Agudat Israel Party, but we decided not to include those kibbutzim in our sampling, because with them other issues, such as religious practices, override the basic issue of social equality versus personal freedom that is of interest to us.

Most of the interviews for this book were conducted in English. In the few instances where the interviewees spoke Hebrew, translation was done by Gary Brenner in consultation with Jo-Ann Mort. As scholars are aware, there are many ways to transliterate Hebrew. We have attempted to achieve a reasonable level of consistency. We followed *Merriam-Webster's Collegiate Dictionary*, 10th ed., in the spelling of common words, proper names, and places. For all other words and for the names of some places such as kibbutzim or small Israeli cities or towns not listed in *Webster's*, our spelling and transliteration is loosely based on the guidelines established by the journal *Studies in Contemporary Jewry* of the Avraham Harman Institute of Contemporary Jewry at Hebrew University.

Israel uses the metric system and we have followed that usage throughout our book. There is also a uniquely Israeli way of measuring land, the *dunam*, which we have also used where appropriate. One dunam equals .25 acres (or 1,012 sq. meters or .10 hectares).

We realize that the reader could use some guidance on how many shekels equal a dollar. However, exchange rate fluctuations, especially for the shekel, are significant, particularly in the decades discussed. As a guide, we offer this: the Israeli shekel (NIS) was depreciated sharply, mainly because of hyperinflation, during the period 1978–1985. In 1977 the value of the dollar was 0.0015 shekel. At the end of the hyperinflation period the rate of exchange was about 1,000 times higher at around 1.5 shekels per dollar. The Israeli consumer price index was multiplied by a factor of 1,300 during this period. In 1990 the rate of exchange was about 2 shekels to a dollar, reaching 4 in 2000, and approaching almost 5 NIS per dollar in 2003.

Throughout the book, we refer to monetary amounts in both U.S. dollars and Israeli shekels (NIS). This reflects the way the Israeli economy is structured and the way we gathered information. The shekel fluctuates to such a degree that often amounts in Israel are simply calculated in dollars or both dollars and shekels. Visitors can experience this phenomenon when they stay at a hotel. The hotel bill is almost always calculated in U.S. dollars, but on the same bill, food charges are often in shekels. All land issues, including house prices and rents for apartments, are, in Israel, discussed in dollars, and we have also followed that practice here. Of course, references to actual U.S. dollars are given in dollars.

We thank several people without whom this book could not have been written. We thank the many people on Gesher Haziv, Hatzor, Gan Shmuel, and elsewhere who opened their homes and their hearts to us, giving graciously of their time and their thoughts in a transparent and frank manner. We did not conceal the identities of the kibbutzim or the kibbutz members—*kibbutznikim*—and we are grateful that those whom we interviewed were not inhibited by the discussions. We hope we did justice to their concerns. Our aim was to tell as complete a story as possible, not to disparage any path chosen by a particular kibbutz or kibbutz member.

We especially want to thank Aliza Elkon and Riffi Schlossberg from Kibbutz Gesher Haziv and Omri Kenan from Kibbutz Gan Shmuel, who helped us in arranging interviews with their neighbors. We thank

Ariel Halperin for sharing his wealth of information and insight with us. Tali Tamir's excellent retrospective of the artist Yohanan Simon at the Tel Aviv Museum of Art was an inspiration to us, and we thank her for helping us locate Simon's daughters, Aya Ben Tzedef and Nitza Simon, who graciously allowed us to use their father's artwork. We thank Samuel Bacharach, Menachem Brinker, and Michael Walzer for reading the text with such care. We are grateful to our editor, Fran Benson, and the incredible staff at Cornell University Press, who believed in this book and worked so hard to make it a reality. And, for their generous support, we thank Bernard and Audre Rapoport and Fred Howard, without whom this book could not have been written.

Our Hearts Invented a Place

# SETTING THE STAGE

## Kibbutzim on a Continuum

> To repeat to the young people, morning, noon and night: kibbutz, kibbutz, kibbutz, is useless; we must not turn living endeavors into dogma.
> —Berl Katznelson, at the 1927 Hashomer Hatzair conference

The story of the kibbutzim—their successes and their failures—is a significant chapter in the larger story of Israel. It mirrors Israel's evolution—socially, culturally, politically, and, of course, economically.

In the period preceding the establishment of the state of Israel, while the entire Zionist movement was involved in rallying diplomatic support for the new state, it was mainly the labor movement that prepared the infrastructure for the fledgling country. The placement of kibbutzim and moshavim in the first half of the twentieth century actually delineated the future borders. The Histadrut, which was founded to represent Jewish workers who had come to Israel to fulfill their socialist-Zionist goals (today, Histadrut represents Israeli workers who are Jewish and non-Jewish), was responsible for the creation of a central organization of self-defense called the Haganah (Hebrew for "defense"). Both the Histadrut and the Haganah were established in 1921. The Haganah was illegal during the time of the British Mandate. From World War II through the creation of Israel there was a need to prepare young Jews for combat. To hide these activities from the eyes of the British, two thousand young people joined various kibbutzim as "workers" where they were trained for combat. They became the soldiers of the Palmach, a paramilitary elite unit of the prestate army that conducted almost all the major battles for independence during 1947 and 1948. The kibbutz movement was widely admired for their contribution to the country's security.

But this was perhaps the last creative innovation of national significance that the movement introduced into Israeli life. This is why some have argued that with the creation of the Israel Defense Forces (IDF) by Israel's first prime minister, David Ben-Gurion, in 1948, the kibbutz mission was fulfilled.

From the mid-nineteen forties, a *pilug*—or split—developed in the labor movement, which was mainly caused by different attitudes toward the Soviet Union. The majority of the Mapai Party (which later became the Labor Party), made up of both city dwellers and kibbutz members, opposed the pro-Soviet attitude of the minority. As a result, the latter created its own faction called the Achdut Avodah Party, which was supported by a majority of kibbutz members. By 1951, a pilug also took place in the kibbutz movement. Ideological debates raged around such esoteric concerns as which anthem to sing first, the "Internationale" or "Hatikvah" (the Israeli national anthem). These ideological battles led to bitter fights that sometimes split families and kibbutzim down the middle. Many kibbutzim shared the same name but joined opposing federations. For example, Givat Haim Ichud and Givat Haim Meuchad, Ein Harod Ichud and Ein Harod Meuchad.

A couple of decades—and a few crises—later the suspension of collective child rearing (raising kibbutz children in communal homes away from their parents with the idea that this would create better human beings) led doomsayers to declare the demise of kibbutz. Similarly, when outside workers were hired to do the work of the kibbutznikim, against the declared ideology of not employing (and thereby not exploiting) outsiders, or when farming was replaced by industry as the principal business of the kibbutz, choruses declared the kibbutzim to be history. Each of these changes represents a redefinition of kibbutz but not the demise of the kibbutz project.

Today, at the dawning of a new century, the kibbutzim are going through an even more profound cycle of change. Once again, voices are heralding the end of this grand communal experiment. There is no question that this round of change is different from all that came before. Israel is no longer a nation struggling with scarcity. It is a thriving modern state with a per capita gross national product that aspires to match that of the European Union. The kibbutz mission, which had historically been placed in the context of building a nation and creating a better world, has now been reduced to surviving as an indigenous community.

Undoubtedly, some kibbutzim will end. Others may change so as to loosely resemble their original form. Some are trying a middle ground. And a handful are attempting to keep to the traditional form. But rather than decrying the end of the kibbutz experiment, we choose to explore the current reality with an eye toward the next phase. Today's kibbutzim are home to 120,000 men, women, and children. Their fate is intimately tied up with the decisions made on each individual kibbutz as to how to move forward into a new phase.

Kibbutzim predate the modern state of Israel. The first kibbutz, Degania, was founded near the Kinneret—the Sea of Galilee—in 1910 by a handful of *chalutzim* (or pioneers) from Romania. The kibbutzim were born out of a combination of ideology, necessity, and scarcity as part of the socialist-Zionist enterprise. They thrived as long as they were considered integral to the goals of the Zionist movement and Israel. The broader kibbutz movement served the Zionist enterprise in various ways: settling new kibbutzim in regions that were considered fit for shaping the borders of the future state (sometimes with no consideration for the economic viability of the individual kibbutz); supplying men to lead the illegal immigration to Israel of refugees from Europe and Holocaust survivors (between 1939 and 1947, during the British Mandate); and organizing the Haganah and other political, economic, and cultural institutions of the labor movement and the Yishuv, as the pre-1948 Jewish community in Palestine was called. "The kibbutz was the full-fledged servant of Zionism twenty-four hours a day," observed Hebrew University professor of philosophy Menachem Brinker when we interviewed him in Jerusalem in July 2000.

The idea of the kibbutz emerged at the end of the nineteenth century and the early part of the twentieth as thousands of young people, mostly from Europe, Russia, and North America, flocked to the land of Palestine.[1] They were committed to a unique form of socialist

Zionism that would invert the social and economic pyramid of the Jewish people from one where professionals—lawyers, doctors, and business people—were on the top to one where the top positions would be held by workers and farmers in the historic land of Israel.

Though they have been compared to other grand communal experiments, the kibbutzim are uniquely Israeli. As Israeli journalist Amos Elon noted in 1972 in his seminal book *The Israelis: Founders and Sons:*

> "Morally perfect" communal communities dedicated to this or that utopian ideal—from the Essenes of antiquity to the Doukhobors of Russia, the Harmonists or Mormons of America, and the Flower children of today—have appeared regularly in history at times of crisis and during marked transitory periods. In the case of the kibbutz, practical and ideological factors of varying force combined to give it a longevity and a place in the general community.[2]

Kibbutzim were created for their time and were hugely influential in the settlement of the state of Israel and in its early growth. In fact, because the earliest kibbutzim were founded several decades before the creation of contemporary Israel in 1948, some argue that the role and influence of the kibbutzim in Israel's creation was even more important than their influence poststatehood. Others contest this assertion, citing the importance of the kibbutz movement in absorbing new immigrants and building the agricultural and industrial backbone of the fledgling state. Whichever side one chooses in this argument, the salient point is that the kibbutzim played a vital role in the formation of the modern state of Israel. The debate revolves around *if* or *when* that influence ended. We think that the kibbutzim played a vital role not only in the nation's founding but also in the shaping of the modern nation. They can continue to play an important—if decidedly different—role if they adapt skillfully to today's new reality.

From their inception, kibbutzim were both homes and communities for their members, as well as being part of a greater mission dedicated to creating a better society and a nation. In the early days, a typical theme for kibbutz movement discussions was "Kibbutz: A

Movement for Social Change or a Home?" Today, with the kibbutz movement and socialist ideology both severely weakened, a kibbutz is primarily a home, one with important responsibilities for the economic and social welfare of its members.

Ironically, although the kibbutz began as a communal settlement of the young, today, they are often referred to as old-age homes, reflecting their aging populations and their inability to either keep their own young as members or to recruit new ones. Until 2000, when the two large kibbutz movements merged, they recorded their demographic statistics separately. Statistics available in January 2002 show that from 1996 to 2000 there was negative growth in the Takam kibbutzim.[3] There were 58,000 adults and children in 2000. In that year, 581 children were born in Takam kibbutzim; 609 were born in 1999, 850 in 1985, while 1,300 children were born in 1990. In 2000, 3,100 adults took a leave of absence or sabbatical from the kibbutz.[4] (Previous experience indicates that a majority of these people will not return to the kibbutz.) In 2000, there were 5,200 seventy-year-olds, while in 1995 there were 5,000. In 2000 there were 4,300 sixty to sixty-nine years olds, while in 1995 there were 3,700.

Regarding the Kibbutz Artzi numbers, at the end of 2000 there were 33,000 adults and children. In 1996, there were 35,000. In 2000, 361 children were born to Kibbutz Artzi, while in 1996, 439 children were born.

The kibbutzim we are highlighting reflect these statistics. In 2000, Gesher Haziv, a Takam kibbutz, had 290 adults and children with an average age of fifty-five years. Hatzor, a Kibbutz Artzi kibbutz, with 550 adults and children in 2000, had an average age of sixty. And Gan Shmuel, also Kibbutz Artzi, had 848 adults and children in 2000, with an average age of fifty-three.

Before the influx of Holocaust survivors and subsequent groups of immigrants, the Yishuv was an amalgam of the old and the new. There were sparse settlements of Jews who had lived in Palestine for generations long before the First Aliyah (or emigration) that marked the rise of a Jewish movement for national liberation—Zionism—in the late nineteenth century. These people were mostly clustered around Jerusalem and some of the ancient cities such as Safed in the Northern Galilee. They lived side by side with Arabs in the major cities and in neighboring villages throughout the land. Up until the socialist-Zionist *aliyot* (emigrations) of 1904–1913 and 1918–1925, religious Jews came to Israel (usually Jerusalem) to die and to be buried on the Mount of Olives, not to take part in the rebirth of a nation.

The new, youthful immigrants came in three waves out of an idealistic commitment to both Zionism and socialism (prodded by pogroms in czarist Russia). The immigration continued except for interruptions caused by the world wars. During World War II, and soon thereafter, they were joined by survivors from Europe determined to start over and by relatively affluent Zionists from North America, invigorated by the pioneering spirit. In the 1950s, the ingathering of Jews to Israel included waves of immigrants from the Arab nations of North Africa and the Middle East, some leaving a rich Sephardic culture and others escaping abject poverty.

During the 1980s and 1990s, a massive emigration of over one million Jews from the former Soviet Union arrived in search of political, cultural, and economic freedom. A smaller influx of immigrants came from Ethiopia.

Many members of the mass immigrations were older people—Holocaust survivors, Jews from Arab countries, and Russians—whose assimilation into the country was difficult; few settled in kibbutzim. Immigration to kibbutz was pointedly for young people, including the Youth Aliyah for children whose parents were killed in the Holocaust and, later, for Sephardic children from Middle Eastern and North African countries whose families immigrated to Israel but could not take care of them in the difficult new environment.

Jews from Canada and the United States, although in smaller numbers, were part of these aliyot in the beginning of the Zionist movement. Even though the North Americans who came to Israel were steeped in an ethos of social justice and secularism, they were always less dogmatic—influenced by liberal thinkers such as John Dewey—than their comrades from Europe, Israel, and South America.

The Second Aliyah, the immigration wave from 1904 to 1913, was key to the formation of the kibbutzim. It included individuals who would later become the heroes of the socialist-Zionist revolution. These early pioneers were the founders of the labor movement, which laid the foundations for the fledgling state. They established the trade

union movement, the Histadrut; the national health insurance system, Kupat Holim; and the financial holding company for the trade
union infrastructure, the Chevrat Ovdim, out of which most of the
early Israeli economy evolved.

The kibbutz comprised an ideological mission and a pragmatic enterprise. This seemingly contradictory pairing reflected the inherent
tensions of kibbutz life, always apparent from the earliest days and
continuing to the present. Even though the young people who arrived
were infused with ideology, they didn't immediately conceive of the
kibbutz as an ideological ideal. They had a problem to solve and the
creation of the kibbutz framework could solve it for them. As historian Anita Shapira, the biographer of Zionist labor leader Berl Katznelson, put it: "The cardinal problem was: could an educated European
Jewish worker do grueling and monotonous labor and support himself and his family? This was a source of great despair which gripped
the Second Aliyah after 1908."[5] The conditions were severe, and
many people didn't stay. Building a new country by reclaiming desert
land for agriculture, draining the swamps, and fighting off malaria was
too much for many young people, and they left Israel to return to the
countries of their birth and the middle-class way of life they had
vowed to disown.

The young people who came to Israel in the Second Aliyah had a
utopian streak, largely influenced by the *narodnik* non-Marxist Russian socialist movement and the Chibat Zion ("Lovers of Zion") Rus-
sian-Jewish pro-Zionist movement founded and led by Leon Pinsker
and Ahad Ha'am. Another influential figure in this aliyah was Aaron
David Gordon (A. D. Gordon) who joined it at the age of forty-seven,
leaving his comfortable life in Russia to become an agricultural
worker in Palestine. Gordon preached that outdoor physical work
would cure and "redeem" the Jewish individual and the Jewish people. The young people were influenced by a myriad of other Zionist
thinkers, such as the idealistic socialist Nahman Syrkin, the Marxist
Dov Ber Borochov, and the writer Joseph Hayim Brenner. For them
the return to Zion and becoming a worker were one and the same.
Overriding all other principles, there was one unshakable doctrine,
*hagshama atzmit* or self-realization, meaning not only aliyah but participation as pioneers in the collective life of the kibbutz. It was not

enough to create a Jewish homeland. This was the way to create a Jewish working class and renew the Jewish collective existence.

A. D. Gordon, the legendary figure who lived his last years in Degania, exemplified the sentiment:

> What we seek to create here is life—our own life—in our own spirit and in our own way. Let me put it more bluntly: In Palestine we must do with our own hands all the things that make up the sum total of life. We must ourselves do all the work, from the least strenuous, cleanest, and most sophisticated, to the dirtiest and most difficult. In our own way, we must feel what a worker feels and think what a worker thinks—then, and only then, shall we have a culture of our own, for then we shall have a life of our own.[6]

But, while pioneers of the Second Aliyah arrived in their promised land instilled with ideals, they did not have a blueprint for what daily life would be like, nor did the thousands of young men and women who followed them in the Third Aliyah (1918–1925). How could they? This grand experiment was unlike any that had preceded it. There was little time for existential debates, but these followers of Karl Marx or Leo Tolstoy or Ahad Ha'am debated all the same.

Menachem Brinker, the Hebrew University philosopher, put it this way when we spoke with him in July 2000:

> The kibbutz was founded as an improvisation, not as an ideology. All socialist-Zionists, whose ideology was shaped in the Diaspora, objected to the idea of permanent settlement of workers. They thought it would turn the workers into middle-class people, eliminating the revolutionary elements of both their Zionism and their socialism. The strict Marxists among them thought that kibbutz life would dilute the class struggle by turning workers into landowners. And in retrospect it could be argued that it did. The idealists and the Ahad Ha'amists thought that it would turn the pioneers from people that are committed to working the land themselves—by their own hands—into employers of others, mainly cheap Arab workers, and in this way

betray the aim of Zionism of making the Jewish people into a "nation of workers" (*am oved*). The debate over this issue started when some General Zionist thinkers—such as Franz Oppenheimer and Arthur Ruppin—suggested at the Zionist Congress of 1913 the permanent settlement of workers on land acquired for this purpose by the Zionist movement as a way of overcoming the crisis of the Second Aliyah. In the years preceding these proposals, the number of pioneers leaving the country each year was greater than the number of newcomers. That fact shed serious doubt on the prospect of ever realizing even the most minimalist Zionist projects. The debates within the labor movement on accepting or rejecting the proposals took at least five or six years. At the end, the supporters of the idea of permanent settlements, people like Berl Katznelson and the kibbutz movement leader Yitzhak Tabenkin, succeeded in persuading the labor movement to accept the idea. They were helped by the influential writer Josef Hayim Brenner, who insisted that if land and the means of production are not given to them, the chalutzim of the Second Aliyah would leave the country, because the salaries they earned were not sufficient to raise a family. Another factor that helped those that pleaded for permanent settlement of workers was the beginning of the Third Aliyah in 1918, and the decision to save this new aliyah from the crises and disappointments of the Second Aliyah. In that way, the unique Israeli version of socialism, 'constructive socialism' was founded.

The kibbutz structure made sense. It reflected both the ideals and the reality of these new *olim*, as those who had made aliyah were called. The communal kitchen could feed lots of mouths. Food rationing—a necessity—was easier to do that way. While some members of the community were feeding and caring for the community as a whole, others could drain the swamps and build the farm sheds. Pooling clothes was economical, but it also fit an ideology that rebelled against bourgeois customs. Kibbutz folklore includes stories of the *communa*, or kibbutz laundry, which, in order to eliminate any sense of private possession, would issue work clothes on a first-come-

*Revolution*, 1949 mural by Yohanan Simon in the classroom at Givat Haviva Kibbutz Institute. Today the mural is covered. (Reprinted from Tali Tamir, *Yohanan Simon: Dual Portrait.* Courtesy of the family of the artist.)

first-served basis, leaving hefty people wearing clothes too tight for them and smaller people swimming in their clothes.

The American veterans of Kibbutz Hatzor tell about how they had to turn over their best Shabbat clothes to the *communa*, giving up the last remnant of their *galut*, or diaspora, lives. Other kibbutz veterans tell of the odd sensation of seeing people they barely knew, comrades in their new environment, wearing clothes they brought with them from home—perhaps a favorite dress or a present from a parent. But everyone went along with the system because conforming to ideology became a social norm.

Indeed, the work clothes and lack of style became a part of the Israeli mystique, demonstrating young people's rebellion against their parents and grandparents, while also reflecting the economic realities of the time and the prevailing social and cultural norms of the broader Israeli society. Clothing allowances were small, and makeup, jewelry, and all types of fashion were shunned as part of the kibbutz ethos. The photo image of the Israeli kibbutznik in sandals and shorts was the image of Israel as a pioneering state. Only since the mid 1980s have Israelis followed the latest European or American fashions. Today, there is an Israeli fashion industry that stresses a hip, young attitude, and the kibbutz population, especially the young, appear no different from the general Israeli population. Kibbutz teenagers have pierced eyebrows and noses like Israeli teenagers from the cities. Their hair is streaked all colors of the rainbow, and they wear the latest outfits.

Until Menachem Begin came to power in 1977, not only representing a right-wing, revisionist Zionism but also wearing a suit and tie, the Israeli fashion, even for prime ministers, was an open shirt and sandals. Through the latter part of the twentieth century, it was considered acceptable for a man to wear an open shirt and collar almost anywhere. In 2001, however, a sign (of the times) in front of the Knesset entrance forbade men from wearing sandals.

Although the pioneers of the Second and Third Aliyot in general postponed having children because of the rugged conditions, some who did have children found a way to synthesize their ideology and pragmatic needs. With the adults sleeping in tents until proper housing was built, it was important to figure out how to shield the infants and children from malaria and typhus. So, the first housing that was built was collective housing for children. Parents were, for the most part, free from child care and were available for work. This was reinforced ideologically by a vision of creating a better human being by taking children out of the nuclear family to raise them collectively in an educational system that reflected socialist values.

North American immigrants, who came to Israel through participation in socialist-Zionist youth movements such as Kibbutz Artzi Federation's Hashomer Hatzair and Takam's Habonim (composed of the Ichud and Meuchad Federations), were prepared in advance for life in their new environs.[7] The stories North American immigrants told in our interviews emphasized the conscious—and conscientious—efforts made to adjust to the harsh surroundings.

Sylvia and Yitzhak Kedem of Kibbutz Hatzor, both eighty-three years old and both from Brooklyn, described their preparation for making aliyah to kibbutz in an interview with Jo-Ann Mort in their home. Yitzhak has a master's degree in economics from Brooklyn College, and Sylvia has degrees from Brooklyn College and Columbia University. They were among the founding generation of the kibbutz. As Sylvia told us:

> In 1939, we were in the *hachshara* [Hashomer Hatzair training farm in Hightstown, New Jersey where teenagers prepared for life on kibbutz]. We were very active in Crown Heights and Brownsville, Brooklyn. We decided to retain a communal identity and *garin* [core group that would move together to kibbutz]. Most of the men went to the army and the women stayed at a commune the group had near Grand Army Plaza in Park Slope, Brooklyn. The movement also established communal houses in New York, Baltimore, and in Canada. We had many couples in the kibbutz [each communal home was called a kibbutz], people who were married or planning to be.

The Kedems were committed to Hashomer Hatzair and willingly followed its dictates. Sylvia continued:

> There was no family life. We lived in the same house and had a ban on couples sleeping together. Couples were only allowed to come if they separated. This was all preparation for aliyah, for the new life in Israel, and we thought that if anything smacked of permanence it would threaten us. We were really nuts!

Upon arriving in Israel, many couples were forced to share their tiny rooms with a third inhabitant, partly because of the shortage of buildings but also to enforce the point about couples threatening the collective. Sylvia said, "In 1946, we came to conditions that we never dreamt of. We came by boat. I was nine months pregnant."

Sylvia Kedem's situation points to the constant tension between ideology and real life that made the kibbutz experience absurd, fascinating, self-destructive, humanistic, possible, and impossible, all at the same time. Reality tripped up even the best-laid plans, and even the most committed comrades found life seeping into their ideological calendars.

Sylvia recalled:

> There was nothing here when we came but tents and a few very small shacks. There was a communal shower, oriental toilets, something we never dreamed we'd have. No toilet paper, or newspapers. I brought a carton of Gerber's baby food in bottles, and the woman who received me, a very nice woman with good intentions, said we don't use this, we use all fresh food, and she threw out the baby food.

Aliza Elkon, seventy-one years old, hails from Jersey City, New Jersey. She arrived in Israel in 1949 as part of a Habonim garin that came to Kibbutz Gesher Haziv, which is north of the city of Nahariya, just ten kilometers from the Lebanese border. She arrived just two days after the kibbutz was established:

> There was a Quonset hut or two at the entrance. We lived in tents for around a year. When we came, we started building the kibbutz. We had to build houses to live in, to house the children. The children stayed at a hotel in Shavez Zion [a *moshav shitufi*, or family-based agricultural collective, just south of Nahariya] until the first children's houses were built, which were wooden bungalows more than houses. We were an American group, and also Canadian Habonim people. We had to work the land. There were a few orchards. I was nineteen and got married here to someone from Atlanta.

As Israel prospered, the kibbutzim became integral to its economy, national spirit, and national identity. Although they were always a minority population, until the early 1980s the kibbutzim and their members were perceived to be the vanguard of Israeli society in agriculture, politics, and the military. A significant portion of the labor-oriented leadership was drawn from the kibbutzim, as was the military elite. Even as late as July 2000, 42 percent of the air force, considered the elite of Israel's defense forces, came from kibbutzim or moshavim.

Until the end of the 1970s, most Israelis knew someone on a kibbutz. If you weren't a kibbutznik yourself, you had family on a kibbutz that you visited on holidays; or maybe your parents sent you to spend the summer holiday with the kibbutz cousins. And young people in the city were sent to the youth movements with the possibility of going through the IDF Nahal (agricultural settlement corps) and eventually even becoming a kibbutz member. Kibbutz members saw their communal task as integral to building the new nation.

The kibbutzim hardly ever exceeded 4 percent of the population, but throughout the late 1940s, 1950s, and 1960s especially, as they grew and prospered, they often represented the face of Israel to the outside world.

Yet, as integral as they were to the new and vulnerable Israeli state, the kibbutz leadership naively ignored the nation's changing demographics. David Ben-Gurion, the legendary prime minister, implored the kibbutzim to absorb the new immigrants or at least to employ them in their regional factories and packing facilities for agricultural produce. For a range of reasons, deserving of another book, a rift emerged between the kibbutzim and the new immigrants, who were largely from the Arab countries of North Africa and the Middle East and who were settled in "development towns"[8] or as newly converted farmers in the semiprivate moshavim. They became the kibbutzim's greatest antagonists, politically and culturally.

As the nation grew and prospered so did the kibbutzim. But even when they exhibited relative economic success, first in the agricultural sector and later in industry, their first priority—building the country and serving in the army or public life—inevitably had a negative effect on their economic life. When there was a consensus among social elites and the banks regarding the utility of the kibbutzim, there was a national will to sustain the kibbutzim economically. However, this compact between the kibbutzim and the state began to rupture as national priorities and demographics changed. The story of the kibbutzim is the story of once-revered idealists floundering through a Kafkaesque maze of economic and social crises and being ignored or even disparaged by the new majority. Parts of the story are clearly gloomy, if not tragic. While current demographic and economic realities are not encouraging, we have chosen to focus on and reconstruct the reality of those kibbutzniks who are making a go of it. They are paying the price of relinquishing historic values and principles and focusing on survival. They are strongly criticized from within and from without, but in our view they represent the only future for the kibbutz—that of change in a changing Israel.

# CHAPTER TWO

# FROM ONE CENTURY TO THE NEXT

The men and women of the kibbutzim, and later their children, more than any other group would symbolize the "new Jew" . . . more than any others they have personified the ideals of labor Zionism, which at least up until 1945 were the dominant themes of Israeli nation building.

—Amos Elon

There are 287 kibbutzim in Israel. Most—270—are affiliated with the Kibbutz Movement, newly formed from the merger of the Kibbutz Artzi Federation and the United Kibbutz Movement (Takam). Seventeen are religious kibbutzim, sixteen belonging to the Kibbutz Hadati Movement and one to the ultra-Orthodox Poalei Agudat Israel (the kibbutz arm of the Agudat Israel Party). All the kibbutzim have been affected by a sea change in Israeli daily life and by economic and cultural globalization. From our interviews, anecdotal evidence, and newspaper reports, we conclude that the religious kibbutzim are struggling with many of the same questions as the secular ones, with the added dimension of having to impart orthodox religious conventions from one generation to the next.

What makes a kibbutz a kibbutz cannot be defined only in sociological and anthropological terms. "Kibbutz" is not just a sociopolitical community; it is a legal term, enforced by the Israel Land Authority (ILA) in conjunction with the kibbutz movement. There are seventy Israeli laws that mention the legal entity "kibbutz." The principles of the kibbutz are clearly outlined in the Articles of Association, a legal document representing the law of the communal settlements, first written in the 1920s and modified in the 1970s. The kibbutz Articles state that "the kibbutz is a free association of people with common goals, including settlement, absorption, maintaining an organized communal society on foundations of collective ownership of all property, self-labor [meaning that the entire workforce of the kibbutz is made up of members, with no hired labor], equality and sharing at all levels of production, consumption and education."[1] Furthermore, "a member of the kibbutz must act in accordance with the norms of the kibbutz society . . . giving his labor to the kibbutz and agreeing to the kibbutz supremacy when it comes to educating children . . . acknowledging its authority by way of the general assembly of the kibbutz."[2]

The social and legal foundations of the kibbutz are grounded in the principles of collective ownership of the means of production; a complete separation between what a member contributes to the kibbutz and what he receives from it; complete collective responsibility for health, education, and social welfare; self-labor; direct participatory democracy by way of the general assembly; cooperation and equality; and commitment to fulfilling the missions of the surrounding society. Yet at the beginning of the twenty-first century, these foundations have been dramatically shaken.

Although many factors contributed to the kibbutzim's current situation, location has been an important factor—and, for the most part, not something over which a kibbutz has had much control. Most of Israel's land is publicly owned, approximately 22 million dunam (or 2 million hectares) within the 1967 pre–Six-Day War borders. Prior to 1948, the Jewish National Fund (JNF), a legal entity of the Zionist movement, was responsible for purchasing land to facilitate the settlement of new immigrants. The kibbutzim were allocated plots for both agriculture and their fledgling communities. Some kibbutzim waited as long as a decade before being allowed to settle at a permanent location. For example, the founders of Kibbutz Hatzor lived in a nearby town, Rishon Letzion, for ten years (1936 to 1946) before finally being allocated land. During that period, members worked as hired laborers doing farming and road construction. They were also called upon by the movement to send a group of their strongest members to establish a new kibbutz in the Negev Desert.[3] Like almost all of the pioneer kibbutzim, an important part of Hatzor's heritage lies outside the internal community in its public contribution to the building of the state of Israel.

With the 1949 armistice agreements came international recognition of Israel's boarders. Kibbutzim lying along the new borders were not only ideological communities and important agricultural producers they were also military outposts. Members worked during the day in the fields, carrying their rifles, and did guard duty at night. Today, the Israeli army assumes most security responsibilities. Even so, members of kibbutzim on the borders still do regular turns of guard duty. Other kibbutzim, which were initially positioned by the Jewish Agency (the Zionist movement's operational arm set up to administer the Yishuv) as border settlements, found themselves in the center of the country after the War of Independence, when the Arab armies were pushed back to what became the 1949 borders.

The strategic positions of Gesher Haziv and Gan Shmuel were unchanged by the War of Independence. However, under the 1947 United Nations partition plan, Hatzor was a border settlement. In May 1948, just a day after Israel's Declaration of Independence, the Egyptian army invaded from the south. They were eventually stopped about eight kilometers west of Hatzor (not before shelling the kibbutz a few times) and pushed backed to the lines of Gaza and Rafiach. As a result, in 1949 Hatzor found itself no longer a border settlement but situated in the middle of the country. Today Hatzor is sandwiched into an area of increasing suburbanization, much like Gan Shmuel. Gesher Haziv, near the northern Lebanese border, is considered more on the periphery.

Although Israel achieved statehood in 1948, it was not until 1960 that all the public lands (public lands include JNF land, state-owned land, and former Arab property) were placed under the responsibility of the Israel Land Authority. The ILA still owns most of the kibbutz land. The ILA, in effect, rents land to the kibbutzim under forty-nine-year, renewable leases.

Historically, the kibbutz movements participated in devising this plan. The movements created a collective association called Nir Shitufi to be the legal owners of the kibbutzim. This meant that in case a kibbutz disbanded, the movements could claim the land for a new kibbutz settlement in the future. And, in fact, groups of people were sometimes moved around and resettled in mix-and-match arrangements by the kibbutz movements.

As Micha Drori, legal director for the Kibbutz Movement, explained it, "The *nikudah*, the plot itself, was the sacred thing. If the people were not working, they were replaced. The plot was more important than the people."[4] In the context of a struggling economy in a precarious military situation, such thinking was not outrageous. There are examples in the history of kibbutz where groups disbanded as a result of economic failure or internal social unrest. In the 1950s, one kibbutz of the KAF—Harel—was disbanded by the federation (and later reconfigured) because the KAF considered the members to have extreme leftist tendencies. This was a period when the movement leadership was highly charismatic and functioned in an ideological, centralized manner. Politics were an inherent part of the kibbutz identity, but political pluralism was not. A familiar slogan of the Kibbutz Artzi Federation was "freedom of debate, unity of action." It affected the daily decisions of the kibbutz, from economic and social programs to child rearing.

Plots were allocated based on each family receiving from ten to twenty dunam for a house, barn, workshop, and farm. Therefore, a kibbutz of one hundred families would be allocated one hundred plots.

The part of the plot where the members lived and congregated was called the *machane*, or encampment (without a military connotation). Within the typical machane was the kibbutz "house," which included a water tower, a public dining room, buildings for services such as the laundry and local store, children's houses, the *moadon* (clubhouse), and small homes for the members. The private home was last in the order of priorities. Instead of having a larger private dwelling that would include a kitchen, laundry, living room, and bedrooms, the individual kibbutz house was about thirty-eight to fifty square meters, with a kitchenette, living room, bedroom for the adults, and not much else.

It was a priority for members to have suitable facilities to congregate together, in order to cultivate the sense of community. The importance of communal life generated "historic" debates such as whether or not a member should have a *koom koom* (tea kettle) in his home because such an appliance—used on the hot plate—might lead to his not joining other members in the dining room for the afternoon meal.

Today, the children's houses are used as playrooms, and the water tower—long since replaced by modern plumbing—stands rusted as a reminder of a heroic past. A factory off to the side may have replaced the farm animals, but the general physical outline of the machane remains the same from generation to generation. Even in this era of privatization and change, a stranger entering any kibbutz will see a similar layout at the center of the kibbutz geography.

There's a story, well known among kibbutz members, about an American tourist visiting Israel for the first time in the 1960s. While touring the kibbutz machane, and viewing the landscaped public and private gardens, he comments on the intelligent kibbutznikim who built their homes in such beautiful parks and not in the adjacent desert wasteland. Of course, the reality was quite different. Whether it was Gesher Haziv on a rocky plain alongside the Mediterranean, Gan Shmuel on the swampland alongside a farming town called Hadera, or Hatzor on the northern border of the Negev Desert, these "public parks" were actually cultivated with a great deal of hardship and individual devotion.

Historically, kibbutz settlements were positioned in hostile areas alongside borders, which, at first, had little agricultural potential. The swamps of the Hefer Valley where Gan Shmuel is situated and the former wasteland of the Negev Desert that houses Hatzor may look like national parks, but the price of success was high, very high. Because of the innovation, advanced scientific methods, and stubborn diligence of their members, the kibbutzim should be the pride of the State of Israel and a symbol for underdeveloped countries. However, Israel has changed, and so has its way of measuring success.

Economically and socially, Israeli society changed profoundly from the early 1950s to the late 1990s. The population increased from 700,000 to six million. From an era of scarcity and almost extreme self-denial (especially in the case of the kibbutzim), Israel has developed the highest standard of living per capita in the Middle East. As late as 1990, Israel had only one television station. But in the early twenty-first century, Israelis watch dozens of channels and programs, including the latest American sitcoms, MTV, ESPN, and the ubiquitous CNN, via cable and satellite networks. A growing percentage of Israelis own home computers. Israelis, who love gadgets and whose phone system used to be notoriously expensive and difficult to use,

Kibbutz Gan Shmuel *machane* in the late 1930s. (Reprinted from Tali Tamir, *Yohanan Simon: Dual Portrait*. Courtesy of Kibbutz Gan Shmuel.)

are among the world's largest users of cell phones. Israeli young people dye their hair purple and blue and travel in droves to India and Bangkok to try to discover the meaning of life. They attend raves near the Dead Sea and in Tel Aviv, a city that rivals New York for twenty-four-hour nightlife. Until the 2000 al-Aqsa Intifada, which paralleled a worldwide recession, Israel's economy was booming, boasting many new young millionaires from the burgeoning high-tech corridors of Israel's three largest cities.

From its inception, many perceived Israel to be a socialist state with the kibbutzim as its idealistic hard core. Along with the Histadrut, the kibbutzim were leaders in fostering the values and goals of Israeli socialism. In actuality, the interdependence of state and socialist institutions was closer to a "political economy of intervention" as described by kibbutz sociologist Daniel Rosolio, in his seminal study, *System and Crisis: Crises, Adjustments, and Changes in the Kibbutz Movement.*[5] This was largely the result of the labor-controlled economy via the Chevrat Ovdim (business enterprises owned and managed by the Histadrut trade union), Kupat Holim (public health clincs and insurance owned by the public sector), and other governmental and nongovernmental institutions. Of course, there was always a capitalist sector, but the social elite of Israel typically came from the labor movement, and the leaders of industry nearly always identified with the parties comprising the Labor Alignment.[6]

As the Israeli writer Amos Elon notes, "With all their hairsplitting the socialist Zionists shared the aim of not only reconstructing a land and creating a haven for the persecuted, but of establishing a 'good,' 'just,' even 'morally perfect' society as well."[7]

The kibbutz movement, strongly allied with the labor movement, was considered to be its vanguard in agriculture, some forms of industry, the army, culture, and political life. It represented a socialist hegemony now gone from Israeli life. In all cases, the early kibbutz members and, later, their sons and daughters filled a disproportionately high percentage of positions in each of the above sectors in comparison with their actual numbers in society (never more than 4 to 5 percent of the population, and less than 2 percent in 2002).

When one adds to the above the number of former kibbutznikim, those who were born or raised on kibbutz and left the communal setting for other walks of life, the obvious impact of kibbutz becomes even more impressive. Labor Party leaders including Yitzhak Rabin, Shimon Peres, and Ehud Barak all had kibbutz backgrounds. In industry or culture, if key public figures were not kibbutznikim or ex-kibbutznikim, then they were certainly raised in one of the pioneer socialist-Zionist youth movements.

In one sense, the success of the kibbutz is also the reason for its demise, as demonstrated by the statistics in chapter 1. The founders invested their limited wealth in their children by educating them in quality schools that taught the value of hard work and the importance of cooperating with peers. The younger generation was expected to serve in the military in elite units and as officers. When they returned home, they were guaranteed university education. During their military service and in the university, the kibbutz youth met others who were choosing walks of life that often appeared more attractive and were certainly more lucrative than what was offered on the kibbutz. Lured by the opportunity to choose, many young people left the kibbutz after finishing their university education or army duty. This resulted in a severe brain drain from a relatively small community. Ironically, it was also a direct testament to the founders, whose children became leaders in all spheres of Israeli life, making their contribution to society—but outside the kibbutz. Also, the distance from the urban centers was an obstacle to the new careerism (although this may be changing as a new generation is attracted to the quality of life of the countryside).

In many cases the attraction of outside society negatively affected the nuclear family, as demonstrated by the story of a couple who were founding members of a kibbutz. In the early 1960s, the kibbutz committee for higher education approved Jacob Farhi's request to study architecture at the university, even though this was not considered to be a "functional" profession (that is, something needed by the kibbutz). Returning from his studies, Farhi found that the real personal challenges for him were in the city. He believed in the kibbutz, its values and system. But, as a professional (long before the age of modern telecommunications and transportation might have afforded him more flexibility in combining his career with kibbutz life), he was not ready to make the sacrifice. He left the kibbutz to work in Tel Aviv. His wife, Yehudit, on the other hand, was deeply rooted in the kibbutz and its ideology. She was not ready to separate herself from it.

While the sometimes intractable *mazkirut* (secretariat) would not condone Jacob's betrayal of the community, they could not very well prevent the couple from maintaining their family life and raising their children together, at least on the weekends. Years later, after her children were old enough, Yehudit Farhi found a job at the Tel Aviv headquarters of the KAF and returned home to the kibbutz on weekends. She, her husband, and the kibbutz found a compromise (which did not prevent petty jealousies from arising among those who could not find similar solutions). As Jacob Farhi became old and incapable of taking care of himself, the now more accommodating and less judgmental mazkirut voted to accept him back into the kibbutz, taking care of his needs in his last years.[8]

The crises of the kibbutz were not only of a personal nature. The dramatic political and economic changes in Israel in the last twenty-five years of the twentieth century had a major influence on the development of the kibbutz. The 1973 surprise attack on Israel by Egypt and Syria left the country in shock and deeply disillusioned.[9] The failure of the Labor government to foresee and prevent this war, along with the exorbitantly high price Israel paid in human lives, shattered Labor's invincibility. This burst the self-inflated balloon of invulnerability that arose after the 1967 Six-Day War and led to the fall of Labor as the majority power in government after twenty-nine years of political hegemony. The kibbutzim paid a disproportionately high price in the 1973 war, as in all previous Israeli wars. Economically, the workforce disappeared overnight and didn't completely return for a few months.

The army, having lost many of its key officers in the war, called upon the young kibbutz members to sign up for another term of duty; and many eventually did not return to live on kibbutz. Some who did were often shell shocked from the war, from the once infallible Israeli army being caught off guard and the incredibly high number of their friends who were killed in action.

The effect in many kibbutzim with only a few hundred members of having two, three, and sometimes more fallen soldiers was profound. It still had an impact at the end of the seven or thirty days of mourning when life was supposed to return to normal.[10] The mazkirut, along with the educational and health committees, are continuing to address deeply personal problems resulting from the tragedy of war. All this contributed to an overall disillusionment with those held responsible for the collapse of what was called the "conceptzia," the confidence that post-1967 Israel was strong enough to deter any enemy attack.

In 1977, the new Likud Party prime minister, Menachem Begin, put together a coalition of right-wing and religious parties that were traditionally outside of the political consensus of Israel. With the exception of members of the National Religious Party, which had its own kibbutz movement, Likud supporters did not plough the fields nor were they prominent in the army. (In the early 1970s, when the Likud was created by merging the veteran Herut and Liberal Parties, the two military leaders to join were Ezer Weizman and Ariel Sharon. In later years, the two split politically with Weizman taking a more dovish course and Sharon—Israel's prime minister in 2003—remaining the eternal hawk.) The Likud regarded the existing social and economic elites with disdain, and the kibbutzim were a convenient target. Menachim Begin often denounced the kibbutznikim as millionaires with swimming pools. This kind of demagoguery was particularly effective in that the largely Sephardic (or Mizrachi) population of the development towns was employed in regional industries owned and operated by the kibbutzim.

During the 1950s, the government of Israel, under the leadership of Prime Minister Ben-Gurion, initiated massive work projects in these development towns. The kibbutzim built the factories, sent the agricultural produce to be processed and packaged, and managed the operations. In the first two decades of Israel's existence, both the planning and the implementation of these projects were largely successful, and when they were not the government subsidized them. Beginning in the late 1970s and continuing throughout the 1980s and 1990s, these enterprises became increasingly less viable, which resulted not only in the economic crisis of the kibbutzim but also a major social crisis when it came to the employees of these kibbutz-run enterprises. Because of this situation, it was easy for Likud leaders, including former prime minister Benjamin Netanyahu, to attack the kibbutzim and the labor movement and further polarize the populations while gaining political support.

The Likud and its satellite parties, in the eyes of many in Israel, personified nationalistic war mongering, while Labor and its supporters were presumed to represent the values of peace and eventual coexistence with Israel's Arab neighbors. However, the 1979 peace treaty with Egypt signed by Prime Minister Begin, following President Sadat's historic visit to Jerusalem in 1977, demonstrated to a younger generation of Israelis that it was not only Labor that could make peace. The younger generation who "didn't know Joseph" were suspicious—if not outright disdainful—of the Labor Alignment leaders. ("Didn't know Joseph" is a commonly used expression in Israel. It typically refers to the younger generation that didn't experience the building of the nation, its trials and hardships, and therefore didn't have the same regard for the pioneer leaders.) Except in the the area of extraparliamentary politics, such as the protests of Peace Now in support of the peace process (beginning in 1978) and against the War in Lebanon (1982), fewer and fewer kibbutznikim wielded political power.[11]

The war in Lebanon convinced many of the disenchanted Laborites that the Likud's real priority was not a historic compromise with the Arab states that included withdrawal from the territories conquered in 1967 but its spiritual commitment to a Greater Israel that encompassed the territories conquered by Israel in the 1967 war. While the continuing occupation of the West Bank and the Gaza Strip and the war in Lebanon had no direct bearing on the economic crisis of the kibbutzim, the social and economic revolution introduced by the Likud definitely did.

The Likud was committed to a neoliberal economic policy, including extensive privatization and reducing the power of the Histadrut. The policy, according to Daniel Rosolio, "produced a rapid rise in the standard of living, but failed to produce a parallel economic growth."[12] It also spoke to the frustrations of the Mizrachi Jews who had emigrated from North Africa and Yemen, and who blamed the Labor Party and Labor's allies for their lack of progress in Israeli society.

Partly because of the costs of the war in Lebanon and partly because of Israel's economic policies, hyperinflation developed in Israel. By 1984–85 inflation rates reached almost 1,000 percent. In 1985 the national unity government led by Prime Minister Yitzhak Shamir and Finance Minister Shimon Peres declared an economic policy aimed at reducing inflation and stabilizing the economy. According to Rosolio,

"The price of this policy and its achievements was paid primarily by the productive sector of the Israeli economy . . . including the kibbutzim."[13]

Stanley Maron, a researcher at the Yad Tabenkin Research and Documentation Center of the United Kibbutz Movement and a member of Kibbutz Mayan Tzvi, described the situation of the kibbutzim in an article published in the *Journal of Rural Cooperation:*

> At the beginning of the 1980s, the kibbutz economy had an annual turnover of U.S.$2 billion and a surplus of more than U.S.$120 million, with more assets than debts. Then came a crisis in the Israeli economy with soaring inflation, excessive interest rates, and a drop in exports. The productive sectors of the economy were hit especially hard because of their dependence on a high ratio of working capital that must be at low interest rates, particularly in agriculture.
>
> Since the kibbutz economy is based almost entirely on agriculture and industry, and interest rates at one point reached 100% in real terms, it didn't take long for the kibbutzim to find themselves deep in a financial crisis. To make matters worse, just at that point there was a sharp [global] drop in the price of cotton, the main cash crop, and kibbutz agriculture turned from profit to loss.
>
> By 1984, the annual surplus had turned into an annual deficit of 165 million dollars, with the high interest rates creating a geometric increase in the debt load. Credit became more and more scarce, and that crippled the current operations, particularly in industry where factories had difficulty filling orders because they did not have the credit to buy raw materials. Within four years the debt load almost quadrupled and reached 5 billion dollars. Other large parts of the Israeli economy found themselves in similar difficulties. The major banks in the country were faced with collapse and the government was compelled to intervene.[14]

But the hyperinflation in the 1980s is only part of the story. The kibbutzim did not react to the economic situation in a timely fashion. The high level of investments in non-income-generating projects, such as expanding the members' homes to include room for their children; the failure of the kibbutz industries to meet expectations; and mismanagement of regional enterprises were also partly responsible for the collapse.

From 1992 to 2000, Ariel Halperin was the trustee for the Israeli government, the banking system, and the kibbutzim for the Administration for Implementing the Arrangement for the Kibbutzim.[15] This was a commission set up by the government, the banks, and the kibbutzim to settle the kibbutz debt crisis so that the kibbutzim would not all default on their huge debts and cripple the Israeli economy. The first debt arrangement wiped out $2 billion in debt and spread out the debt repayment. A supplementary kibbutzim arrangement followed to relieve additional debt. The supplementary arrangement included provisions calling for the kibbutzim to relinquish as much as 40 percent of their agricultural land in order to dissolve their debt. In a July 25, 2000 interview with the authors in a café near Tel Aviv University Halperin described the unique and complex relationship between kibbutz member, kibbutz community, kibbutz movement, government, and economic institutions as a series of concentric circles:

> We find the kibbutz member in the center with the kibbutz as an encircling sphere. In the next wider sphere stood the kibbutz movement. It promised the kibbutzim mutual guarantees: We will not let you fail and will help in every way possible. This is what actually happened—when a kibbutz was in financial trouble, the kibbutz movement poured in funds, set up capital guarantees, sent families to support the weaker kibbutzim. The movement actively supported the kibbutzim wherever possible. It took the best of the youth from veteran kibbutzim to help form *garinim* [plural of garin, or core group sent to fulfill a mission] to establish new ones.
>
>     There were additional spheres—the Zionist institutions, the political establishment, the banking establishment, and the Histadrut. Each time the kibbutz went into debt, the government and the banks found another way to supply the loans, the credit lines, and the debt settlements to erase debts. Once it was

accomplished through the Histadrut and other state-run businesses. Other times it was the banks that intervened on behalf of the kibbutzim.

Rosolio, the kibbutz sociologist and a member of Kibbutz Kabri in the Western Galilee not far from the Lebanese border, claims that the history of the kibbutz movement has been replete with financial crises. The first crisis occurred in the 1920s, the second in the 1930s, the third from 1951 to 1952, the fourth in the early 1960s, and the fifth in the 1970s. In short, the history of the kibbutz movement is the story of crisis after crisis after crisis. Rosolio's thesis, based on a number of well-known economic and sociological theories of political economies combined with his own intimate knowledge of the labor movement enterprises, helps clarify the character of the kibbutz crises.[16]

Rosolio refers to two kinds of economic systems—hard constraints and soft constraints—that were also used to document models of change within the old communist systems by economists such as the Hungarian Janos Kornai and others.[17] Hard constraints describes a situation in which the economic system, whatever it may be (family, firm, nonprofit, any kind of ownership), has fixed resources that cannot be increased by creating a deficit or by a flow of funds from outside sources (government, grants, credit). In a system of soft constraints there is the possibility of creating a deficit, receiving protection, or having outside financial support. State socialism, of whatever kind, may best characterize this system.[18] The outer spheres in Halperin's illustration, the kibbutz movement, the government, the Histadrut, and the banks provided the soft constraints needed by the kibbutzim.

The kibbutz economy from the late 1920s until the middle of the 1980s was essentially conducted under soft constraints, as a component of the socialist-Zionist program for establishing the State of Israel and absorbing Jewish immigrations from around the world. Every government has its own social and economic agenda and will do what it can to promote that program within the framework of the law. During the Depression, the Roosevelt administration implemented its New Deal to jump-start the American economy. The recurrent crises of the kibbutzim are the result of the creation of the state and the absorption of new immigrants, after which it was expected that hard constraints would be created. The kibbutzim were not prepared to gradually wean themselves away from government support, nor was the Labor government ready to forgo the kibbutz contribution to building the nation. This, of course, abruptly ended with Likud's rise to power and the sudden imposition of hard constraints. However, the following factors are equally important in the deep financial crisis of the kibbutzim: the lack of contemporary management skills, the changing expectations of the members (including the decision to raise children in the parents' home), and meager economic resources.

In addition to the soft constraints, Rosolio describes another characteristic of the kibbutz economy—a paradox of scarcity. Permanent scarcity is a characteristic of socialist economies, not the result of a mistake in planning or production but rather a structural situation, where the economic system grants unlimited resources to the productive system unconnected to any market demand. This includes capital, labor, and raw materials. Inasmuch as the demands from the system supplying the resources are unending, they create a kind of permanent scarcity. The agricultural production targets of the kibbutzim and moshavim were always based on maximizing cultivation, regardless of market demands. Produce was brought to a central depository that was organized and operated by the kibbutz and moshav movements where it was sold in Israel and for export by a single centralized marketing outlet owned by the labor movement, with the kibbutzim and moshavim as the only shareholders. The people in the development towns were the workers in these central depositories, and their continued employment was also a consideration. In instances where Israel lost its relative advantage, such as with the profitable field crop cotton (known as "white gold"), the kibbutzim had to dramatically reduce the number of dunam planted by more than 50 percent and revert to alternatives such as fruit orchards and livestock. In the early years, increased agricultural output in a society that was growing by leaps and bounds could usually be absorbed in the marketplace. That was not the case at the end of the twentieth century, when the Israeli consumer could buy less expensive imported fruits and vegetables.

The introduction of industry to kibbutz during the 1960s was a kind of anomaly, antithetical to the kibbutz ideology of returning to the land. Engaging in industrial projects requires heavy capital investment, essential skills in varied technologies, and, ultimately, the ability to market one's product. It required hiring outside labor, both high-paid experts and inexpensive line workers, because of the small size and limited specialized skills of the kibbutz members. The idea of using hired labor was also anathema to the kibbutz principles. However, it was inevitable if industry was to be adopted.

Competition in world markets was a factor in undermining the value of labor as part of the ethos of kibbutz. At first, kibbutzim searched for industrial projects that would give work to members. Kibbutzim even established industries for veteran members who could no longer endure the hardships of agriculture, so that they could continue to be productive. In some cases, the concept of making a profit and using the income to sustain the community and guarantee its future was almost secondary to providing jobs. While this may appear to be an extreme representation of the reality, at kibbutz meetings the question of providing jobs was inevitably posed. In any case, as opposed to the Soviet economies where the paradox of scarcity extended to industry, the kibbutzim, which entered industry relatively late—sometimes only in the 1980s and 1990s—had to learn to compete in the world marketplace, and usually with limited capital resources. The main problem of kibbutz industries in the 1980s was the price of capital—extremely high interest rates combined with an unlimited supply of credit—which created a situation in which non-high-tech industries were financed with no equity and real interest rates of 15 to 30 percent.

None of these commitments were economically viable in the strict sense of the word. The kibbutz was able to subsist and even flourish to a certain extent as long as the corporatist arrangement between the kibbutz and the state was maintained. Because there was an identity of interest between the national government, the economic institutions, and the kibbutz, there was no apparent conflict. The kibbutz members perceived their community as a beachhead from which the country went forth to fulfill its goals. And the country was expected to make sure it was kept secure.

As we have explained, these arrangements were neither sinister nor the result of a lack of vision. The kibbutzim and the kibbutz movement served an important historical role in the creation and development of the state. In line with the definition of corporatism, they represented the hegemonic interests of the Zionist movement and, later on, the State of Israel.[19] The kibbutzim and the kibbutz movement served as subcontractors, implementing the social, economic, and security goals of the Zionist movement and, then, the State of Israel.[20] The individual kibbutz member was part of a social elite, ready to serve the nation at all levels. The kibbutz and the movement were institutional elites in terms of their position in society and how they perceived themselves, if not by their economic standing. As one contemporary kibbutz intellectual, Avishai Grossman, said on various occasions, *"Tamid l'pekuda anachnu"* ("We are always at the command") of the kibbutz, the army, the greater society.[21] In Hebrew the expression rings almost fatalistically true, epitomizing an elite body destined to eternally serve the society.

Halperin and Rosolio are both critical of the kibbutz movement for its failure to correctly read the sociopolitical map following the upheaval of 1977. In a 1994 article, Rosolio wrote, "The movement failed to perceive the real changes around them, that the rules of the game and the political culture had changed."[22] Amazing now to consider, as late as 1985 the Takam still proposed a five-year settlement plan that included the establishment of twenty-one new kibbutzim in various parts of Israel.[23] In the early 1980s, as a response to the hostile government and as a guarantee of alternative funding sources to the existing soft constraints, the Kibbutz Artzi Federation's mazkirut prepared to invest in a foreign bank. (This never came to fruition.)

Halperin stressed that in the 1980s the kibbutzim spent enormous sums on construction during the switch to familial sleeping arrangements and other changes. These sums were far out of proportion to available resources and resulted in the accumulation of debt. During the time of hyperinflation there was total chaos in the financial system of Israel. Yet, the movements and the kibbutzim continued to lend money to themselves in huge amounts to develop industry and phase out the children's houses. The need for additional housing and improvements was real, as was the need for establishing new industries because the kibbutzim needed new sources of income. However, the financial resources to underpin these projects were no longer available. The paternalistic relationship between the government and the kibbutz system, and between the kibbutz movement leadership and the kibbutzim, had come to an end.

Even so, this is not the whole story. Researchers at the Institute for Research of the Kibbutz and the Cooperative Idea reviewed the relative importance of each of the factors that led to the increase in the kibbutz debt and in 1989 wrote that 40 percent of the kibbutz debt was the result of the government's inflationary policies. The rest was a result of endogenous factors such as ineffective investments and debts of the central kibbutz financing bodies distributed among the kibbutzim according to the recovery plan agreement signed by the government, banks and the kibbutzim.[24] This report indicated other factors that increased the debt, including inefficient investments in industry and agriculture, debts of the movement and regional organizations, an increase of active capital for production, an increase of active and nonactive capital for consumption, and other factors adjusted after profits, grants, and revenues.[25] We agree with Halperin that there could be no possible solution other than implementing fundamental changes that come from within the kibbutz itself.

As Halperin told us:

[At first] I thought some settlement of these debts and a financial restructuring and a minor reorganization plan for the kibbutzim themselves would create an atmosphere in which the kibbutzim would continue to grow and live for another generation. [The first debt settlement plan in 1989 erased $2 million in debt.] After a few years, I slowly changed my views. I understood that the crisis here is much more profound, and the basics of the kibbutz agreement will not in any way solve the problem.

After the individual kibbutz member finished blaming his own kibbutz leadership, and after the kibbutz finished blaming the movement, and after the movement finished blaming the government and the banks, it came down to the individual kibbutz and its members having to make a fundamental adjustment in order to continue to exist within a new Israel.

CHAPTER    THREE

# THE CRISIS AND THE SEARCH FOR SOLUTIONS

> In the past, the system worked despite the flaws, because people
> within the system had unbounded faith in it.
> —Ariel Halperin, 1997

Although there have been crises for the kibbutz enterprise before, today's situation is profoundly different. The current crisis of the kibbutzim is rooted in the fundamental shift within Israeli society from
a political economy of intervention to a neoliberal economy favoring
privatization, with little government intervention in the economic
process. All of the previous economic crises of the kibbutzim were resolved by arrangements sponsored in part by the government and supported in part by the banks. These corporatist arrangements allowed
the kibbutzim to continue to fulfill their mission. As we discussed in
the last chapter, the changes—social, political, and economic—in Israel have put the kibbutzim at a grave disadvantage.

The severe debt—$6 billion—of the kibbutzim and the kibbutz
movements (through their regional economic organizations) finally
could not be ignored, since they seriously threatened the stability of
the Israeli banking system. Now under the shadow of Israel's high-
tech start-up companies, the kibbutzim had little to offer beyond
their celebrated history. However, most of Israel no longer cared
much about the history and even considered the kibbutzim obsolete.
Many in Israel became highly resentful of having to bail out the kibbutzim.

As the 1996 annual report of the Administration for Implementing
the Arrangement of the Kibbutzim concluded:

The combination of stagnating population growth, low growth rate, low per capita production, and a severe labor crisis in the kibbutz work force points to a profound structural crisis in the kibbutz sector. The kibbutzim and the kibbutz movement should consider structural changes, including a redefinition of the relationship between the member and the kibbutz, in order to create the conditions needed to emerge from the crisis.[1]

The combined debt along with the process of privatization was forcing the new economic reality on kibbutz members in a stark way. As highlighted in *Ha'aretz* newspaper, the new economics of the kibbutz meant that except for members on the richest kibbutzim economic change was a necessity:

In the Israel of 2000, there are thousands of poor kibbutzniks. . . . More than 30 percent of all kibbutz members are living below the poverty line . . . most kibbutz families still live in apartments of less than sixty square meters in which the furnishings are modest at best and do not even begin to compare with the contents of the average city dwelling. . . . The average per capita standard of living on the kibbutz has declined by 30 to 40 percent. In the age of privatization, kibbutzniks subsist on a monthly budget of between NIS 2,000 and NIS 4,000 per person—depending on the financial status of the kibbutz. For 70 percent of the kibbutniks, the monthly budget does not exceed NIS 3,000, and there are a few kibbutzim where it is below NIS 2,000.[2]

The crisis of the 1980s and 1990s raised many new questions: Can you liquidate a community in which social and economic aspects of people's lives are so entwined? How can you resolve a multibillion dollar debt by selling a cow (which has little or no commercial value) or foreclosing on an apartment (which has no real estate value)? What do you do with workers in a failing factory? Can they be fired? Who will pay the unemployment checks when there is no social security or pension fund? Should the kibbutz switch from a once profitable industrial crop like cotton to manual labor crops like vegetables and fruits, and employ foreign laborers? Should kibbutz electricians, carpenters, and plumbers be required to sell services at market prices to reduce community overhead, and, if they don't—or can't—should they be replaced by cheaper and sometimes more efficient workers from outside the kibbutz? Does the kibbutz need to provide alternative forms of labor (income) for its members, or is it the responsibility of the individual member to support himself? If medical care and education are still to be guaranteed, what happens to alternative forms of medicine or special education? Can a community holding a debt of $25 million still afford to give the most expensive medical treatments and schooling? And: Whose responsibility is it to support the old people (pensioners without pension funds) who were the founders of the kibbutz? Should it be the younger generation of kibbutz members who are struggling for survival? Or should their children, most of whom left the kibbutz long ago, have some responsibility for their elderly parents?

According to Ariel Halperin, the kibbutzim settlement arrangement was designed because from the early 1990s "we needed some sort of 'chapter 11' arrangement combining organizational plans for the kibbutzim and a creditors' arrangement for each separate kibbutz. This was necessary to allow the kibbutzim to continue to operate as ongoing concerns."[3]

If the social contract was quite emphatic about the guarantees the kibbutz confers upon its members, it was equally clear about the individual having no property of his own. In Halperin's words:

> What do I mean by "nothing"? The community is committed to its members, but the member has nothing concrete—no inheritance rights, no social welfare rights. He is defenseless against decisions taken by 51 percent of the kibbutz general meeting. For example, a majority of 51 percent can decide to enlarge the homes of younger members rather than older members. This affects the older members' property values. The kibbutz member has no absolute certainty regarding his future, which does not exist independent of the kibbutz system.[4]

Some opponents of fundamental changes in such areas as differential salaries, privatization, and property rights claim that the problem lies in a lack of leadership. Gary Brenner recalled that in conversations that he had had over a three-year period with Moshe Nachtomi, a veteran kibbutz member of Hatzor, Nachtomi always blamed the *mosadot* (the governing institutions of the kibbutz) or the mazkirut. If a member didn't conform to the community's expectations, it was held to be the job of the mazkirut to call him to task. If the factory didn't produce the expected profits, the mazkirut should call on the coordinator (in the early kibbutz idiom managers were called "coordinators," as a sign of their limited authority) to do a better job. If children's caretakers and parents were disappointed and frustrated with the system of collective child rearing, the mosadot should convene the members to work out the differences. The system didn't need changing . . . the mosadot needed to function better. In the words of Yaakov Gadish, a member of the religious kibbutz Kvutzat Yavne and a former director of the budget in the Ministry of Finance in previous Labor governments (and, as will be described below, a leader of the conservative faction within the kibbutz movement), "The system didn't fail, the people did."[5]

On one level, this argument is valid. Not every community of four hundred members can be expected to maintain the same high level of leadership from generation to generation. Achieving a proper mix of economists and managers, social leaders and educators, creators of local culture and community planners is sometimes impossible. Although the founders of pioneering Israel were a generation of revolutionaries ready to make the sacrifices a revolutionary must make, subsequent generations were satisfied with being good kibbutzniks and not imposing themselves on their fellow members. To paraphrase Micha Harari, one of the central figures in Hatzor's process of change: What motivated the founders was either a well-defined ideology or the shame of not fulfilling the expectations of the kibbutz. Today, there is no ideology and very little shame. Therefore, fundamental changes are essential.

Moreover, the social matrix of a kibbutz can often be too provincial to provide enough positive reinforcement (let alone financial rewards) to hold on to qualified leaders. Traditionally, leadership in the kibbutz was rotated once every two to three years. This was true for the social functions of the community (health, education, and welfare) and the economic ones (farm and coordinators). In fact, qualified people would often rotate from one key position to another with time off for a few months to wash dishes in the communal dining room or work on the factory assembly line. Local cynics would call this "the difference between rotation and circulation." Nevertheless, advocates of this system of rotation claimed that it would help preserve the democratic nature of the society by not concentrating power in the hands of a few.

Whether the intentions underlying the principle of rotation were realized is questionable. Kibbutzim that have successfully implemented a process of change typically owe this to a hard core of leaders who were prepared to make a long-term commitment to the renewal of the kibbutz. Learning new management skills, negotiating with banks, lawyers, and tax authorities, and promoting real estate ventures such as suburban housing projects and shopping centers requires a level of complex professional skills unknown to the pioneer founders. This eventually led to the question of rewards and differentiation.

But, like Ariel Halperin, we do not think that the failure of the kibbutz is simply a matter of poor leaders or undisciplined members. Rather, we agree with him that "the system went out of equilibrium, and the members of the kibbutz could not function anymore as one unit because the interest of the individual belongs to property rights, social security, and freedom and could no longer be integrated into the interests of the kibbutz."[6] Reengineering the system would require an intense process of learning, a high level of self-criticism, and a readiness to break from ideologies that were the the reason why many chose to live on the kibbutz. All this would need to be done under a magnifying glass held by both creditors and suspicious members.

Sometimes the attacks came from within, as demonstrated in a response by Menachem Rosner, a sociologist at the Institute for Research of the Kibbutz and a veteran member of Kibbutz Reshefim, to an article we published in *Dissent*:

> Many of those hurt by the reforms had played central roles in the establishment of the economic foundations of the kibbutz. They are now workers who need a "committee" to represent them in front of the new managers. The latter reached their positions on the basis of general trust. Now they have been leading, as the case of Hatzor illustrates, a stubborn struggle to

introduce "reforms" that reflect their managerial views and ensure their privileges.[7]

Part of the process of creating a new equilibrium between the member and the kibbutz was a change in language. The new vocabulary
represented a fundamental shift from the rights of the community to
the rights of the individual that included issues never dealt with before by the kibbutz, like the concept of inheritance. Kibbutz veterans
often had as much difficulty accepting the new lexicon as the changes
themselves. The traditional branch or sector became a profit center,
or ceased to exist altogether. The *merekez* (coordinator) became a
manager, and work coordinators became "human resource managers," since they no longer placed members in jobs but instead ad-
vised them about market salaries and labor rights. The *hanhala
rachava* (expanded factory committee) was transformed into a board
of directors with a clear mandate of authority and responsibility. As
late as the middle of the 1980s, the factory merekez had to appear
before the general kibbutz meeting for approval to make a business
trip abroad. The factory manager said that on returning home, the
merekez of one kibbutz factory was asked if he "brought back any orders" from customers. He replied that of course he "brought back orders." He brought back the hand phone ordered by Ruchama and the
sneakers ordered by Shlomo. This joke reflected the truth that on almost every trip abroad the manager was asked to bring some member
a particular appliance or pair of shoes or something more easily at-
tainable abroad.[8]

The relationship between the kibbutz and the individual member
changed because of a lack of security about the future. It also changed
as the kibbutz became a more mobile society in response to the need
to find work outside or as small local schools were closed in favor of
larger and better-equipped regional schools. Shlomo Getz, a sociologist at the Institute for Research of the Kibbutz, characterizes this mobility as another way of measuring change on the kibbutz as the
"social borders" of the kibbutz fluctuated.

A member of Kibbutz Gadot (located in the Hula Valley in the
Northern Galilee), Getz described the population of the night and the
population of the morning in his kibbutz. "I feel like a stranger in my
own place. In the morning, about 25 percent of Gadot's members are

going to work outside the kibbutz."[9] This includes kids going to the regional school and their teachers, who are also members. As the cars go out, others are coming in, service workers and other hired workers (approximately one hundred altogether at Gadot) who bring younger children to attend Gadot's kindergarten. In Getz's words, "The kibbutz has completely changed without even needing to pay differential salaries or adopting new norms or without even deciding about the shifts or changes." The conversion of the kibbutz from an integrated society of workplaces, schools, and social services interacting on a daily basis to a bedroom community is a much more visible change than the economic ones that are the primary subject of this book.

In the early years, a day in the life of a kibbutz member revolved around a small apartment, the public dining room, the workplace, the children's house, and the moadon. A story of a day in the lives of Hatzor members Haim and Tzippi Amitai gives a sense of the kibbutz as it once was.[10]

Haim and Tzippi met on the kibbutz in the early 1970s. He made aliyah from Argentina, and she came from a garin of Hashomer Hatzair in Haifa. From day one, Haim worked in agriculture with the field crops. Tzippi worked in the children's house, eventually becoming a kindergarten teacher. Haim got up before sunrise to walk over to the garage where the tractors were parked for his morning coffee before going to plow the fields. At around 7:30, he and his coworkers drove back to the dining room for breakfast.

Tzippi arrived at the kindergarten around 6:30 as the children were waking up. (This was when children were raised collectively and slept in the children's houses where the kindergarten was.) The night guard had finished his last tour of the children's houses at 6 A.M. and wrote notes on a pad about any children who woke up at night for whatever reason. Tzippi checked to see that all was in order and prepared the morning tea and cookies for the children and helped them get dressed before the day's activities. She ate breakfast with her kindergarten children. At 10 every morning she took off a half hour to visit her son, Roy, who was living in another children's house. (The collective child rearing was divided according to age groups. Tzippi and Haim later had three more children.)

Haim returned to the fields after breakfast. Sometime in the morning hours the caretaker of Roy's group would take the children on a *tiul* (walk or trek) through the kibbutz, often to the parking area for the tractors and other agriculture equipment, which the children always loved. Haim would have an opportunity to see Roy on these occasions. At noontime, he returned to the dining room for a hot meal. Tzippi's work week was divided in such a way that one day she worked from 6:30 to noon, took an afternoon rest, and returned to the kindergarten from two to four in the afternoon, before the children went to visit their parents' home. Other days she worked from 6:30 in the morning until two in the afternoon and then put in another hour in the evening when the children were returned to the kindergarten by their parents. She made sure they all went to sleep properly and quietly.

At four in the afternoon, Tzippi and Haim were free to be with Roy (and, later, their other three children) at their home. They played outside, enjoyed a light meal, and were totally devoted to one another. During the harvest season, Tzippi would bring Roy to the fields, and he would join Haim on the tractor.

Around eight in the evening, after Roy went to bed in the children's house, Tzippi and Haim would meet in the dining room together with their friends and fellow members. At least a couple of times a week, Haim would attend an evening meeting of the farm committee or some other social committee of which he was a member. Tzippi, too, served on committees, usually one of the educational committees. Every Saturday evening, the general kibbutz meeting would take place in the moadon and most kibbutz members would attend. The mazkirut prepared this meeting carefully with both economic and social issues of the day to be discussed and voted on.

This may sound quite lackluster to some, merely the lives of provincial farming families. But this was how people lived in one of the most ideological communities that ever existed. Life was simple and quite fulfilling. There was quality time to spend with one's children. Of course, Haim served his thirty to forty days a year in a paratrooper unit of the Israel Defense Forces.[11] As a reserve soldier, he fought in two wars (1967 and 1973). But, Tzippi and Haim didn't have to pay rent or taxes. She was sent by the kibbutz to study education and took periodic refresher coursers. The major intrusion on their lives was a turn serving food or washing dishes in the dining room on a Friday night or Saturday, once a month. In their middle fifties,

Tzippi and Haim were certainly not prepared for the changes they were about to face.

As Shlomo Getz explained, the breakdown of the social borders—when people like Haim and Tzippi began to work outside the kibbutz, when outsiders came in to work the fields and take care of the children, when children from outside began to fill the empty spaces of the children's houses and were educated along with their new kibbutz friends in day schools, when the dining room was closed in the evenings, if not altogether, and meals were taken in the home or at the workplace, and when many of the social services were sourced elsewhere—affected the social structure of the kibbutz, well before differential salaries and other economic changes.

Social borders were broken down because a growing number of kibbutz members were not willing to work in existing employment, primarily in kibbutz factories, agriculture, and service divisions. In addition, the kibbutz's ability to compel a member to accept everything connected with the type and character of his job had weakened or disappeared in the majority of kibbutzim. This resulted in a massive exodus of members to outside jobs and a corresponding rise in hired labor.

However, wanting to begin a second career and being prepared for this challenge are not always the same. Kibbutz members in their forties and fifties began entering the job market at a low level, and their salaries were in accordance with their positions. At first, the kibbutz did not insist on high salaries. It was enough that people were finding jobs.

The 1996 annual report of the Administration for Implementing the Arrangement of the Kibbutzim concluded that "income from members working outside the kibbutz during 1991 to 1994 did not cover the rising costs of hired workers, who occupied the positions left by kibbutz members."[12] In his 1997 lecture at Kibbutz Saad, Halperin was even more categorical about "the collapse of the kibbutz labor system":

> In many kibbutzim we are witnessing a mass desertion by kibbutz members of the workplace and the hiring of outside labor to fill the gap. According to the latest statistics of the Kibbutz Industry Association, in the beginning of the 1990s 30 percent

of the kibbutz workforce consisted of outside workers. Today the number has reached 60 percent. The nominal number of kibbutz members working on kibbutz is decreasing, while the number of hired workers is increasing. This is true not only on the factory floor. Hired managers in every department are now running kibbutz factories. The salaries of kibbutz members working outside the kibbutz don't cover the expense incurred by hiring outside workers. Income levels are going down.

We are witnessing the erosion of the kibbutz work ethic and the collapse of the labor system, both of which are taking their toll on kibbutz life. The kibbutz work ethos was as integral to kibbutz ideology as the ethos of cooperation and equality. Lacking the work ethos, the kibbutz community cannot survive. In Israel as a whole, perhaps 1 to 2 percent of the population can live off its assets without having to work. This is not true of the kibbutz. The kibbutz has lost its capacity to support itself. This problem is even more serious than those I described previously. Low per capita income is an index of the crisis.[13]

Halperin's comments, along with those of the settlement administration, were made in 1996 and 1997. From our interviews in the three kibbutzim, we conclude that the situation has improved somewhat. Kibbutznikim are learning to find suitable positions and to negotiate reasonable salaries. Kibbutz managers are demonstrating greater mobility and assuming positions in neighboring kibbutz industries as well as on newly established boards of directors. Undoubtedly, the linkage between salaries and income has helped motivate people to find better-paying jobs.

Yisrael Tsufim was born on Kibbutz Kiryat Anavim near Jerusalem of parents who came to Israel from Russia. Tsufim, now in his middle forties, was trained in organizational psychology at the University of Sussex in England. He is now a member of Kibbutz Harduf, a unique kibbutz organized around the principles of Austrian philosopher Rudolf Steiner. It is set on a hilltop in the Western Galilee near the cities of Ma'alot and Karmiel. He is one of several change consultants who emerged in the 1990s to guide the kibbutzim in their changes.

According to Tsufim, there are three core models for change in the kibbutz movement—the *meshulav,* the *reshet bitachon,* and the *yishuv kehillati.*[14] We would add a fourth model—the kibbutz that is against change, the *shitufi* or collectivist model that most closely resembles the classic kibbutz. The three kibbutzim we will shortly profile fit loosely within these four models, although, as will be seen, they are incredibly fluid. Only a magician with the ability to foresee the future could accurately say whether or not these models will remain for more than a few years or whether they will morph into each other.

Meshulav, which we translate as "composite," is an amalgamation of components that maintain basic kibbutz values but still change the system. The components include allocation based on seniority, allocation based on a community decision regarding which parts should be privatized and which should be preserved as communal, and allocation derived from differential salaries after progressive taxation.

The second model, reshet bitachon, is easily translated as "a safety net." Here, the system has changed completely, but provisions are made so that no member can end up impoverished or without property. It is based on differential salaries paid directly to the members, with progressive taxation financing membership in the community. Private property (homes) is integral to the system.

The third model, yishuv kehillati, or "collective neighborhood," is almost complete privatization. By privatization we mean that part of the economy that is in the individual's control. For instance, the communal dining room might still be opened—as it is at Hatzor every meal of the week and at Gan Shmuel for most lunches and dinners—but each kibbutz has privatized the meal allowance. (Hatzor has cash registers in the dining room that ring up food against a member's food allowance, and Gan Shmuel instituted a food allowance for each member in 2002. Gesher Haziv has no dining room—all members take care of their own food from their salaries or from the solidarity fund provided for the founding generation who are no longer able to work.)

At the beginning of the twenty-first century, Gan Shmuel is a shitufi kibbutz. In our opinion, it is on the way to becoming a meshulav kibbutz. Hatzor is a meshulav kibbutz on the way to becoming a reshet bitachon kibbutz. And Gesher Haziv is a reshet bitachon kibbutz well on the way to becoming a yishuv kehillati.

According to Tsufim, there are five parameters for evaluating the changes in kibbutz: *takziv* or budget; a connection between salary, social security, and standard of living; collective social services; welfare (pension fund, compensation, and education); and ownership. Tsufim's paradigm is a far cry from the Articles of Association of the 1920s.

In the composite model the personal budget (or allowance) is relatively egalitarian; in the security net there is no budget whatsoever. In both cases, the playing field is leveled by progressive taxes that are collectively decided on by the members—they are much more extensive than those in the most extreme Scandinavian social democratic system.

In the composite model there is no direct connection between salary, social security, and standard of living. Although the system varies from kibbutz to kibbutz, we found that the differentiation in standard of living is, so far, not more than 20 percent. In the security net model there is a direct connection between the three, but once again there is a leveling tax that narrows the differences. In the third model, standards of living could, presumably, differ as widely as elsewhere in the "outside" world.

In the meshulav model there are many collective social services, including health, education, dining room, and laundry. The *kehillah* (or community) of the kibbutz subsidizes all of these. In the reshet bitachon model municipal services are subsidized directly by the members. In the yishuv kehillati model there are basically no collective services, although, as we learned from Gesher Haziv, there will always be a security net for veteran members.

For Tsufim, in the composite model there is no private ownership, while in the security net model, ownership is an important component. But we found this not to be entirely accurate. Even some of the most shitufi kibbutzim, like Gan Shmuel and Ma'agan Michael (located on the coast thirty kilometers south of Haifa), have instituted sleeper clauses for private ownership in the event that the kibbutz undergoes fundamental changes in the future. (This might be considered to be a different kind of security net, designed just in case the socialist experiment really does fail.) And, Hatzor, which is still operating under the meshulav model, is engaged in parcelization of land in advance of eventual home ownership and reshet bitachon.

In 1996 the Administration for Implementing the Arrangement of the Kibbutzim recommended that "the kibbutzim and the kibbutz movement should consider structural changes, including a redefinition of the relationship between the member and the kibbutz, in order to create the conditions needed to emerge from the crisis." Indeed, by the time the report was published, many kibbutzim were well on their way to fundamental change. Five years after Halperin came up with these conclusions, which were bitterly fought by some of leaders of the movement and grudgingly acknowledged by others, the weekly newspaper *Kibbutz* published data gathered by Yeshayahu Gavish, a researcher and organizational consultant to many kibbutzim and himself a member of Kibbutz Yiftach.[15]

Out of 287 kibbutzim, only sixty-eight defined themselves as shitufim. Forty-four were engaged in discussions about fundamental changes, having established a committee to brainstorm different alternatives. Forty kibbutzim had instituted various systems of "rewards and punishments" or bonuses. Forty had instituted the meshulav or composite model (egalitarian allowance, with incentives for work); eighty-six the reshet bitachon or security net model (differential salaries, taxes to the kehillah or community, and *ezra hadadit* [collective responsibility for health, education, and welfare]). And nine had converted to a yishuv kehillati (suburban community) with private salaries and property. No matter how one takes an accounting of the kibbutzim, by 2001 a critical mass of them had passed the stage of no return from a purely collectivist society to a community bringing together various degrees of socialism with private salaries and property.

One reason these models are fluid is that every kibbutz undergoing a process of fundamental change is defined by unique demographics (total population and number of members of working age), economics (extent to which the kibbutz has income-generating businesses— agriculture, industry, services), geography (proximity to the center of the country and real estate value of the land), and leadership (a group of members who have the intellectual ability and the commitment to see through the process).

Among the kibbutzim today, a group of traditionalists have formed an organization—Zerem Shitufi, or collectivist movement. Among the prominent leaders of this movement is Yaakov Gadish.

The Zerem Shitufi movement is also called Kibbutz Tamid. This movement adheres to the notion of *tamid*, which aspires to some form of continuity, although tamid's literal translation is "always." This movement arose in response to an indigenous movement for change within the kibbutzim, which later on retaliated, calling itself "kibbutz atid," meaning "future." The proponents of fundamental changes were reacting to the collapse of the economic infrastructure, the lack of any substantive tools to correct the situation, the departure of the younger generation, and the absence of a pension fund for those in their forties and fifties who were carrying the major burden of the kibbutz.

In response to the demand for fundamental and structural changes, the Zerem Shitufi proposes to narrow the kibbutz principles to three: The member contributes his labor to the kibbutz and receives from the kibbutz according to his needs (pure Marxism). All property, that is, means of production, public buildings, and family homes, belong to the kibbutz. And health, education, and welfare are guaranteed by the kibbutz. Notions of pure self-labor and participatory democracy have been replaced with recognition that certain forms of outside labor and representative democracy are necessary evils.[16] In addition, the Zerem Shitufi makes a distinction between public and private property, so that a move to parcel out homes is well within its current consensus, as demonstrated by the example of Gan Shmuel and Ma'agan Michael.

Leaders like Yaakov Gadish believe that "the kibbutz doesn't depend upon any external situation. If people believe in this system and seriously want to continue living it, they will."[17] These leaders believe the kibbutzim's troubles are a result of a failure of will.

Indeed, the Kibbutz Tamid movement takes a hard-line position when it comes to defining "kibbutz." According to them, if there is any deviation from the above three principles, a kibbutz ceases to be a kibbutz. They have gone as far as to appeal to the Israeli courts to uphold the correct definition of "kibbutz."

One of the notable characteristics of the kibbutzim associated with Kibbutz Tamid is that they are almost all well-off economically, usually as a result of a successful industrial enterprise.[18] Therefore, members have none of the insecurities of kibbutzim floundering in economic crisis. They enjoy high living standards (at least relative to members of other kibbutzim), and they have confidence that their leaders will maintain their ship on an even keel. The leaders of Kibbutz Tamid, many of them former leaders of the Kibbutz Artzi and Takam movements, begrudge the current heads of the recently unified Kibbutz Movement for openly advocating change and for supporting kibbutzim that go through the process.

   The collision of the Kibbutz Tamid and kibbutz atid factions is a bit reminiscent of the old ideological battles over the "correct" definition of "kibbutz" (whether to have one hundred, three hundred, or a thousand members, collective or private child rearing, an agricultural economy alone or also industry). One might expect a dwindling community to spend more of its energies searching out commonality and pluralism in order to recreate a kibbutz movement with both continuity and a future, rather than parsing differences along ideological fault lines.

   As change occurs, the public debate intensifies inside the kibbutzim (including in the two kibbutz weeklies, *Kibbutz* and *Daf Ha-Yarok*, where reports from the field and editorial comments are the regular sustenance of concerned members from both sides) and among the general Israeli public. Leaders of the Kibbutz Movement are regular targets, hit either for doing too much to promote change or for doing too little, depending on who is doing the shooting.

   However, Gavri Bar Gil, who became co-leader of the Kibbutz Movement in 2001 and who comes from the Kibbutz Artzi Federation, understands that the changed atmosphere means a changed kibbutz movement:

> People will make changes whether or not the movement makes a formal decision. As the gap grew, the movement became irrelevant. The process of change inside each kibbutz is taking place. Some don't want to face it, but it's true. The question is will the movement help or not? The kibbutz movement must function as a pluralistic movement, otherwise it will be irrelevant. Besides, each kibbutz will do what's good for itself anyway. Kibbutz Artzi has to build tools for the classic kibbutzim and for the change kibbutzim. I truly believe that the only way to survive is to make changes. The movement has no redlines. There is a connection between work and money today. We are moving from total equality to basic equality.[19]

One reason that the various models of change are morphing into one another has to do with the timing of the change. Those kibbutzim that made changes before the end of the 1990s had no choice but to experiment. They had no new kibbutz bible to follow but, rather, had to create their own models. They were constrained by financial failures, internal social unrest, and an extreme lack of what is called in Yiddish *firgun*, or equanimity, for those undertaking the burden of leading the kibbutz out of its desperate situation.

Following a decade of searching in a wilderness of economic and social ideas, kibbutzim are increasingly moving straight to the reshet bitachon model, where members largely take control of their own lives and where there are limited mutually agreed-on responsibilities toward the community. While it took a kibbutz like Hatzor seven years to reach the composite meshulav model, a kibbutz like Ramot Menashe (where Kibbutz Movement leader Gavri Bar Gil was born) voted in the spring of 2002, after a recent decision to embark on change, to move directly to the reshet bitachon model. Indeed, when each kibbutz makes changes, new versions of one of these models is born. As the need for change becomes a matter of consensus, the questions asked are more how? and when? than why? In this sense, the painful process undergone by Gesher Haziv and Hatzor should make it easier for other kibbutzim who are now beginning structural change. But the change process probably will still be difficult—even with the collective learning curve—because each kibbutz is a world unto itself and so can only partially learn from the experience of others.

All change is dependent on the precarious nature of the economy of each individual kibbutz. How each kibbutz adapts to one of these basic models also has to do with its own financial situation. If a kibbutz begins the change process when the community is already in financial distress, the nature of the change will be different from those made by a community that has the luxury to make changes in a more generous, thought-out fashion.

Gesher Haziv, for example, had to make radical changes because its income was less than its debt. The desperate situation in which the kibbutz found itself forced a quick phasing out of the kibbutz. Hatzor, although in financial trouble that was nearly as bad as Gesher Haziv's, had the foresight to make changes in time to retool its economy and increase its income, while reinventing the kibbutz. Gan Shmuel, still resisting major change, has the luxury to resist, although social forces may overtake the lack of economic incentives.

In that each kibbutz is a unique case, the narratives of three kibbutzim—Gesher Haziv, Gan Shmuel, and Hatzor—cannot begin to describe the entire gamut of change in kibbutzim today. Rather, we hope to tell a story of the process, the trials and tribulations of a struggle to create a society not from *b'rashit* ("in the beginning, God created . . .") but, rather, to reinvent it in midcourse, with the idealistic founders still very present and the youngest generations sitting on the fence watching and waiting before they decide whether to remain in their homes or move on. We hope to do so by choosing three kibbutzim that are as representative as possible of the Israel of the new century.

Indeed, the catalysts for change are not university radicals but middle-aged veterans who tried doing kibbutz by the textbook until it was almost too late. These narratives catch each kibbutz at a particular stage of its history: during an economic crisis with no light at the end of the tunnel or with relative prosperity and security; with a cohesive group of leaders or as a divisive gathering of highly capable individuals; located on the periphery near Israel's violent borders or surrounded by thriving industries and sprawling suburbia. Each is just a story of a small community, once the vanguard of socialist Zionism and now existing in a normalizing nation-state of changing priorities and changing values.

We found that our interviews interestingly reflected the way in which each kibbutz faced change. Despite our asking the same set of questions to each person we interviewed on each kibbutz, we got very different answers. The leaders of Gesher Haziv have tried to make an organized retreat from collective ownership. Hatzor is trying to reinvent itself. And Gan Shmuel is attempting to preserve the traditional kibbutz values.

# GESHER HAZIV

## A Kibbutz Privatizes

Just as in the past, solutions have not been influenced by the particular composition and atmosphere of Gesher Haziv, but have reflected the trends in the country and in the kibbutz movement; so it will be in the future. The next decade will, no doubt, bring its own set of new problems. The kibbutz has, since its inception, been a dynamic form, constantly adapting itself to meet changing conditions, as will Gesher Haziv, being part of the kibbutz movement. In some things it will probably be the initiator and forerunner, and in others it will be a follower.

—Menucha Kraines, 1959

Gesher Haziv is a forty-five minute drive north of Haifa, Israel's third largest city, on the main highway that runs parallel to the Mediterranean. The highway is increasingly clogged as a result of suburban sprawl. You first pass through Akko, a mixed Jewish and Arab city. Between Akko and Nahariya there are high rises, low rises, shopping malls, fast food outlets, and factories sprouting up amid bits of a Roman aqueduct that runs between Kibbutz Shomrat and Kibbutz Lochmei Hagetaot. Nahariya is experiencing a building boom to accommodate its new residents, who are mostly from the former Soviet Union. There are kibbutzim, moshavim, and a scattering of Arab villages, which light up the night like beads on a necklace. The mountains of Lebanon and the cliffs of Rosh Haniqra loom before you. North of Nahariya, near the popular Achziv Beach and just ten kilometers from the Lebanese border, you reach Kibbutz Gesher Haziv.

By any estimation, the kibbutzim in this part of Israel are considered on the periphery. While malls filled with triplexes and superstores pop up along the highway (sometimes owned and operated by kibbutzim and moshavim), the close proximity to Lebanon means that any time there are hostilities across the border this population is primed for katyusha missile attacks. The Club Med at Achziv Beach, a popular resort along the Mediterranean just north of Nahariya, was hit twice by katyushas, both times in the dining room, an offense the chef was rumored to take personally. Members of Kibbutz Gesher Haziv spent time in bomb shelters as recently as the autumn of 2000. Facing intermittent dangers for much of the last three decades, the only perks (if you can call them such) offered to kibbutzim, moshavim, and towns and cities on the periphery are certain tax breaks and government incentives for investment.

Summers are hot up here. In August, it's difficult to be outside in the middle of the day. The humid air feels so close you can hardly breathe, and sometimes even a swim in the glistening Mediterranean doesn't offer necessary relief—plus you may have to dodge the medusas (jellyfish) that abound in the summer months. The winters bring the rains (except in the case of drought as there has been for the last several years). But, to be sure, the land in the Western Galilee is also painfully and ruggedly beautiful.

In the summer of 2001, a year after our first visit, we arrive at a roadside stand where a handful of reserve soldiers in their thirties and forties sit sipping espresso and eating pastry, their guns by their sides and their jeeps parked outside. The café is next to a gas station and small supermarket, 51 percent of which is owned by Kibbutz Gesher Haziv, at whose foot this tiny shopping complex lies.

The first thing a visitor notices after driving up the hill to the kibbutz parking lot (passing a factory and a school on the way) is the stunning lack of people. Most kibbutzim have people milling around the machane—what to Americans would be considered the town square—but not at Gesher Haziv. It's possible to walk around for as much as a half hour before seeing even one person. In the summer, that surely is partly a consequence of the extreme heat—after all, the houses and other structures have people inside them, busy with their lives. But, it is something more. It's a sign that Gesher Haziv has

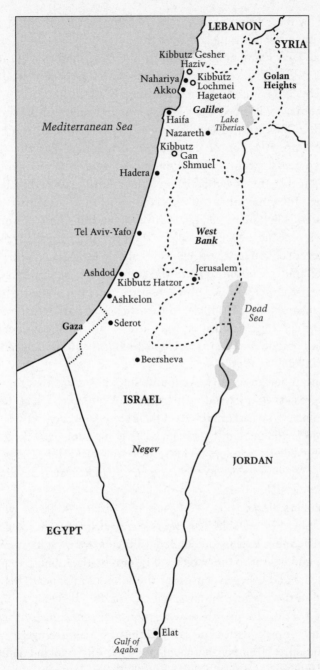

Map of Israel with Gesher Haziv, Hatzor, and Gan Shmuel

shifted its life as a community from a communal to a private one. People get up in the morning and drive their cars out of the kibbutz to go to work. They come home at night to their tiny homes and eat with their families. The communal dining room has been closed since 1999. This is a community in transition.

Gesher Haziv has become synonymous in Israel with kibbutz privatization. This struggling kibbutz was one of the first to begin a near complete privatization of its communal holdings. Early on in the change process, twenty kibbutz members were so distressed by the transition that they even petitioned the courts against the changes. Although the government never acted on it, the petition received a lot of press. Obviously, change is difficult, and this kind of immense change is especially so. For people in their seventies and eighties, who have never cooked for themselves or balanced a checkbook let alone arranged transportation to go to the store (under the classic system, the kibbutz store provided all necessities and even some frills), this can be intimidating. For those in their fifties and sixties, the change is also unnerving. It's difficult for those who have always depended on the kibbutz to find them work and provide for all their needs to adjust to the new reality.

Yet, from our interviews, we found that allegations that members' fates were cast to the wind were baseless. There is a social safety net for members who can't make it on their own. However, only one person, who is 100 percent handicapped, is being supported by the kibbutz. No one else has applied for it. Everyone else who can't work or who is of pension age receives *bituach leumi* (national social security) plus some pension money from the kibbutz.

Pensioners are getting 3,400 shekels a month, 2,000 of which is from Gesher Haziv itself. The rest is social security from the government. The kibbutz pension contribution gets drawn from members' salaries and is sent to the bank each month by the kibbutz to pay for health care and other expenses for the kibbutz member. This is enthroned in the kibbutz by-laws, which can only be changed by a 90 percent vote of the members who vote. Pensioners also have their own club for gymnastics and other activities. This arrangement will continue until 2011, so that people who are fifty-five and older now will be included.

Today, Gesher Haziv is well on its way toward privatization—that's true. Most of what remains communal is their debt—their financial debt and their debt to each other through a minimal social safety net. They are closer already to a kehillah, or community model, than to a classic kibbutz. They would be familiar to Americans as something similar to a planned community or even a small town or township where services are provided by local taxes. Everything from housing to health care that was previously communal has been transferred, or is in the process of being transferred, to the individual's responsibility. Members now earn outside salaries and keep almost all of their earnings.

But, it wasn't for lack of trying to hold on to its traditional ways that Gesher Haziv made the changes it did. True, it was never as rigidly ideological as either Hatzor or Gan Shmuel; in fact, it was less ideological than most kibbutzim, but the founders and subsequent members of the kibbutz did join out of socialist belief, a belief they thought useful—perhaps necessary—to adapt in a pragmatic manner, even decades ago.

The current process of change at Gesher Haziv began in 1996, although discussion began as early as 1986 among some members, in that by the 1980s the kibbutz was essentially bankrupt and living on loans. They had no choice but to take drastic measures.

As Aharon Sharif, the community financial manager, told us bluntly in the summer of 2000, "This particular community was not able to continue on the basis of the classic kibbutz."

In 1996, the kibbutz separated its community from its economy. Similar actions were taken in almost all of the kibbutzim in Israel beginning in the early 1990s. These actions were based on the new assumption that all business enterprises should be organized according to criteria of profit and loss alone, while the community has social, welfare, and cultural priorities that cannot (and should not) necessarily be measured monetarily, although they still must be budgeted with complete accountability. Gesher Haziv created separate bank accounts for all the profit centers or departments of the kibbutz, and each economic branch paid rent to the kibbutz as a whole. Each member received an internal bank account, but it was almost immediately frozen because of the debt crisis. (In May 2000, the account funds were released to the members.)

By 1998, Gesher Haziv had established a pension fund and differential salaries. The pension and internal unemployment insurance were intentionally similar to those offered by the State of Israel, so that the kibbutz could "behave like all citizens of Israel," in the words of one member. Gesher Haziv, unlike most kibbutzim, always allowed members to have private money. Outside funds, or private monies, were left untouched by the collective.

Some kibbutzim, whether for lack of entrepreneurship, managerial skills, or bad luck, were never able to succeed financially. In these cases, financial woes inevitably trickled into social woes that undermined the stability of the community. This was true of Gesher Haziv. Under such circumstances it would have been irresponsible for the core leaders at a kibbutz like Gesher Haziv not to act—and act in an economically radical fashion.

Those in the press or in the kibbutz movement who have opposed the change at Gesher Haziv, arguing that the kibbutz has reneged on its commitments to its members (especially its elder population), should note the current economic numbers. In 2001, for the first time since its establishment as a kibbutz, Gesher Haziv turned a profit—and dedicated most of it to care for the founding generation and to an economic safety net for those members who can't adequately support themselves.

Gesher Haziv didn't make these changes based on a well-thought-out plan or a specific ideology. They didn't have that luxury. Their struggle was much more utilitarian and pragmatic. Had they not made these changes, it's likely that the entire community would have remained bankrupt, unable to pay pensions or to provide the most basic services such as health coverage. Any member who could afford to leave would have, and those who remained would have been nearly destitute, saddled with a big debt in their declining years.

Riffi Schlossberg is the leader for change at Gesher Haziv. A forty-something, sharp, intense, pragmatic, striking, dark-haired sabra, she married a *ben kibbutz*[1] in 1977, a member of the large Schlossberg clan of three brothers and their families, along with the parents. The Schlossberg parents were founding members hailing from the Habonim youth movement in Canada. It was under her reign as *mazkira*, or general secretary, that the kibbutz made its major changes. Today, Schlossberg is part of a trend among her generation of kibbutzniks. She is a management consultant, working with other kibbutzim to implement their changes by using her experience at Gesher Haziv.

"A vision of the future didn't bring us to where we are," she told us when we visited her in the summer of 2001. "We are coping with where we are. We would like to be like Kibbutz Be'eri [a rich kibbutz in the Negev that has avoided making changes, perhaps because of its very successful printing business and financial well-being], but we are not." She, however, made a point to let us know that "by the way, in Be'eri there are also fewer young people. Even there, they are beginning small, slow changes.

"My preference would have been to remain a kibbutz, but I began to see that the majority of the people who live in this community are not going to be those who want a kibbutz. I would like to find something that will work with the problems and the realities of this place." And, that is what she and the others are doing.

Gesher Haziv was established in 1949 with a garin, a group, from Kibbutz Bet Ha'Arava, a kibbutz in the Arava Desert near the Dead Sea that was evacuated and left for the Jordanians after Israel's War of Independence and the drawing of the 1948 Armistice borders. Half went to Kibbutz Kabri, which sits directly adjacent to Gesher Haziv, half to Gesher Haziv. The Bet Ha'Arava group was made up of German refugees from Nazi Germany and other Jews who lived in Israel before 1948. The Habonim groups from Canada and the United States joined them shortly after the war. The kibbutz became a favorite stop for Habonim youth groups, something that added to their absorption pool through the years.

There were 182 members of Gesher Haziv in the summer of 2001. At its peak, there were 250. One-third of the membership is of retirement age. Of the 130 working members, fifty are between fifty and sixty years old, eighty are between thirty and fifty. Today, over seventy members work outside of the kibbutz, and their income provides for themselves and for the modest safety net for all established by the kibbutz. In 1997, only 46 percent worked outside; by 1999, this had increased to 54 percent. In the classic kibbutz model, the ideal was for almost everyone to work inside the kibbutz, though "outside" sometimes included a kibbutz-owned factory located in the regional industrial zone or a teacher in a kibbutz regional school that happened to be located on kibbutz property. In earlier days, the vast majority of members worked inside Gesher Haziv. Gesher Haziv is a good example of Shlomo Getz's description of the "night and day" populations at his kibbutz, Gadot. Even if Gesher Haziv hadn't privatized to the extent it did, the fact that so many of its members—essentially all of its working-age members—work outside the kibbutz would have forced a monumental change on the kibbutz.

Aliza Elkon was one of the first members. She arrived at Gesher Haziv from Jersey City as part of a Habonim group in 1949, just two days after the kibbutz was established. Instead of an espresso bar and shopping mart on the corner, there were Quonset huts at the entrance left over from the previous inhabitants (the site had been a British army camp). Living in tents, they set about building housing and common spaces. Aliza was nineteen when she arrived. The Americans and Canadians merged with the German group from Bet Ha'Arava, although to this day, the Americans call the Germans "yekkes," a Yiddish term for German Jews that invokes the sense of superiority that the German Jews project toward others.[2]

The first houses built by the kibbutz were the children's houses, "more wooden bungalows than houses," as Aliza Elkon recalls. Even with the communal children's houses, Gesher Haziv was one of the first kibbutzim to allow children to sleep at night with their parents. Soon after they could afford it, the kibbutz veered away from communal child rearing. The predominance of North Americans on the kibbutz won out over the kibbutz ideology of communal housing. Even the German Jews on the kibbutz agreed to it. It was one of the ways in which Gesher Haziv exhibited individualistic tendencies earlier than other kibbutzim.

Another example of individualism on the kibbutz was the lack of strictness when it came to pooling private funds. In contrast to Gan Shmuel and Hatzor, for example, the norm at Gesher Haziv was not to put personal monies into the communal pot. (Although some kibbutzim were stricter about this than others, one result of the changes on the kibbutzim is that the black-market-style existence of private monies that were supposed to be pooled collectively was finally brought into the open.) Additionally, the *renta*, or remuneration monies paid by the German government to Holocaust survivors, was not pooled. These substantial funds, when added to the common pool, aided some kibbutzim in strengthening their financial status (for instance, at Kibbutz Kvutzat Yavne, the home of Zeram Shitufi leader Yaacov Gadish). But at Gesher Haziv it was accepted practice to keep out the funds for personal use instead of putting them in the collective draw.

Dancing on the kibbutz in the late 1940s or early 1950s. (Photo courtesy of Kibbutz Gesher Haziv.)

Peter Braun, who manages the kibbutz factory, Polyziv, which designs, develops, and manufactures plastic pallets, told us: "When I got here [from the United States] in 1969, I didn't have any great illusions that Kibbutz Gesher Haziv was in the forefront of the kibbutz movement either in ideology or economic success, but it was a very easy place for us to come into, and the framework was a compromise that also made it easy for us to come in." When we visited in July 2001, Polyziv was being sold to a German company. By the beginning of 2002, the sale had been completed. The money was used to settle much of Gesher Haziv's debt as part of the kibbutzim settlement arrangement.

Peter Braun told us:

The kids were already living at home until age thirteen or fourteen, although, theoretically, I was in favor of kids not being at home. There were lots of Americans from an older generation. When we came, we asked questions like what we should bring or shouldn't bring, and they said, don't worry. So, there was a gray area of equality. Although there were no televisions and no private cars, there were more gray areas than at Hatzor, I'm sure. People had personal possessions, and people lived with it. The compromise between ideology and getting along was about making life livable. There were divisions between the Israelis [of German descent] and the Americans, but in general we were growing. There was immigration with more families coming in. We grew from about 160 to 200 in the period of 1968 to 1970, 1972. This was big growth then. It leveled off in the 1980s.

Braun, who as factory manager now earns one of the highest salaries on the kibbutz (a fact mentioned to us by several others we interviewed who resent the unequal salaries in the new system), was born in Chicago in 1946 to a nonreligious, non-Zionist family. His parents were American leftists who owned a thriving family business. He joined Habonim when he was ten, continuing in summer camp through the Habonim "workshop" (a year in Israel set up to encourage aliyah among the Habonim young people). After returning to the States for a degree from Roosevelt University in Chicago and postgraduate work in history, he worked for Habonim and the student Zionist movement in the United States, while being marginally active in the antiwar movement. In 1969, he came to Israel, eventually marrying a woman who was born in Israel of American parents. In 1970, he joined Gesher Haziv as part of a garin from the United States. "I always considered myself a socialist, and coming here was very important—the socialist part probably as important as the Zionist part," he told us.

Braun continued:

When we got here, coming from Chicago and settling here in the far north, it felt more isolated. I remember that after being here a year, we went out to Nahariya to barbecue meat on the beach with another couple because we were hungry for meat.[3]

There was nothing I wasn't prepared for. I adjusted fairly easily, learned the language, worked in field crops, and loved it. That's what I wanted to do. The first years on the kibbutz were everything they were supposed to be, even though we came from a house to live in one small room. It didn't seem to bother us. I worked in agriculture until 1979, for about ten years. Then I became *merekez meshek* [farm manager] in 1979.

We always had a guesthouse in addition to agriculture, and in

1976 we started a plastics factory. [The guesthouse was closed in the early 1996, because of unrecoverable financial losses.]

We have capital today, Kibbutz Gesher Haziv has capital, but the community doesn't have the will to invest the capital in a factory with a record of losses.[4] The real value of the factory to us today is that it will go against two-thirds of our debt, which is about 40 million shekels, and make the debt management of Gesher Haziv a piece of cake.

These are the types of choices faced by kibbutzim today. To compare Gesher Haziv's decision with Hatzor's, for instance, Gesher Haziv is choosing to live on the salaries generated by the individuals who live there, which means a relatively low standard of living. Hatzor has decided to raise the standard of living for everyone who is a kibbutz member through the capital investment of their main moneymaker, the soybean extraction factory, Solbar. Hatzor's members enjoy a higher standard of living than those at Gesher Haziv. Gan Shmuel, which has more collective wealth than Hatzor and much more than Gesher Haziv had when it was incorporated collectively, chooses to pool more of its wealth to benefit the community rather than the individual. (Although, as we shall soon see, there are rumblings among the members of Gan Shmuel who desire a higher personal standard of living.)

Gesher Haziv is a community that no longer has the will to develop a sustaining communal economy. As Braun explained, "Certainly part of the change in Gesher Haziv is that in the long term people feel that they will be either owners of rental property or of pieces of the gas station."

Gesher Haziv is banking on any new revenues, separate from outside salaries, to come from properties on their land that they rent out—everything from the dining hall to the swimming pool to the empty tiny houses of former kibbutz members. The most interesting venture is using kibbutz land to build a new neighborhood of single-family homes called Ziv Estates that is open to nonmembers. It's not too much of an exaggeration to say that the fate of the almost two hundred kibbutz members is tied up with a plot of land and the homes that may be built there, although the exact value of this project remains to be determined.

The Israeli laws relating to kibbutzim and land are among the biggest bones of contention in the struggle to revamp Israel's collectives.[5] However, because of Gesher Haziv's status of being on the periphery, it has been able to move forward more quickly with renting out its uninhabited houses, and even with the plan to build the new housing development on kibbutz land. Kibbutzim in parts of the country where land is more valuable (the Tel Aviv surburbs for instance) have been stymied in the courts as a result of political opposition to their transforming agricultural lands into income-generating residential and commercial real estate.

"There is certainly less economic return on real estate in the north than in the center of the country," Braun said, "but the value we have to pay for land to the land authority is zero, and that makes a big difference." As he talks, he points to a trailer outside the office window. "That's supposed to be the new neighborhood of two hundred houses," he tells us. He hopes that people want the quality of life that can be found in the far north, away from the city. By early 2002, the kibbutz had already sold sixty plots. This was the critical mass needed for the Israel Land Authority to approve the entire project and use the revenue to erase all of Gesher Haziv's debt.

The group that led the change at Gesher Haziv dreams that their children will want to move back home to live in the new neighborhood, but Peter Braun is pessimistic. "I'll be surprised if 20 percent will be sons and daughters of Gesher Haziv," he sighs. "I have three children. A daughter in Tel Aviv works with computers; one son is in the center of the country; and my youngest son works in a factory in Ma'alot. He may be interested in buying something here rather than in Ma'alot. But the older kids want to be where the action is, not here."

Riffi Schlossberg has similar wishes but is realistic: "The kids don't want to buy in. We don't have something to offer them. Kibbutz Be'eri or Kibbutz Ma'agan Michael [both wealthy] has something to offer them, but we don't."

But she is optimistic about new families coming to the community to live among them:

> In ten years, Gesher Haziv will have another two hundred families here in the neighborhood. It will be a very good place to live. Our location is good—by the sea, by a city. The municipality is

talking about building a small airport that will connect us to the center of the country. Our *moatza* [regional council] is working very hard to increase population of the kibbutzim in the area.

There are over half a dozen kibbutzim and moshavim nearby; several are very wealthy—Lochmei Hagetaot,[6] Regba, and Shavei Zion. These last two are moshav shitufim, cooperatives that are similar to kibbutzim, all of which are privatizing. Regba is building a big shopping mall of superstores on the main highway, and Shavei Zion has an extablished adjacent neighborhood that is one of the richest in Israel.[7] It's likely that Gesher Haziv's new neighborhood will draw former kibbutz members and the children of kibbutz members in the surrounding region who want to be close to their parents.

Listening to Riffi Schlossberg talking in the kibbutz office, with the mountains of Lebanon glistening in the distance through the window, it's easy to imagine—for a moment—that when peace comes to the region Gesher Haziv could, indeed, be sitting on valuable property. A municipal airport and a superhighway could make the kibbutz more accessible not only to the center of Israel but also to Lebanon and even Damascus. But with a regional peace an illusive dream for the moment, Gesher Haziv's lot is still a difficult one, despite the optimism of its leadership. While some people choose to live in private homes in the northwestern Galilee because of its beauty, without peace with Lebanon and Syria, it is not as desirable a location as it could be.

The kibbutz is in need of young blood. As Schlossberg explains, "We have a kindergarten here, but we don't have children."[8] The school building sits across from the factory as you drive through the kibbutz entrance. It's not simply that Gesher Haziv doesn't attract new members—although it doesn't. As with other kibbutzim, once the process of change started, Gesher Haziv stopped taking new members. "We don't know what being a member means," Schlossberg laments. "It's a totally different meaning now on both sides—the responsibility we have to members and they have to the community."

Indeed, this is a paradox faced by most kibbutzim. What do you do about a new generation of young people, even your own kids, when you are still trying to determine your own identity as a community? Tell them to go away and put their lives on hold until a decision is made? This existential question is being addressed by nearly all kib-

Typical housing at Kibbutz Gesher Haziv in 2002. Pictured here are four units, like a garden apartment complex. (Photo courtesy of Kibbutz Gesher Haziv.)

butzim—rich or poor, traditional or in a process of change. According to Natan Tal, the secretary general of the sector of the Takam kibbutz movement to which Gesher Haziv belongs, in the last ten years, 14,000 sons and daughters of Takam kibbutzim didn't come back.[9] It is not simply that the kibbutz is not attractive to the younger generation. The kibbutz itself, in a quandary over its own future, doesn't know how to absorb a new generation.

In a poor kibbutz like Gesher Haziv, where most of the remaining communal apparatus exists to dissolve past debt, it's hard to lure new members anyway. "No one will live under the living standard we decided for ourselves," Schlossberg explains.

Gesher Haziv's standard of living was always low. In the years when there was general scarcity in the country, no one noticed it, but as Israel's economy expanded and the general standard of living rose, the kibbutz members realized theirs wasn't rising with it. By the 1980s, they were realizing that their standard of living was not as high as that of other people in Israel with comparable interests and education. And, while some kibbutzim in a similar situation were willing to go deeper and deeper into debt to finance their collectivity, Gesher Haziv wasn't.

Brochure advertising the new Kibbutz Gesher Haziv neighborhood, Ziv Estates. The headline reads: "Ziv Estates: Choose a Home of Your Own." Each model is named after a different bird. (Courtesy of Kibbutz Gesher Haziv.)

Braun talked about the personal choices that he and others faced:

The standard of living on the kibbutz went down steadily from early 1980 on. Everybody else in Israel was on a fairly rapid upwards spiral, and in general we were static or going down—from food to education to, of course, pocket money and cars. We were able to send our children to university, but it was a hard row to hoe; it was always very difficult.

Until 1986, we were still heating water by lighting a kerosene water heater in the bathroom. So, the changes in the 1980s were not about ideology but about money, nothing else.

I didn't think about leaving—maybe it was inertia, thinking things will get better. But the bottom line is I want to be a kibbutznik. I was probably afraid that I wouldn't get along outside the kibbutz. But I went through different phases. I actually did have a job lined up outside and just at the last minute decided not to go. My wife said, "Get up and go." In my opinion, if we hadn't made changes at the end of the 1990s, we would have left. I just couldn't see any future for the kibbutz. It was just so bleak. I was ready. That would be it.

Forty-six-year-old Asher Koren is a ben kibbutz. His father, David, a former Knesset member, was an original Gesher Haziv founder from Bet Ha'Arava. Koren's wife is from the United States. She came to the kibbutz as a volunteer and today teaches in the regional college. They have three children. The oldest is fourteen. Koren echoes Braun's words:

When I was growing up here it was a different period of time. It was a new country. You always had hope that things will get better. Israel of the 1970s is not the Israel of today.

It was very good growing up here, the best childhood. It was a great time in Israel, not just on the kibbutz. . . . Gesher Haziv was never in a good situation, but I came to the realization in 1996 or 1997 that we needed to change. My father lived here for fifty-three years. But I was close to leaving before the changes.

Koren managed the turkey farm after graduation from the Technion in Haifa (a university often called "Israel's MIT"), where he studied computers. Today, he works in software development.

Koren, Braun, Schlossberg, and others—twenty families in total—
came together in 1996 to elect Riffi Schlossberg mazkira, having decided that change was necessary for the future of the kibbutz—and
for their own willingness to remain on the kibbutz with their families. Koren puts it most starkly: "I would risk my family by staying
here. There was no pension for the members. If I stayed two or three
years more, we would have been completely bankrupt, and we would
have had nothing."

Not all kibbutzim undergo change under the threat of social dis-
ruption and mass departures. In Hatzor, for instance, this wasn't the
case. But this turmoil is symptomatic of kibbutzim that are in the
kind of financial and social distress faced by Gesher Haziv.

Koren continued:

> Riffi thought she was going to lead a long process. She started
> with an organizational structure with a flowchart. When we saw
> the flowchart we decided that we weren't going to have change.
> The process would be too long. We said, this is not what we
> mean—we need major change now, otherwise, we will have
> nothing to do with it.

Asher Koren was impatient with the way the process began at
Gesher Haziv. But from what we learned about changes in the kibbutzim we are convinced that unless the organizational structure is
transformed in a methodical way, the other necessary changes can't
be made.

Even before Riffi Schlossberg's election as mazkira, the kibbutz had
tried to reorganize some of its economy by bringing in an advisor—
economist Yeshiyahu Gavish—from the United Kibbutz Movement.
The advisor didn't work out, but he did jump-start the process of
change. The kibbutz no longer found work for people; they were responsible for finding their own work. The definition of work changed.
As Peter Braun put it, "We got certain days off like every worker in
the world." (Kibbutz members used to work without traditional days
off.) And the kibbutz began on a route that Gavish had rejected. Braun
continued:

> We got together and he said, "I think you are on the wrong track,
> and I won't work with you. You're on the way to wage differ-

entials and breaking up the kibbutz framework." He didn't want
to go in that direction, so he left. The kibbutz members found
other consultants to work with and were well on their way to
change.

Today the atmosphere is civil. All the years we have lived
here, people have been basically civil with each other. There
haven't been large fights between groups that have polarized the
kibbutz, like on other kibbutzim.

At Gesher Haziv, there are very few conflicts. We had an *asafa*
[general assembly], but few attended. But most of the important
votes we do and did are by ballot, so everyone votes.

Asher Koren told us that just before the change, his family went on
*chofesh* from the kibbutz "as a way of dealing with it. We thought to
go out for a year. We got permission, and we started to look for places
to move. If the change hadn't started, we would have left. We had already decided it." Israelis translate "chofesh" as "vacation." In this
context, it's not a vacation but more like a sabbatical from the kibbutz. Many kibbutz members who are frustrated by the lack of change
on their kibbutz, but aren't ready to make the extreme move of leaving the kibbutz, take chofesh as a way of dealing with it, hoping that
when they return things will be different.

For the sixty-year-olds on the kibbutz, it wasn't so cut and dried.
Batya and Uri Amitai both came to the kibbutz in the 1950s. Their
daughter is married to Yehuda Etzman, the former kibbutz *gizbar*
(treasurer), who is now in charge of developing real estate ventures on
the kibbutz. Their family is four generations strong at Gesher Haziv;
Uri's eighty-seven-year-old father also lives on the kibbutz, as do
Batya and Uri's grandchildren.

Batya Amitai reminisces with us about the good old days. She is un-
perturbed about the poverty but has other concerns:

In the 1950s, there was a nicer atmosphere, a feeling of the tribe
that we were all together. The standard of living was lower. I
lived in a wooden tent. There was no water. We had to walk to
the communal shower. There were two sides—one for men, one
for women.

I can do anything I want now. I don't want much. I don't want to travel. We buy each other presents sometimes, sure, and buy presents for our grandchildren. I never had so much money as I have now. But money isn't everything, is it?

I miss the communal cultural activities. We have no more combined Pesach anymore.[10] We have a big family here, but what about those who don't have family? It's all fallen apart. The cultural activities are getting a little better again, but I miss all that. The shinui changed the combined celebrations.

Batya Amitai's lament for the loss of communally celebrated holidays, collective cultural activities, and, indeed, the general communal kibbutz spirit is typical of those on all the kibbutzim who are hesitant about the change. They tend to blame the change for the communal drop off; but those who have embraced the change see it the other way. They see the change partly as a result of the collapse of the communal infrastructure and the increasing privatization of people's personal and social spheres.

In any case, cultural and social activities are beginning again. In today's privatized universe, volunteers take it upon themselves to organize what used to be done as a matter of course on the kibbutz. A cultural committee—to plan everything from bar mitzvahs to seders to Friday night activities—used to be as much a part of the kibbutz infrastructure as a work committee. Today, social and culture committees have to be organized and maintained at the initiative of a member, since they are no longer mandated by the community.

Uri Amitai studied at a vocational school and spent his years on the kibbutz working in agriculture, until the 1970s when he began working in the factory. When the factory was sold, he was laid off. He wasn't the only one to lose his job. The factory no longer employed as many kibbutz members as possible; rather, it only employed the number of people necessary for production.

Uri and Batya tried to resist the change. They loved the old-style kibbutz and wanted it to remain. At first, Uri was resentful:

Families who weren't born here called for change. It was very difficult for me to accept it. The consultants took a lot of money. But it took the farm manager from Beit Oren to show us what we were living from. I was impressed, but not convinced, by change. But Yisrael Tsufim and the managers put the reality in front of the kibbutz, what we had, what we were living from.[11]

Batya elaborates, "It was a utopia of fools. We would never have gone so deep into debt, if we had known. The change was inevitable, and we still have debts, but the fact that each person is living according to his means is a good thing."

Batya and Uri Amitai kept hesitating when we talked to them about their pension, either unsure of what is due them or nervous about finding out. Indeed, we discovered that people aren't sure of their rights under the new system. It is unclear exactly why. It could be because they are afraid to find out. It could be the fear of the new. Or, perhaps, it is simply that they don't believe whatever they are told— they don't believe that monies will be there for their future. The irony is that under the old system, what the kibbutzniks didn't know didn't harm them. Their community could fall deeper and deeper into debt, but as long as the social contract between the kibbutzim and the country was intact, there would always be money for tomorrow. With that contract broken, and with the privatization making clear that there isn't much money to go around, many kibbutz members feel unsure of their future, no matter what the reality.

Even though we were told in no uncertain terms that there is a guaranteed pension for the founding generation, negative newspaper stories to the contrary created a perception among anxious kibbutz members on other kibbutzim that the Gesher Haziv pensioners were left wanting. This is important because at a time of radical change in the kibbutzim—and with no existing road map—one kibbutz looks to another for ideas on how to change. Gossip and rumors add to an already unsettled atmosphere.

Neither Batya nor Uri Amitai appeared bitter. Rather, they grieve for the old days, missing the communal spirit evocative of an earlier Israel. Batya said:

The bad thing is that we're not a commune anymore in terms of the feeling of the people. Everything else was trampled in the way. People work very hard and have time for their family, and that's understandable, but it's not a communal family feeling anymore. It's not what I came here for, but I'm not going anywhere. At age sixty-seven, can I start somewhere new? And I like it here with my children and grandchildren.

One change instituted by the Amitais' son-in-law was a personal credit card for each member. There was an expectation that something like a credit card—with a personal credit line—could stave off massive changes on the kibbutz. But, since the credit line had to be secured by the kibbutz, there was never enough money to go around, and the urge for a raised standard of living wasn't satisfied. The kibbutz returned to hashing out the difficult process of change. "What convinced members to change was the guaranteed pension for old people, because there was lots of insecurity among the old people," Batya Amitai admitted.

Zmira Lapidot, a former mazkira, is a generation behind Batya and Uri. Born in Baghdad, she grew up in Jerusalem and came to Gesher Haziv to marry a man from whom she is now divorced. An artist who is active in the cultural life of the Galilee, Lapidot creates environmental sculptures two to three meters high, life-size figures with roots in Canaanite and Mesopotamian sources. She has three sons, one of whom is renting an apartment at Gesher Haziv with his wife. The other two, she hopes, will buy apartments at the kibbutz, but as part of the new neighborhood, not as kibbutz members. She is grateful to her former husband—who lives at Kibbutz Lotan in the Negev—for paying for their sons' education, as it would have been impossible for her to do so under the current Gesher Haziv system. Because Gesher Haziv doesn't have the money, they no longer pay for the college education of members' children, although everyone we interviewed said they would like to if they could. Had the kibbutz not privatized, it's unlikely they would have been able to pay for their children's higher education either, inasmuch as the kibbutz was broke.

Lapidot's insecurity is typical of the generation in their fifties and sixties who are worried about the future. She told us:

I realized we had trouble when we couldn't make our budget or get out of debt, so in the beginning I was part of the group that

supported change. I didn't want to leave. I have no other security but being here; my age is such that I have nowhere to go.
Anyway, I didn't want to go. I preferred changing and dealing
with the economic problems. In the beginning the change was
okay, but then it turned into something different. People began
saying "if you don't do this" we are leaving.

I felt there was a big influence from an outside consultant who
brought his ideas here. It was too fast, too extreme, and didn't
take into account the forty-five- to sixty-year-old middle-age
group. There were many problems with that age group. Some
aren't capable of earning as much money; and, on the other
hand, they aren't protected with pensions. I felt that many
things were unfair. On the other hand, the government didn't
defend us. The young people said, if you don't do it, we will
leave, and then we would have no one to depend on.

After Zmira Lapidot ended her time as mazkira and moved from
supporting change to the opposition, she joined with nineteen others
on the kibbutz to send a letter to the Ministry of Agriculture, re-
questing legal action by the government to stop the privatization. "I
started to be very active with the people who were against these types
of changes," she said. "I got hate letters in my mailbox from people
who wanted change that said, 'Fuck you,' and it was like being in Russia. I was very upset about it. But we weren't defended by outside law,
and the inside law is broken, so what were we supposed to do?"

Lapidot's concerns point out one of the most difficult aspects of this
era of change. Since their founding, the kibbutzim functioned like
separate fiefdoms. Not only did each kibbutz maintain norms by
which the society functioned but each kibbutz movement maintained laws relating to strict ideology. When that social structure
began to break down, because the kibbutz was organized as a cooperative and governed by the national laws of cooperatives regarding
housing and distribution of wealth, individual members had no guaranteed retirement money.

As the changes progress, many kibbutz members are caught in
limbo waiting for the laws of the country to catch up to the kibbutz
changes in areas such as taxation and the parceling of land. Old laws
remain on the government books. Basically, joining (and especially

founding) a kibbutz meant that each member took a great leap of faith, assuming that the kibbutz would survive forever and care for them and for future generations. This also took into account the national social compact between the kibbutz and the state. When there was a national consensus that the cooperative kibbutz was needed for the good of the country, for the mission of building Israel—whether placing kibbutzim like Gesher Haziv on the peripheries to define the borders, or producing large amounts of agricultural products, or living strict ideological lives that taught new generations to accept scarcity and to value cooperation, socialism, and serving in the elite military units—then the kibbutz was protected by the state. No one in the national government ever asked any kibbutz for a budget, and the kibbutzim never produced one. But they got government subsidies for all sorts of things, and they were frontloaded funds to produce water-sensitive crops like cotton and their water costs were subsidized.

So, it isn't unusual or unreasonable for someone of Zamira' Lapidot's generation to assume that she had a lifelong social safety net by being a kibbutz member. Nor was it unreasonable for her to think that even when Gesher Haziv wasn't doing well financially, her future would be secure.

Still, she insists:

> I don't see myself against the change. I thought the process was undemocratic; there was no way of hearing people who had other ideas. Others told us, we are the strongest, we will tell you what to do.
>
> I don't get any financial support from the outside, and I wanted to continue living here, so I had no choice. I said, okay, I'll do my own thing but not continue to fight. I didn't believe that I would win.

In the old days, Gesher Haziv supported Zmira Lapidot to produce her art, and, in return, she was active in the life of the community, not only as mazkira but also editing the kibbutz newspaper, creating art for communal celebrations, and serving on the cultural committee. Today, she teaches high school outside in Ma'alot, a city in the north-central Galilee, and elsewhere. She misses the time she spent doing her own art. But she has created a good support system of friends outside of the kibbutz: "From being disappointed by some people, I have created my own network from outside."

There are also, she has discovered, some good things about the shinui. "I like having a salary. I'm independent. The old style was a kind of summer camp."

Still, the negative aspects of the new life gnaw at her:

> You felt secure. It wasn't a true life, but people met together in the dining room and elsewhere. Now, it's broke. Everyone doesn't have time. I don't have time myself. I don't feel secure now. I trust my family, not the kibbutz. I feel okay about the pension. I think it's low and that we should make it higher. I hope it will be continued. If I had my pension as a teacher, it would be much higher than what I have from the kibbutz. I gave that up because of the kibbutz system. Even at the kibbutz high school, we didn't pay pensions for the teachers. So, now, some have outside pensions and some don't. For the next five to six years, we have to see what will happen.[12]
>
> I believe that if a woman is a single parent, it's worse. It used to not be a problem on the kibbutz, but now it's worse because we are not defended by outside law. The kibbutz doesn't care for my children. If I had three small children, and I was alone, that would be a problem. Also, with the loss of central services like laundry, dining room, a woman has two jobs.

Lapidot, as upset as she is about the changes, appears to be not only resigned to the change but also realistic about the changes. Unlike others who believed that participation in the communal life of the kibbutz as represented by the asafa or a communal holiday celebration dropped away as a result of the changes, Lapidot acknowledged that the communal celebrations and participation had been gradually declining through the years. "The shinui didn't save the kibbutz," she says bluntly, "but maybe it saved the people. The way they want it now, we have to create a new *chevra* [circle of friends], a new society based on everyone being independent.

It's difficult because we're not starting from the beginning. I put all my effort into the kibbutz, but it broke down. Today, it's not a kibbutz. It's not a city. We will see what we are going to do, what kind of festivals we are going to celebrate together."

Zmira Lapidot has decided to make peace with her neighbors.

Marcia Greenfeld is a former American and a member of Zmira Lapidot's generation. She's a graphic designer working outside the kibbutz, who came to Israel and the kibbutz as a result of her youth movement activity. Her husband is a drug addiction counselor; he, too, works outside of the kibbutz. Greenfeld told us:

> I studied art and have a degree in graphic design. I didn't finish university before coming to kibbutz, because I knew I was coming to kibbutz and you didn't need a degree for kibbutz. So, before the change but after the [kibbutz] sewing shop fell apart, at age forty-eight, I went to the WIZO School of Design in Haifa. Now, I work in a print shop across the road from the kibbutz. I started working there in the mid-1990s. When I started, I put my salary in the kibbutz; now, I put my salary in the kibbutz and get it back.

Today, each member's salary goes to the kibbutz, which takes out taxes for the meager social safety net and returns the remainder to the member. Previously, the entire outside salary was used to finance the kibbutz, and each person would get an identical amount of money. The differential only applied to inheritance or family money, or German reparation money, the renta, which, as we mentioned before, was never pooled.

Greenfeld explained the effect:

> I was in shock at first, especially with ideas like differential salaries. We started charging to send kids to school. Materially, it's definitely good—but it's not a pie . . . it's a lot of cupcakes. With the changes, a lot of the hypocrisy went out the window. People don't have to hide anymore.

Marcia Greenfeld was one of several to acknowledge the hypocrisy on Gesher Haziv (not uncommon on most kibbutzim) where people would hide a private income they didn't want to share with the collective, giving the false impression that everyone was living equally. Unlike Zmira Lapidot, she isn't sure that the changes are worse for women:

> I remember when we voted for women to have a six-hour work-day. We thought we were being really progressive, but we were being really regressive. We thought that if you only work six hours, you could be home for the kids. But what happened was that if you can only work six hours, you couldn't take certain jobs that need longer hours. We didn't think of it then. They assumed that if you are a woman, you have to work in education or take care of children. Today, it's economic. Now, women are out in the real world market, so they have the same problems of any women in the real world; they aren't in the bubble of the kibbutz. I make a pretty low wage. I don't know if I were a man if I would make a higher wage, but that's not a kibbutz issue at all.

Marcia Greenfeld's idealism still hasn't faded, even if Gesher Haziv's collectivity has. We asked her if she was bothered about others earning more money on the kibbutz than she and her husband with their combined salaries:

> You mean Pete [the factory manager] makes a lot more money than we do? Okay. That doesn't bother me. It bothers a lot of people, but not me. So some are adding on to their houses and others aren't. Okay.
>
> In general, living on kibbutz, every five years or so, you turn around and think, What are we doing here? Is this really the one and only place where we want to live? I don't think it's something you do when you live in a normal society. You may think, is this the job I want, but being a kibbutznik means you change your life so drastically—so you review it. But I never felt a crisis point.
>
> Maybe I'm stupid, but I felt so much a part of this community that even when it was bad—and it was bad—we didn't really talk about leaving. Maybe one reason was economic—whether or not we could get up and do it. We never worried about our future, because there was a kibbutz and there would always be a

kibbutz. Gesher Haziv has always been in an economic crisis. When they announce on the radio that the kibbutzim are in crisis and aren't serving rolls for breakfast . . . why, we always only had rolls once a month.

Our personal situation is now definitely better than it was. Our children are all grown. We don't have the burden of education. We can't pay for our youngest daughter's education like we paid for my schooling, because we made an economic decision—as a kibbutz—not to pay for children of the kibbutz if they aren't living here. It was a financial decision. My daughter is going to college with money she got from the army.[13]

In 1995, the kibbutz was paying for higher education, by 1999, they weren't. Some people got caught in midstream, depending on their children's ages. It wasn't that the kibbutz once had the money to pay for higher education and now doesn't. It never had the money, but the kibbutz members used to live by different rules. Now, it's about affordability, not values. Wealthier kibbutzim like Hatzor and Gan Shmuel can afford to pay for their children's higher education and even—as is the case with Gan Shmuel—throw in an incentive sweetener of spending money for the youth during their time between the army and university to try to keep the young people on the kibbutz. Greenfeld continued:

Our children grew up in a closed society and went to camp and hikes all over the country provided for them by the kibbutz and the kibbutz movement. This doesn't have to do with the changes—how our kids live now—it was a different time. When my kids were young going to Nahariya to get an ice cream cone was a real adventure. The country has changed.

After the privatization, we started charging rent to our children who weren't living in their parents' houses. The rent was lower than what we charge to outsiders, but that's when a lot of children moved into their parents' homes, which weren't big enough for adult children living with their parents. That definitely was a crisis—that's when people started enlarging their homes.

I think something in me would like to hope that the shinui was inevitable, because I'm always looking for a justification of what we started. While there were a lot of things that bothered me, there was a lot of good.

Not everyone is better as a result of the changes. Herzl Dobkin, who grew up in Washington, D.C., was in Habonim from the age of thirteen. He came to Gesher Haziv with a Habonim workshop in 1960 and made aliyah in 1969. Today, he is fifty-nine years old with two sons from a previous marriage. He lives with a woman who used to be a member of another kibbutz. With money from a small inheritance, he and his girlfriend tried to start a Mail Boxes Etc. franchise in nearby Nahariya, but he told us that it failed, and they were in the process of shutting it down. Now, he works on the assembly line in a factory belonging to a neighboring kibbutz. Dobkin is very bitter:

> The motivating factor for the change was the families that threatened to leave. They were in their mid-thirties and forties. I had helped pay for their education, and they had much better jobs. Change was inevitable, but it could be a little fairer to everyone all around. I put thirty-two years into this place. I have nothing to show for it. I'm a simple grunt in an assembly plant. I was the bookkeeper for the kibbutz guesthouse. When it closed down I went looking for a job and found that difficult. Six of us from Gesher Haziv work at the Kibbutz Evron factory.

Both of his sons are in the United States. One is driving a truck in California, and the other is an industrial psychologist in New York. He hopes that at least one son will return to Israel, but not to Gesher Haziv:

> There's nothing here. I'm very bitter and very disappointed. It was all socialism and kibbutz in Habonim, and the next step was to make aliyah to Israel. I made the next step, but they didn't tell us the whole truth.
> Even then, it was not the equality that was exact equality. First of all, equality can't be complete equality. Second, Gesher Haziv made a decision early on that inheritances didn't have to go into the kibbutz. Then, when the German government paid renta, there was a whole big thing. Well, if you're not turning in

inheritances, we're not turning in renta. Some did, but that was very glaring. Then, you couldn't build on to your house, so people went on vacations in the 1970s, 1980s, outside of Israel. It was no small thing for a poor kibbutz to send members outside Israel. Those members who had family in the U.S. who could pay for it were allowed to go. The Israelis said, "Just because my family is in Tel Aviv, it's not fair." So, we adjusted. I had what I needed—a good education for my children for which the kibbutz paid through high school. In 1995, my mother died and I inherited enough money to help my older son through university.

I was actively against the changes. We had gotten to the point where the salaries were so skewed between the people working in the service branches and the plant manager, that it was hundreds of times more. It wasn't following any of the principles. Promises were made that weren't fulfilled. My whole contention is that we did it too fast, with no time to mull over major decisions that would affect our lives for the rest of our lives. Everything was pushed through. They would hand out a proposal in writing on Friday, discuss it on Sunday, and vote on Wednesday and Thursday and Friday. On Sunday we got the decision, and then the whole thing started next week.

No one at Gesher Haziv said they were opposed to change, just to the process. Herzl Dobkin, who was the most adamant of all those we interviewed, said he would support change, just a different change.

I'm not saying we shouldn't have done it. Now I'm seeing it had to be done, but my problem is the time element. At first I was completely opposed to change. We didn't know all the facts. Not all of the treasurers told us these years that we were bankrupt. It wasn't clear, in spite of the fact that I was a bookkeeper, because we could always get loans. The problem was it all stopped when the government changed.[14]

Dobkin said that he didn't organize the petition to the government but did help get signatures for it. The *rasham* (government registrar in charge of kibbutzim) refused to rule on the petition, insisting that the community had to make its own decisions.

The rasham said you are a minority group, so work it out for yourselves. It wasn't a group as such. Most of the things went by on majority vote. One vote, according to the model we chose, had to be 70 percent. All those who signed the petition are still here, for the same reason I am—nowhere else to go. There really is nowhere else to go. We had a standard of living on the kibbutz, even if it was beyond our means, and it is very difficult—when the ideology collapses you become poor.

Herzl Dobkin remains suspicious of those in charge of the kibbutz. He says he doesn't know if he has a pension. When we tell him that he does, and when we tell him the numbers, he says, "In theory, yes. I hope that is true. No one has shown me a balance sheet. I don't trust the community. I've become so cynical."

Still, he says, "Today I accept the changes. I don't particularly like some of the results, but it was inevitable. Yes, I know what's coming to me, quote, unquote, but I have my doubts. Things change so fast and so drastically that it wouldn't surprise me if we just voted ourselves out of existence."

Yehuda Schlossberg, Riffi's brother-in-law, was the first son of the kibbutz, born in 1949, after his parents emigrated from Canada. "It was great growing up here. To stay in kibbutz is to be complete, to be satisfied in a way of living," he explains. And, while he wasn't a leader in the changes, he said that he "held Riffi's hand throughout." He is clearly determined—and very successful. Today, he is a marketing manager of Plasgod, a German-owned factory at nearby Kibbutz Gadot. But for him the change isn't just about money. "All that I need is this Omega watch, nothing else," he says, holding up his wrist to show off his watch.

Yehuda Schlossberg speculates:

I think that if we didn't make the change nobody would stay. The kibbutz wouldn't stay. The kibbutz movement as a whole is growing older each year. In order to stay alive, the kibbutz has to have an internal and external reason to live. The people of Israel were proud of the kibbutzim, and the kibbutzim are one of the reasons there is a state. We were going to the frontier. When

I was young that was the atmosphere. Until the beginning of the 1980s, there was no TV, no cars. There was no big gap between kibbutz and nonkibbutz.

There was a crisis in our community. Life doesn't compare to the economic situation before. Three or four years ago there was no tomorrow.

With the shinui our aim was to get up to the average cost of living in Israel. Everyone has to work. Before we had lots of unnecessary jobs and it was costly, like eighteen people working in the laundry. People we never thought could work are now working. It was an economic revolution. Nothing changed our community like closing the dining room, but it wasn't economical to keep it opened—it was like eating three times a day in a restaurant.

The strong kibbutzim, when they hit a problem, they cover it over with money. Today, I'm living the way of life that I think is the right one. At the end of the day, we are a *yishuv kehillati* [cooperative community]. And we want to build roads near our houses.

Indeed, Gesher Haziv is on a building spree. Anyone who can afford it (and many can) are building additions to their homes. So far, disputes regarding building and land use of the tiny plots that surround each private parcel have been minimal. When they have arisen, the kibbutz brought in an outside mediator. But it's easy to imagine that the kinds of zoning laws that govern all neighborhoods will someday govern Gesher Haziv.

Asher Koren is one who is busy building:

I am adding to my house, and my neighbors will do the same. We are building now because we know we will have an income. We can afford it. We want to invest in our house. The children used to live outside when they were teenagers, but now they are staying with us and even staying after the army. We can build up to 140 meters. There is an organized kibbutz committee, and you do have to get approval by your neighbors. Not design, though. Everyone does his own design.

In addition to building additions to their homes, each member, as Yehuda Schlossberg remarked, wants a driveway or parking space in their own front yard. This is sure to lead to problems. Each kibbutz was laid out with no street names or street signs. Roads were mostly kept to the area around the machane and rarely, if ever, extended into the living quarters or tiny neighborhoods. Instead, there are paths only large enough for bicycles, strollers, and, increasingly, motorized carts. Rather than acknowledge this as a positive thing—something that doesn't need changing—the trend among the kibbutzim today is to make all the same ecological mistakes that modern Western society has made, things like destroying the internal layout of the community with a road system just so that each family can park its car next to their house instead of walking nine meters from the public parking lot.

In 2002, ground was broken for the new housing development, from which the kibbutz hopes to earn enough to sustain itself in a modest future. The intermixing between young families who come to live in the new neighborhood and current kibbutz members will be the next phase of the experiment. No one on the kibbutz expects their potential neighbors to salvage the kibbutz, but they do think it will improve the quality of life for the community and ease them into the future. Riffi Schlossberg is sanguine and realistic:

> The kibbutz will be a very small part of the new community. There will be a committee to decide who will buy in. But it will be a limited committee—not like in the old kibbutz [when committees decided everything]. The new neighborhood is for money, but also for us. We are an aging community. That's one of the problems. There are a lot of empty apartments being rented because members have died—and the renters are transitory. We want people to live here. We want to have a community where people feel like it's their home.
>
> The kibbutz will become smaller and smaller and the community bigger and bigger. In the end, the kibbutz will disappear—in twenty or thirty years. But, for me, it's very important that it be a community. It means that my children know the people, that I now them. Not moneywise, but socially. Not

to support people financially. There won't be social security. There will be a community tax for holidays and such, but it doesn't mean that if somebody has a problem I have to solve this problem. I'm not sure we will succeed in it, but that's what I want.

# HATZOR

## A Third Way?

> This conversion recovery is not intended to undermine the princi-
> ples of the kibbutz, such as cooperation, mutual responsibility and
> support, equality, and so on. Rather, it is the recognition of the im-
> portance of the economic needs to ending the crisis, and ensuring
> the ability of the productive/business sector to be competitive.
>
> —Kibbutz Hatzor's "Guiding Principles
> for Economic Conversion Recovery"

On a clear day, while children play in the pool and seniors whir
around the kibbutz grounds in their motor carts, you can hear the
F-16s as they take off from the adjacent air force base. Tamar Brenner,
Gary Brenner's wife, born and bred at Kibbutz Hatzor, once remarked
to the authors that in times of military tensions, Hatzorniks know
that Israel is preparing an air strike before it gets reported on the news
because they hear the piercing noise of fighter jets flying above their
homes. (Tamar's father's Polish religious-Zionist parents came to
Palestine when he was six; her father later rebelled to become a secular socialist and part of the founding Israeli garin of Kibbutz Hatzor.
Her mother emigrated from Bulgaria in 1946.)

A different kind of noise emanates from Hatzor if it's Friday or Saturday night. That's when Metroc, the disco started in a former grain
silo by some of the young people who are past army age, is open for
business. From late in the evening until sunrise, hundreds of young

people from the surrounding area as far north as Tel Aviv and as far south as Ashkelon dance to the latest music beneath the swirl of colored lights.

Unlike the atmosphere at Gesher Haziv (but similar to Gan Shmuel), it's obvious as soon as a visitor enters Hatzor that there is a vibrant communal life here. In fact, although privatized, the kibbutz dining room remains open for all meals and is a center of kibbutz life. (As we shall see, Gan Shmuel, which hasn't privatized its dining room, has closed its communal dining room for evening meals, except for the eve of the Shabbat dinner.)

Like other kibbutzim, Hatzor was once a tranquil rural outpost. Today, it's a community of six hundred people (350 members) in transition, on its way to economic well-being. The kibbutz was founded in 1936 as the third settlement of the left-wing Kibbutz Artzi Federation at its interim location in Rishon Letzion, near Tel Aviv. In 1946, it was allocated land on what would have been a border post had the 1947 UN partition plan been realized. The kibbutz is located forty-four kilometers south of Tel Aviv (reachable from there in only thirty minutes thanks to a new superhighway—except during rush hour). Fifty-three years later, Hatzor's expansive fields are surrounded by suburban communities sprouting from a sleepy Yemenite and German-Jewish town called Gan Yavne. The closest city (six kilometers east) is Ashdod, which was founded in 1956 by a younger generation of Israeli-born pioneers. Immigrants from North Africa and other Arab countries quickly populated Ashdod. Today, it is a thriving port city, with a population that dramatically increased in the 1980s and 1990s with the arrival of immigrants from the former Soviet Union.

Hatzor's founding members came from the Yishuv, North America, and Bulgaria. In the 1950s, members of the Swiss and French Hashomer Hatzair youth movement joined. They were followed by young people from North Africa, Iran, and Iraq. In the 1960s and 1970s, North American and Western European volunteers came to study Hebrew on the kibbutz and stayed, including one of the authors of this study, Gary Brenner, who came from Los Angeles. Hatzor's membership peaked in the late 1970s with four hundred members. Out of today's 350 members, roughly one third—114—are over age sixty-five. The next largest age group is between forty and sixty-five. Only ten members are under forty, which is typical of most kibbutzim.

In the last five years, about thirty young adults under twenty-eight returned to the kibbutz to live, but they haven't joined. They are called *toshavim*, technically translated as "residents," and have no formal rights as members. They live more like renters in their parents' community, and like thousands of Israelis in their twenties they are in between travels to India, Australia, North and South America, or the university. Whether they remain at Hatzor, either as members of the kibbutz or as something resembling associate members, depends on what a restructured Hatzor can offer them. Unlike Gesher Haziv, Hatzor has determined that it will remain a kibbutz. Unlike Gan Shmuel, Hatzor was willing to tackle serious change. It had no choice. To survive, it had to do something about its economic and social structure. But the kibbutz also made a decision to improve its social fabric, with the hope of retaining the middle generation and their children.

As late as the 1970s Hatzor was considered an economically stable kibbutz, with a relatively profitable industry and productive agricultural branches. It had one of the oldest kibbutz industries, established in 1946, Omen Metal Works, a brass and aluminum die casting plant that manufactures automotive, irrigation, and construction parts. A sister company, Omen SafePlace, produces high-tech safety boxes for hotels.

Hatzor's economy was severely undermined by the economic crisis of the 1980s. The struggling factories and weakened agricultural sector, combined with poor financial management, suggested the onset of eventual economic collapse, which hit the vast majority of kibbutzim. That's when Hatzor decided to search for a second industry.

At this stage, the leaders of the kibbutz didn't completely understand the extent of their complex and desperate economic situation. They were primarily trying to anticipate the future needs of the community. They certainly didn't foresee that the addition of a successful enterprise in the 1980s would help catalyze fundamental changes in the kibbutz in the 1990s. In 1987, the kibbutz found both an affordable and available industrial project. The company that was to be named Solbar Hatzor Ltd. was purchased from the Histadrut-owned Koor Industries (now also privatized). It was quickly established as a limited company (a concept once antithetical to kibbutz ideology) in order to separate the kibbutz from potential financial risks.

Solbar crushes soybeans (bought mainly in the United States), extracts oil, and makes soybean meal for animal feed and human use. The heart of the business includes soy protein concentrates used as raw materials for industrial food processing and animal feed. More recently, a second company was established by the kibbutz, Solbar Plant Extracts, which produces soy isoflavones for dietary supplements and health foods.

Solbar first turned a profit in 1995, almost five years after the kibbutz initiated a strategic partnership and sold minority shares to a German company. The strategy of engaging a European partner was necessary for gathering indispensable resources for capital expansion and for bringing the company closer to world market centers. The German partner was subsequently acquired by Archer Daniels Midland (ADM), one of Solbar's main competitors. The new partnership was eventually dissolved in January 2001 when the kibbutz members (who were by then shareholders) purchased back the 49 percent shares

Solbar soybean extraction processing plant. (Photo courtesy of Kibbutz Hatzor.)

held by ADM, following a conflict of interest between the companies. By spring 2002, Solbar Industries Ltd. was preparing for its first public offering on the Tel Aviv Stock Exchange.

Hatzor, beginning in 1989, took over a decade to recover financially. Today, its financial and social structure is sound, although the lifestyle there is far from lavish. During the recovery period, the communal budget was limited to the bare essentials, with investments in essential housing and an ever-so-slightly improved standard of living. This took place when the overall Israeli economy was prospering and Hatzor's children were moved from the children's houses to their parents' tiny, ill-fitted homes.[1]

Today, Hatzor continues to plow its fields and raise its animals, but agriculture is not considered a sufficient source of income, nor can it contribute to the growing expectations of the community it is meant to support. The traditional industrial crops (cotton, corn, potatoes) are being replaced by more sophisticated—but also more labor-intensive—agricultural products. Eventually, some of the land will be turned over to the banks for its real estate value as part of the kibbutzim debt settlement arrangement.

The future of Hatzor, however, is in industry, and its economy would be recognizable to anyone as a mixed market economy. In addition to Solbar and the Omen plants, Hatzor has opened its gates to its neighbors, offering private preschool education, a kindergarten for autistic children, a convalescent and nursing home, the Metroc disco, and Friday night ballroom dancing for those too old to disco. It once operated a therapeutic riding school for children with physical and emotional disabilities, but this wasn't economically solvent. Many of these initiatives are being led by individuals who previously directed their skills and talents only toward the kibbutz community and who now offer important services to outsiders while earning money for the kibbutz.

Hatzor's model of change would be recognized by those familiar with "the third way" in politics, forged by modernizers in the British Labour Party and the European social democratic parties. Its diversified economy not only finds its vibrancy from this mixture but also from the social ingenuity that has been unleashed in the process. And the robust and extensive social safety net provided by the community for the founding generation and others mimics the best social welfare state model. The progressive taxation is enough to offset the inequalities and would be familiar to any Swedish citizen schooled in decades of social democracy. Yet whether the generous safety net will remain will be up to future generations.

Unlike Gesher Haziv, Hatzor made its change at an opportune moment and, therefore, was able to profit intellectually, socially, and economically. It also had a more cohesive initial social network. Unlike Gan Shmuel, as we shall soon see, Hatzor made a calculation that anticipated future trends and decided to go farther in its change process than was desired by some of the founders. To those committed to the classic kibbutz style, Hatzor has crossed a redline by instituting differential wages and salaries. Yaakov Gadish, a member of nearby Kibbutz Kvutzat Yavne and leader of the Tamid group, is very critical of his neighbors. In a 1992 interview in the English-language *Israel Scene* magazine, Gadish stated categorically that "a community which wants to create a link between the contribution of the individual and his income can be anything but a kibbutz." Gadish insists that Hatzor is no longer a kibbutz because of its decision to institute private salaries.[2] The problem with his formulation, however, is that the members of Hatzor still consider themselves to be living on a kibbutz—and a revived one at that.

Since Hatzor went through the changes, its economy has improved, although key players in the process would probably claim there is still a long way to go. And while some resentment lingers among kibbutz members about how the process took shape, signs of increased family incomes are beginning to appear, as families renovate and enlarge their homes and acquire more mobility. For the most part, Hatzor is both more secure financially since the changes and a relatively contented place compared with many other kibbutzim. Much of the trappings of the classic kibbutz remain, albeit altered a bit for the new economic reality. Individual allowances help guide spending in the social and cultural sphere, but communal cultural and social life is still alive and well at Hatzor. The kibbutz celebrates bar and bat mitzvahs, weddings, and holidays together.

The communal dining room—in many ways the cornerstone of the classic kibbutz—is still abuzz with activity at practically every meal. Its evolution, however, illustrates today's changes. Keeping open a huge communal kitchen and dining room that is barely used for weeknight dinners is a drain on the kibbutz economy, and some kibbutzim, like Gesher Haziv, simply can't afford to do it. But at Hatzor, there is no call to close the dining room, nor is there—any longer—economic pressure to do so. The Friday night Shabbat eve dinner is the one time the hall is full, with extended families coming together for the meal. The dining room still serves three meals on weekdays, although almost all families opt for the evening dinner at home. Hatzor's members keep track of their food allowance through a computerized system of cash registers. This system has greatly reduced food waste. In fact, four-fifths of the former Kibbutz Artzi Federation kibbutzim now require payment for meals in the dining hall.[3]

Meanwhile, the food has improved, largely the result of hiring a master chef. Twenty-nine-year-old Noa Tzur, who was born and raised at Hatzor, was weighing whether to become a Hatzor member. During her sojourn off-kibbutz, she trained as a master chef. She married someone from outside who holds an important position in one of Hatzor's factories. The kibbutz hired her to put her talents to use, and she drastically improved the quality of the meals. People now can enjoy their meal in the dining hall and not just fulfill a social commitment. Today, Hatzor's dining room includes an espresso machine, loose herbs for tea that is so popular with Israeli yuppies, and other popular dining amenities. From October to April, people eat dessert and drink their coffee and tea after dinner in an outdoor café set up on the lawn in front of the dining room.

Israeli chefs are well paid, and although Noa Tzur wasn't asking for a fair market rate, she wanted to earn a salary close to what she would get outside, a demand once unheard of on the kibbutz. Eventually, she started her own catering service outside the kibbutz and the kibbutz hired another professional chef to maintain the new standards. Noa and her husband rent their apartment at Hatzor. They may join the kibbutz, if the change process continues; or they will ask to build their own home somewhere on the kibbutz land, in order to be close to Noa's family.

Uri Eshel, born in Hatzor in 1942 when it was still located in Rishon Letzion, was one of those who led the move for changes at Hatzor. He grew up in Hatzor, attending the elementary school that eventually relocated and merged with those of other kibbutzim. He and his peers were sent to the closest kibbutz boarding school (or *mossad hinuchi*), at Kibbutz Ein Hachoresh, about one hundred kilometers north of Hatzor. This institute resembles an English boarding school, without the disciplinary trappings but with a strong commitment to teaching the values of cooperation and community.

Eshel reached the rank of lieutenant colonel in the Israeli Army and served as a battalion commander. He earned a bachelor's degree in agriculture from Hebrew University. In addition to serving as a *shaliach* (an emissary who represents the kibbutz abroad) in the United States for Hashomer Hatzair, the KAF youth movement, he has held various high-level business positions at Hatzor. Today, he is chairman of the board of several companies, including two outside the kibbutz. His wife, born in England, came to the kibbutz as an infant. After years of working as a kindergarten teacher at Hatzor, Mira Eshel became a consultant in the Kibbutz Movement's Division of Education. She travels around the country helping kibbutzim redesign their preschools to contemporary requirements, including becoming more cost effective. Three of their four children (and one grandchild) live outside the kibbutz; only their seventeen-year-old, at pre-army age, remains with them at Hatzor.

Uri Eshel was one of the few representatives of his generation to act forcefully and with a lot of forethought for change in the kibbutz. The hard core of the change advocates was clustered around Solbar. The cynics say that their physical separation from the kibbutz (Solbar is located eight kilometers from the kibbutz in the industrial section of Ashdod) converted them to unconventional thinking. Others, the authors included, believe that the challenge of competing in world markets and contending with multinationals helped to catalyze their thinking.

There is no question in Uri Eshel's mind that he did the right thing. He told Jo-Ann Mort:[4]

> We had to make some changes to survive. The kibbutz is a very unique society where the individuals are not responsible for their economic life. This was very good when you are twenty or thirty years old—in the beginning of the kibbutz when you had plenty of nothing—but when you have to survive and take care of your family, you have to support yourself. There were one or two people who took care of the kibbutz [economically speak-

ing]. They were like the night guard taking care of everyone else, so that every morning when they woke up, most people saw the sun shining, had their breakfast, the children were in the children's houses—and the rest is history.

The founders had a dream. If you look around here . . . see, they fulfilled their dreams a hundred times. To make change is very difficult. So when people realized that we had to do something, they could choose to stay or leave. Many people left kibbutz because at age forty or fifty they thought this was their last moment to care for their families, since they didn't believe that the kibbutz would change and survive.

We were lucky, I believe, because we had a group of people who were willing to fight, meaning we understood that we had to manage Solbar as a private business in the capitalist world that was, in many ways, not against kibbutz ideology but what people thought was against our ideology, because, for me, to take care of your business in the right way is not against kibbutz philosophy. Some people think that if you have a board of directors for your company this is not a democracy and this is against the kibbutz philosophy. The kibbutz general assembly used to make all kibbutz decisions, including business decisions. Now, you nominate people to be directors of the kibbutz and you have to trust them.

To separate the business from the community is very similar to a family company. Most family companies, by the third generation, either collapse or take professional management on board to work with some family members, and they make a separation between the family pocket and the business pocket.

When we started Solbar, we had to import raw material. We got a credit line for the raw material. We sold the products and the gizbar[5] took the money and bought food for the kibbutz members, so we didn't have money to pay for the raw materials. With a separation, you know first of all that you have to pay for the raw material, then pay salaries for the factory workers—including the kibbutz members—and, then, check to see if there is a profit.

Consultants from academia and industry aided the group that initiated change at Hatzor—consultants that were once anathema to the kibbutz culture. In 1990, Hatzor voted in a set of "guiding principles for economic recovery." They included:

1. The purpose of our economic activity is to create the resources needed to fulfill our social goals.

2. The necessary condition for the survival of the kibbutz as a social entity is its ability to become, once again, a viable economic entity.

3. The way out of the crisis into economic prosperity is dependent upon the understanding, agreement, and participation of the kibbutz members in converting the social unit of yesterday into a more efficient and profit-making tool for the productive branches—the business of the kibbutz.

4. This conversion is not intended to undermine the principles of the kibbutz, such as cooperation, mutual responsibility and support, equality, and so on. Rather, it is the recognition of the importance of the economic needs to ending the crisis and ensuring the ability of the productive/business sector to be competitive.

5. The first stage for what is called here "the conversion of the social unit" relates to the conceptual sphere and the following transformations: from an agricultural culture to an industrial one; from a production to a business orientation; from the existing model in which there is a lot of free time and little money for the members to a model where there is less free time and more money—looking toward an end where there is more time and more money; from a culture of amateur organization to professional organization.

6. The second stage of adapting the system is a translation of ideas into action—changing the culture of work in the kibbutz: habits, quality of work, rules and norms, doctrines of management, and systems design.

In the next chapter, we will quote extensively from a statement of principles written for the members of Kibbutz Gan Shmuel. The two documents differ at almost all levels, including their basic premises. Those who are clustered around creating a document at Gan Shmuel want to reach an agreement on a set of principles to guarantee a just and morally acceptable society reflecting the "spirit of Gan

Shmuel."[6] Hatzor first focuses on the economic resources needed to fulfill the social goals in a distributive manner, to be agreed upon by members who share a common heritage and expectation for the future.[7]

Even after Hatzor voted for its manifesto, members had a hard time internalizing the fundamental changes and translating them into daily life. The older generation of founders was unrelenting in its opposition. The generation in their fifties felt threatened, sometimes claiming in retrospect that "I didn't vote for this," though, of course, they did. A pervading intellectual laziness expected business to be conducted as usual, while the leaders for change continued to pursue their goals, one vote after the other. The gap between perception and reality created ever greater friction and might have spun out of control had Hatzor members lost their center of gravity. It was their common dedication to the survival of the community that kept the camps from erupting in a way that would have ruptured the fabric of the kibbutz.

In the summer of 1993, a group who wanted to consider possibilities for change gathered for a series of informal discussions on author Gary Brenner's lawn. Micha Harari and Gary Brenner initiated the weekly meetings. Harari, another son of the kibbutz, who had almost finished a degree in philosophy before joining Uri Eshel in establishing Solbar, was the intellectual and a driving force in Hatzor's process. Together, they sculpted a set of principles (largely authored by Harari) for the next phase of change. These principles—Hatzor's Port Huron Statement, of sorts—were presented to the kibbutz at an electrified *sicha kibbutz* (general assembly) on a traditionally secular Yom Kippur eve. This statement included:

> The economic, social, and demographic crisis plaguing kibbutz society for nearly ten years also underscores an identity crisis and loss of direction. We contend that for those who, like us, feel a sense of responsibility for this community, for the people living here and for its surroundings, there is no alternative but to reflect upon the complex reality and try to influence it with new concepts and ideas. We are aware of the difficulties and dangers ahead, but many of us believe that without the readiness to struggle with fundamental questions the kibbutz will turn into

a home emptied of all inhabitants and a vision emptied of all content. If this is the future to which we are destined, our sense of belonging to this place is to be questioned.

In these last two sentences, there was a subtle threat of "either . . . or" that upset many in the kibbutz who had heard rumors of the summer meetings but were not prepared for what was coming.

The supporters of change went on to reaffirm their commitment to veteran members but also implied that they should consider stepping out of the process to allow a younger generation to make the decisions for them:

We have no intention of undermining the rights and the lifestyle of the founding members as a result of these changes. We propose that the kibbutz initiate a discussion on the following explicit goals:

1. We want a kibbutz that comes closer to prevalent needs and values;
2. We are interested in a society where individuals enjoy a reasonable standard of living, characterized by a uniquely high quality of life;
3. We want an open and attractive society, combining the old kibbutz features with the advantages of the system around us, also attracting the younger generation;
4. We want a society that is limited in its responsibility for the individual to areas such as education, health, and communal welfare services;
5. We are interested in a society in which there is an agreed upon, but limited, degree of collectivism, equality, mutual responsibility, and social security.

This model for change became a living document—debated, revised, voted on, rejected, and finally approved during the years 1994 to 2000. In the end, the Hatzor model was, like all incremental change, a compromise. In many ways, it falls short of meeting even minimal reformist expectations. (Today, kibbutzim that instituted change after Hatzor have begun with much more deep-seated changes.)

On the other hand, reaching a consensus that the existing model was no longer possible, making a break from the maxim "From each according to his ability, to each according to his needs," and accepting the market as the basis for salaries represents a historic turning point. And, as interviews revealed, although the six years of debate created obvious turmoil on the kibbutz, and some ill will, remarkably—or perhaps not—the social fabric of the kibbutz remains healthy, for now. The leaders for change attempted to foster as much inclusion as possible, even when those who opposed the changes didn't always see it. That effort appears to have paid off.

Gary and Tamar Brenner's oldest son, Jonathan, shed some light on this dichotomy when he accompanied Gary on one of his many international business trips. A marketing director inevitably interacts by phone, E-mail, and extensive international travel and has a range of business associates off the kibbutz. During his high school years, Jonathan Brenner—today an aspiring gourmet chef in Tel Aviv—worked in the kibbutz turkey farm, assisting Yaron Syrkin, a veteran paratrooper, in taking four-year-old chicks and nurturing them into full-sized birds, ready for slaughter. Syrkin, born on the kibbutz over fifty years ago and deeply committed to the "old kibbutz values," always had a special relationship with the younger generations. But he argued bitterly with Jonathan about the changing regime. By the end of their father-son business and bonding trip that extended from Hong Kong to Manila to Sydney and Melbourne and back home via Thailand, Jonathan had a very different perpective on kibbutz life. Solbar was becoming an increasingly major part of the kibbutz economy, and Gary Brenner's trips abroad were fueling the community's economy. Loyal to his farm boss and sensitive to Yaron Syrkin's concerns, Jonathan asked his father in Bangkok, "How do you expect Yaron, who travels from one part of the turkey farm to another at the rate you travel from Tel Aviv to Frankfurt or Singapore, ever to understand why you consider change to be not only inevitable but essential for our kibbutz's survival?"

Uri Eshel would have preferred an even more radical change. "I believe the goal of the community has to be limited, and I believe the people need to decide the level of partnership," he explains, reflecting on the Hatzor of 2001. Ultimately, he wants to share in the support of education but little else (aside from support for the founding generation, for which there is unanimity).

We are saying now that the community has to live from the money it gets from the members' salaries. At the beginning, when we told people this, they said, "How come? We can't live from the salaries." I said, "Look outside the kibbutz—all sorts of people live from personal income, from salaries. If they are lucky—they have shares or a successful business or a rich parent—they can live above their salaries, but most people live according to their salaries.

Although receiving a salary for one's labor is not a particularly radical concept, for a community that had little regard for money and still considered itself as part of a vanguard meant to fulfill the goals of a developing nation, this break from the past was quite traumatic. Eshel noted:

The members of the kibbutz didn't feel like the country was subsidizing them. They were sure that they were supporting themselves even if they got cheaper credit or some subsidies here or there. When people say to me, "We're so sorry to see what's going on in the kibbutzim, because we are losing the most important thing that happened to the State of Israel," I say to them, "Listen, we will offer you a deal. We will keep it as is if somebody will pay for us." The government lost interest in the kibbutz movement, and we had to find another way. The State of Israel slowly but surely became a normal state, and the pioneers finished their job. We are living in a new era. We have to make the adjustment."

Eddie Benedikt, who supported change, agrees. He is a thoughtful, soft-spoken, fifty-year-old agronomist, who runs the persimmon orchards at Hatzor and at a neighboring kibbutz that got fed up with losing money and hired Benedikt to turn a profit from its barren fields. He has also worked part time outside the kibbutz for Israel's National Food Board as project manager in charge of all university research done for persimmon growers. Benedikt, who came to Israel from France with his father and brother when he was fifteen, is the only family member who stayed. His mother died in France at a relatively young age, and his father sent him to the kibbutz with his brother to be educated. His wife, an Israeli from Kfar Sava, a relatively well-to-do city northwest of Tel Aviv, came to Hatzor as an elementary school teacher. Their children are eighteen, sixteen, and nine. "I never talk to my kids about staying on kibbutz," he admits. "I do want them to stay here but not for ideological reasons. I want them close to me for very personal reasons."

Benedikt, surprising perhaps to some of those within the traditional ledger of the kibbutz movement, still considers himself a Marxist. He spoke at length about the changes:

> I'm a materialist in the Marxist sense. One can expect that if the surrounding changes, if the conditions change, then the kibbutz or whatever it is will change also. No community survives through the ages; maybe only fanatics keep living the same way, and fortunately the kibbutz movement has been fanatic but only for a very short period of time when maybe it was necessary.[8] It was the only condition to make possible the creation of the kibbutz and, maybe, of Israel in general. The pioneers had to be very strong believers to overcome what they did overcome, but later on, on the contrary, we taught openness. Perhaps the kibbutz led its own suicide.
>
> There was a time when it was okay to assume principles and follow them, but everyone paid a price and had to make many concessions at the most personal level. My generation did too, but much less. At that time it was okay because Israelis and kibbutzniks sacrificed themselves at every level. I can't say they gave up this batch of things, because what they did was great. They created a country. All over the world, you cannot find many people who created a country out of nothing. It's very exceptional. They were the avant-garde of the Zionist movement, and, as such, for many years they were considered the real aristocracy of Israel. We could see the decline of the general attitude in Israel toward kibbutzniks, especially due to the economic crisis [of the late 1980s]. After forty years, we were close to the bottom.
>
> The kibbutz would have no choice but to somehow follow the general changes in Israel. Also, there were changes happening under the surface, and people weren't following kibbutz principles or rules. What convinced me that there was no possibility to go back, maintain, or even freeze the situation was the fact that we started living in a two-tier system.

I would have left the kibbutz if changes hadn't come, even though I miss the old system—not all of it, but I miss its spirit. I used to have a lot of visitors from France, and I always have been proud of showing them the kibbutz. It came to a point where I didn't want to talk about the kibbutz because I didn't know what to say: What about equality? What about wages? I couldn't tell them what the kibbutz was when I, myself, didn't know what it was. Now I know. Everything is defined, and even though it's not the type of kibbutz that I would have joined, I like it the way it is. In fact, I love it mainly because I know on what ground I stand. The rules of the game are clear. I know what I have to do, where to go, and what to tell my kids. I used to say, "Daddy has to work late because he works for the kibbutz," and now I say I work late because I work for the kids— for the kibbutz and for my kids. They know there is a very tight relationship between what I do and what their mother does and what they get.

I always look at the Scandinavian system, with a very strong welfare system, and I think that finally we will have quality of life and very strong mutual assistance. I think that what I fought for these past fifteen years was right. People will have what they want to have here, more or less. It will be up to them. I will make no effort to convince my children that what we have here is the best. I really don't care if they are convinced that what we have here is the best. I do care about Hatzor and my friends. It really doesn't matter if we have more or less privatization. I think that when a community decides it wants roads and public space and some reciprocity and some mutual whatever it is, it's okay, as long as it's democratically done. I hope the kibbutz will prefer to put its money in mutual welfare, because I think it's right.

I'm convinced that with no mission the kibbutz can't survive as a specific community with a specific way of life, because all ways of life in the world are very tightly involved with national priorities. I think the kibbutz will continue to be part of the leadership of the peace movement. Maybe we will become more active in the ecological movement. But without a mission, we cannot exist.

To live in a kibbutz, one has to make sacrifices. I think that even my generation would have been willing to make concessions and sacrifices if there was a good reason to make sacrifices. But since all priorities were changed and the kibbutz movement mission was over, the kibbutzim weren't necessary anymore, not economically, not for the security of the country, not from a Zionist point of view—so we had no more reason to make concessions. With a good reason, I'll make a good sacrifice, but with no good reason, no good sacrifice. This is one of the reasons I was involved in the shinui. I was convinced that the kibbutz had no more message, no more mission for Israel.

Hatzor's new model, which received 64 percent of the total votes the second time around, has three income components: equal distribution, seniority, and differential salaries. Each of these components is calculated separately and then combined. The composite income is issued as an allowance. Members still don't receive their salaries directly. The three components are calculated together and distributed in monthly allotments.

The first component consists of values and services that are equally distributed by the community, based on family size. The kibbutz differentiates between goods such as health, education, and welfare, which are guaranteed under the principle of mutual responsibility and never questioned, and additional subsidies (mainly for children) based on age groupings. The distribution of subsidies is determined by the actual budget of the community, the amount of money available from salaries, social security, tax benefits, dividend payments from business, and so on, after the mutual responsibility goods are guaranteed. Ninety percent of the budget of the members is then divided: $x$ shekels for each member (equal for all) plus $y$ shekels for each child, depending upon age. This further allocation is made possible by extensive privatization of goods that were once distributed freely, that is, food, laundry, certain alternative medicines, higher education, and electricity.

The second component is seniority. Each kibbutz member is granted four points per year of seniority, valued at twenty-five shekels per point. (For instance, twenty years times four times twenty-five equals two thousand shekels per month.) Those kibbutz veterans who are of retirement age receive an alternative allowance to the third salary component, comparable to the median salary in the kibbutz.

The guaranteed allowance for retirees is higher than in their former kibbutz budget, although retirees now receive less than some who are of working age. Health care for the aged is guaranteed, while the working members are rebuilding a pension fund that was decimated in the financial crisis of the 1980s. (The decimation of the kibbutzim's pension funds is a typical by-product of the 1980s financial crisis; kibbutzim "volunteered" to repay debts to the banks from their collective pension fund.) The need to rebuild the pension fund tends to even out real income. Seniority points are currently designed to benefit not only the retired veterans but members who are in their fifties and sixties, still working but hard pressed to make the transition to higher-paying jobs. They receive credits for the years they worked in the old system, whereas the younger generations will see less income from this component.

The third component combines differential salaries with progressive taxes designed to close the income gap. The first principle is that salaries are determined by the market and not by kibbutz values or mores. From businesses to social services, health to education, there is no other method of evaluation. More than fifty of the two hundred members of working age are employed outside the kibbutz. They already know how to negotiate with employers. Some are teachers or nurses, collectively represented by Histadrut-affiliated trade unions. The transition to differential salaries in the kibbutz businesses and services was instituted in 1999, well before this had a bearing on actual allowances. Undoubtedly, some businesses were paying low salaries to show higher profits to the kibbutz, not unlike owners in the capitalist world who are trying to maximize profits. The new model requires that the kibbutz businesses (industry, agriculture, and services) pay fair wages. Their economic viability should not be at the expense of the kibbutz worker, no less than at the expense of the hired workers coming from outside the kibbutz.

The instituting of private salaries hit some on the kibbutz like a blast of cold air. Members who had worked their entire lives without receiving remuneration for their labor all of a sudden learned what they were worth in financial terms. Consultants from outside helped managers determine salaries based on those in the Israeli workplace and also assisted in the mediation process. However, these objective outsiders didn't always succeed in tempering hurt feelings and the damaged self-images of those who had always done what the kibbutz expected of them. The most offended sector were the farm workers, the majority of whom were in their fifties. Their impassioned and organized protests against the salaries recommended by the outside consultants resulted in a meaningful adjustment; it was almost like a union shop. But it also propelled the agricultural branches to undertake a serious economic restructuring.

Managers of one factory also had to explain why they were offering particularly low salaries (to show better profits) and made salary adjustments. A committee was created, appropriately called "workers' representatives," to assist members in improving their salary levels. Suddenly, member workers were forced to negotiate with their peers, their neighbors, their children's caretakers, even their own family members. From the venerable *hatzran* (community caretaker, a kind of kibbutz institution) to the aging farmers in the failing agricultural branches, disappointment and even bitterness became a central motif of the public debate.

But the purpose of the model was not to create income differences. Rather, it was to establish categorically that for the kibbutz to survive work must have an economic value and not just a social one. In order to close the gap, a rather draconian Swedish-style progressive tax on salaries was instituted. For the higher-salaried members, the income tax is as high as 80 percent. There is no tax on the minimum wage, which is also higher than that in the rest of Israel. (The Israeli minimum wage in 2000 was NIS 3,266 per month.) And a subsidy was given to workers in relatively low-income brackets, where for every hour of overtime the community contributes fifteen shekels, paid directly to the member.

The last feature—overtime wages paid to the individual—was the only difference between the model that was originally rejected and the one finally approved. Perhaps it made the difference; perhaps the eventual acceptance of the reform was the result of a long-term psychological adjustment; perhaps it was simply exhaustion after years of debate. In any case, the new model went into effect in March 2000 and was ratified a year later. (Most kibbutzim used this system of provisional votes to alleviate pressures and allow members to get used to the idea of change. Nobody really thought the process could be reversed after being implemented on a trial basis for a year.)

While there were people on either side of the divide during the years
of debate over change at Hatzor, there were also a significant number
who had feet in both camps, uncertain of the change, not necessarily
against it but wary just the same. Chava Tal, who came to Israel in
1970 a few years after graduating from Oberlin College in Ohio, describes feeling "very schizophrenic" about the changes, though with
her excellent English language skills she can now earn good money
as a translator and editor. She said:

> I joined kibbutz because I believed in the ideology, that it was
> possible to create a new generation of people who would not be
> envious of material goods. It was a rejection of the American
> way of life. I was pretty much able to live within the framework
> of the economic policies of the kibbutz. I wasn't the person who
> went out and bought a car or the first to have a new appliance.
> I do buy books, and when I went to the States, I didn't try to live
> on the budget of the kibbutz. My parents were willing to give
> me whatever I wanted, but I wasn't willing to take it. It both-
> ered me very much that others had outside income.[9]

Chava Tal's husband was born at Hatzor, and they have three boys
ages twenty-six to nineteen. The youngest, Yair, has Down's syn-
drome. He attends a special school in Ashdod paid for by the kibbutz.
When the children's houses were still in use, Hatzor put an extra
*metapelet* (caretaker, usually a woman) in the children's house at
night for Yair. "Communal sleeping arrangements saved our family,"
Chava Tal recalls. She continued:

> I think there was a movement on the kibbutz to look outward
> not inward in the beginning of the 1990s or earlier. People
> wanted what the rest of Israel wanted. My generation became
> very materialistic. I'm talking about the generation of Hatzor
> that married in, not the *vatikim* [founding generation]. Before,
> everything had been so Stalinist—one bathing suit every six
> years, new sheets every five years. Nobody was allowed to have
> anything better than anyone else, and then, slowly, the whole
> ideological basis of the kibbutz was eaten away. Nobody voted
> on it.[10]

She's concerned about how the changes have affected women:

> We've given up the privileges we had [under the old system]. We
> were able to work fewer hours. We had more time to devote to
> hobbies and personal things. I'm sure that we will find that
> women's salaries are substantially lower than men's. In Hatzor,
> women are not in management positions, not in high profes-
> sional positions like engineering. They are still in education
> whether it's high school or children's houses. And Hatzor has
> been very forward looking because the salaries in the children's
> houses are good, because they want to have people [from] inside
> the kibbutz working in them.

Part of Chava Tal's ill feelings toward the changes on the kibbutz
has to do with her consternation over the differential salaries. Her
very human reaction is fairly typical of many on the kibbutz who
were used to valuing work for work's sake and didn't do a cost analysis before they performed what they saw as their kibbutz duties.

> The change to differential salaries made me feel inferior. Before,
> I took care of my family, and I spent a lot of time with my son.
> I did my writing. I also felt like I was contributing—I was on lots
> of committees, and the fact that my husband was the chief en-
> gineer of the factory and works longer hours than I do didn't
> make me feel less equal. But I took one look at what salary he
> was getting and what I was getting [when she was working at an
> administrative job at the Omen factory] and I didn't feel like we
> were equal anymore. It still bothers me. I don't care. We can live
> on the salaries, but it was an insult. I was flabbergasted that it
> was that low. So, I went to the outside people we have who are
> our consultants and I told them what we are doing and what
> salary they gave me, and the consultants said, "You're doing all
> this, and this is the salary they gave you?" And so it was ad-
> justed, but not enough.[11]

> It weakened my loyalty to the factory. I had spent extra hours
> working. But now, I think, while I still can, I want to do things
> that challenge me, use my potential, and contribute to Israeli so-
> ciety and not just the bottom line. I don't want to work here on

the kibbutz so that people can buy more electrical appliances and give more people the chance to go abroad. Before, I felt like we were all contributing, all splitting the pie. But now I don't feel that way. I don't see that having more money has made people more responsible. It hasn't made them nicer people nor made them more responsive to what is going on in Israel. I think we have closed ourselves off.

In fact, those who argued for change on the kibbutz didn't think that change would have an impact on kibbutz members' engagement with Israeli society. Nor would it necessarily make people nicer. It would simply get the kibbutz out of bankruptcy, while also offering a future and a decent standard of living to the kibbutz members. It did both of these things, although Tal genuinely didn't seem to mind the economic circumstances in which she lived before the changes. Like most kibbutz members, she didn't know about the serious financial crisis threatening Hatzor before the shinui.

An ancillary goal of the shinui was to provide ways for kibbutz members to find satisfaction in their jobs either inside or outside the kibbutz. In former times, just being a kibbutz member was satisfaction enough, and members who might read Tolstoy at night didn't mind working in the laundry or the chicken coop by day. But in the early years of the twenty-first century, for the most part, that's no longer the case. The satisfaction Tal has achieved by realizing her potential in new arenas (she works part time as a grant writer for a nonprofit foundation) is exactly the type of positive return for which the change instigators had hoped.

Indeed, in the case of those who fought for the change, they thought that a higher standard of living and more career satisfaction would be factors that could keep a new generation on the kibbutz. In this regard, differential salaries were considered a key element of the economic change. Chava Tal, however, remains skeptical in this regard: "We could have made changes without differential salaries. I think people leaving has nothing to do with differential salaries. Differences in housing is a very big problem. It causes a lot of jealousy because of the age system, which is so rooted here."[12]

Yet for all of her concerns, Tal has more nostalgia for the old ways than a real wish for them to return:

I did see that the opposition group had no model for change and no things to give the kibbutz. I thought that the change people were innovative, creative, contributing throughout their lives to the kibbutz. I am at a time when I want that freedom. On the one hand, I'm really sorry that we couldn't make a go of it. On the other hand, I'm happy we have more. My husband earns a lot. I don't have to ask my parents for money.[13] I sincerely hope we can make a go of it, but I am worried about women—I think the kibbutz system failed women.

Nitza Nadil disagrees. Nearly twenty years younger than Chava Tal, she belongs to the last generation to become members at Hatzor. She came to Hatzor from Jerusalem as a member of an army unit, and she married Atar Nadil, who was born on Hatzor. She is thirty-three and her husband is forty-three. They have two young sons. Nitza has a master's degree in education administration. From 2000 to 2002 she was spending 80 percent of her time working in the Department for Children and Youth at a neighboring regional council (a council comprised mostly of kibbutzim) and 20 percent in charge of Hatzor's educational program. She is also a member of Hatzor's mazkirut. Atar is manager of a company that is an offshoot of Hatzor's safety box business.

Nitza Nadil thinks that the changes have meant "higher positions" with "higher salaries" for women. But she adds: "A woman needs to break down barriers. It is a fact that in Hatzor there are no women in decision-making positions among the businesses. There is a kind of machismo that doesn't allow this. But the women also don't aspire to this."

Sylvia Kedem was one of the vatikim who supported most of the changes. One thing she doesn't miss at all is the children's houses. It's been decades since she has had children to raise, and none of the Kedem children live on the kibbutz today. One granddaughter lives about a half hour away in Beersheva. She speculates that the end of the children's houses was the first chink in the armor:[14]

Personally, I was for raising children at home. I thought it was a wonderful idea. I remember attending a group here—Uri Eshel's wife, Mira, invited me. We were two older women because our children were already grown and out, and I said I thought we should change the system. I remember two young women came over to me—they were crying—and said, thank you.

When Sylvia and her husband Yitzhak and young son took the boat trip from New York to Israel and landed at Hatzor in 1946, Hatzor was only a few tents and some shacks. She recalls:

There was a communal shower, oriental toilets. We never dreamed we'd have no toilet paper. We didn't know, and we didn't want to rock the boat. We accepted the children's houses as part of the whole package. We adjusted to it for the good of the kibbutz and kibbutz ideals that we believed in. But, personally, we didn't like it.

Sylvia and Yitzhak Kedem were very committed socialist Zionists. They joined Hashomer Hatzair in Brooklyn before they were in their teens. During World War II, most of the men went into the U.S. Army

Weekly kibbutz meeting (or *sicha*) at Hatzor, 1980s. (Photo courtesy of Kibbutz Hatzor.)

and the women lived in a movement commune near Grand Army Plaza in Park Slope, Brooklyn. "This may sound nutty today, but we decided that people who were married would not have children because we felt that we were too transitory. There was no family life. We lived in the same house and had a ban on couples sleeping together. This was all preparation for aliyah, for the new life in Israel," Sylvia Kedem recalls in July 2001 at age eighty-three, sitting in their tiny kitchen. However, they did manage to sneak in some private time befitting a young married couple. Before they arrived in Israel, they had managed to spend at least one night together—they arrived with their year-and-a-half-year-old son. Today, he lives in Kochav Yair.[15] The Kedems also have two daughters, one living in Switzerland and the other in the United States. Both married young men who volunteered to work on the kibbutz and later chose to return to their homelands.

Even though they had a hard time adjusting to their new life, the Kedems made friends at the kibbutz and even today feel that they had a good support system through the years. Sylvia managed the communal kitchen. Yitzhak, who has a master's degree in economics from Brooklyn College, worked in industry, for years managing Omen, the kibbutz die casting factory.

Sylvia commented:

> I didn't support all the changes, but I just felt that this could not go on. Working in the kitchen I had a lot of contact with people, and I felt that something had to be done, but I didn't know what. I thought that there should be a way of recognizing the difference of effort, talent, and voluntary activity, what a person gave of himself. I didn't know what. It wasn't concretized in my mind. It even made me cynical about the whole thing. This was in the 1980s.

Yitzhak, however, isn't thrilled with the changes, even though he has been a full participant in the discussions and decision making. He was upset by the hypocrisy of the past decades, but he misses the old-style kibbutz.

> I don't remember whether or not I voted for the changes, it's not important. I'm one of the few vatikim on committees with the

young people.[16] Unfortunately, it will not be a kibbutz. It will be what they call in Hebrew yishuv kehillati. It might be very, very nice. It will have within it many of the characteristics of the kibbutz. But call it the "new kibbutz" or the "revised kibbutz."

These changes are going to be very major. There has been a great regression in management procedures of the kehilla, of the factories, of industry—everything connected with management. We've been trying for many years—not successfully—to have participatory management. That's the big thing today in modern capitalistic management, but we are going backwards. Now there are secrets, worse than before. I don't know how much you make; you don't know how much I make. Also, less and less people are working on the kibbutz. More and more are working outside. A lot of capable people didn't find good expression on the kibbutz. Today, if we don't hire someone to cook, there won't be anyone to cook.

While Sylvia Kedem was more open to the changes, Yitzhak, too, realized there was need for change. But he wishes it could have maintained more of the traditional socialist trappings, including a more inclusive management structure. And while both Sylvia and Yitzhak say they feel secure today, they also say they felt secure before the changes. It's a fairly typical contradiction among the founding generation on the kibbutz. After all, they built something monumental. It was their home for decades. Basically, it provided a good life for them and their children. It's hard for them to imagine it all disappearing, although, without the economic changes, Hatzor would have had a difficult time continuing to provide for the founding generation.

The hint of crisis came when the kibbutz used the Kedems' pension fund—together with that of the entire membership—to make up for financial shortfalls. Yitzhak says, "We thought the return on the pension fund would be greater than the regular pension fund. There was also a theory in the kibbutz movement that since the kibbutz would take care of us, there was no need to establish a pension fund."

That the Hatzor blueprint for change made very clear that the vatikim would be protected offers welcomed relief to the Kedems, but it doesn't stop them from having some continued anxiety about their future, which is only natural. Because news—and gossip—

spreads quickly in a nation as small as Israel, and especially throughout the kibbutz movement, the Kedems were hearing and reading a
lot about other change models on other kibbutzim. "I'll tell you about
Gesher Haziv," Yitzhak said. "At one point, the vatikim organized
and signed a letter. They said they weren't being taken care of."

When one of the authors told him that this isn't true, that the
vatikim were cared for, he and his wife still appeared a bit worried,
but they are resigned to the changes at their kibbutz. Sylvia Kedem
put it succinctly:

> I saw the handwriting on the wall. The caliber of the young peo-
> ple who were leaving was very high. Our children left too. We
> would become an old-age home without leadership. I, person-
> ally, think that if we had not made these changes the leadership
> would not have remained, and we would have been left holding
> the bag. The older people who were the leaders can't function:
> age is limiting. Therefore, change is necessary, and thank the
> good lord that we made it in time.

Whether the new generation will decide to live at Hatzor, even with
the changes, is still a very big question. An afternoon discussion with
several young people of postarmy age in the summer of 2000 at Tamar
and Gary Brenner's home brought forth some honest comments. We
sat around eating watermelon with a pile of cell phones in the center
of the table—at least one per person. The young people, all Hatzor
born and bred, were very respectful—and appreciative—of the generations that came before but, perhaps not so unlike the earlier kibbutz
generations, they want to find their own way in the world. And, like
the Israel of today, they are anti-ideological and individualistic.

One young person we interviewed at that gathering was Neva Zerach, a spirited redhead whose parents were actively engaged against
the changes. Neva was bold in her assessment of the changes. She
lives with her boyfriend who pays rent to the kibbutz. "Israel is an an-
tisystem society today, and kibbutz is a big system. I have no senti-
ments to the communal way of life, only to the grass on which I ran
as a child. I want to keep the community going for that reason and no
other. My friends went to school in order to leave the kibbutz."

Jo-Ann Mort talked with Neva Zerach again in July 2001 at her parents' home. Like many other kibbutz families, there was disagreement between the generations. The interview took place around a table in the corner of the living room, while we all munched on cookies and drank coffee that was heated on a hot plate.

When Binnie, Neva's mother, first came to Israel as a tourist in 1964, she arrived at Hatzor on an *ulpan*, an intensive study course to learn Hebrew. That was where she met Jonathan Zerach, a Hashomer Hatzair youth leader who taught French and history in his native Tunisia before coming to Hatzor with several family members in 1962. Jonathan holds a master's degree in history and is a veteran of the poultry farm, where he is responsible for raising the young chicks. Binnie smiles: "He was quite a romantic cocktail for a student who had just finished Berkeley."

Jonathan Zerach remembers the early 1960s:

Hatzor was very orthodox, even more than other kibbutzim. Today, you would call it conservative, but it was very close to hard line, and especially strict about private possessions and equality. It was forbidden to smoke in the dining room or in public

Hatzor *machane* in the early 1950s. (Photo courtesy of Kibbutz Hatzor.)

Hatzor housing, 2002. Two family units. (Photo courtesy of Kibbutz Hatzor.)

places. They were very strict about what you had in your house. Everyone had to have the same. My professor wanted me to be a Sorbonne professor, but I was ideological about Zionism and socialism.

At that time, the founders of this kibbutz were forty-four, forty-five years old, an age when you are very strong and sure of yourself. They were against hired labor, against outside work, very strict and very Marxist. I was never a kind of Stalinist. I was not a Russian lover. I was more of a French socialist than a Bolshevik. Yaakov Hazan said our second homeland is Russia. I will never forget it.[17]

Binnie Zerach remembers her own beginning at Hatzor:

I was in the New Left at the University of Wisconsin at Madison, and then at Berkeley. It was a time of change, SNCC [Student Nonviolent Coordinating Committee, the civil rights organization], but I also had Jewish roots and wanted that combination. A friend told me to go to a Kibbutz Artzi kibbutz to see the real thing. The kibbutz was very idealistic, and, strangely, there was also a small-town feel about it. I found that disappointing—the gossip. I couldn't believe people were still Stalinist and that no one had heard of the welfare state. I was a bohemian, but here, if someone went into the dining room in bare feet, people said, wow, that showed disrespect.

It was the genuineness that I grew to like on the kibbutz. I found kibbutzniks to be very admirable people, more admirable than I considered myself to be, and I found it hard to keep up with them and their willingness to sacrifice. This was a totalitarian society . . . building a community and building a country based on consensus. So, if you wanted to visit your mother for seven days, and the kibbutz said you could only do it for five days, and you had a cheaper ticket for seven days . . . that was a problem.[18] That's how much the kibbutz seeped into your life.

One day at a meeting, it was decided that my husband and I were going to have to go as pioneers to another kibbutz and leave my mother-in-law alone here. The only reason it didn't happen was that I got up and walked out of the meeting, because that was my American way of saying that I wasn't going to do that. Nobody expected me to have the discipline of the youth movement. I was considered a little weird, but I do have some very good friends here, and I respect the people very much.

Binnie Zerach was in her late thirties in the early 1980s. The kibbutz began having meetings for second-generation members to discuss how their goals would be differentiated from those of their elders, the founders.

I think there was a feeling for some people that the relevance of the kibbutz had been reduced. The things that were hurting hurt a little more. A lot of sacrifice was demanded of people— they didn't call it sacrifice, but you had to cut your wings. There are people here who are very talented, who could have done many magnificent things, and they didn't do them. And there were a lot of things that were petty and small done in the name of the community, and as young people grew up they wanted more of a sense of individual control of their destiny. When the kibbutz was much richer, it was much easier to get a feeling of progress. You're moving forward; you're building something, creating a different kind of educational system. Of course, the collapse of communism certainly had a lot to do with it. And I think a combination of the world scene, the country scene, and an individual sense of a kind of discomfort came together and made people say maybe there's something immoral about everybody getting the same thing no matter what they do.

For Jonathan Zerach, what he calls "the malaise" began when Hatzor experienced financial troubles and when the young people began leaving.

This situation was creating a feeling among the middle generation—late thirties, forties—that something has to be done, and they were connecting the situation to the problem of the structure of the society inside the kibbutz.

The kibbutz was split in two camps. We were in the camp that said this is the wrong analysis of the situation. The young people don't stay here not because of financial problems but for other reasons.

In 1986, the kibbutz decided to discuss limited economic change. We never talked about living on a different level inside. We never touched that. We just wanted to be more economical. A branch that was losing money should be shut. That was the first change.

That made sense to Jonathan, but not to his wife:

In those days, if there were changes made I thought they had to be on a social level, not economic level. Many of the social institutions of the kibbutz were crumbling, and the lines of communication between the different groups living on the kibbutz were becoming rotten. And a community like this could not function if the people didn't care about each other.

Jonathan Zerach doesn't support differential salaries, but he understood the need for some extra income for kibbutz members, and he thought that there was a way to achieve this goal.

People were hiring outside people to do simple jobs. Instead, let kibbutz members do these jobs for a little money. Some of the managers of the factory said, "No, we don't have time to do extra work, but we are diligent. We work for the community when some people do nothing during the day," and they were moving slowly toward different salaries.

"I thought that eventually the government would help us out," Binnie said. "Yes, the economic output had to be monitored because a lot of money was reinvested in ways that were very wasteful. But that is different from a setup where every person in the kibbutz is part of a unit that is supposed to be profitable." For Jonathan, though, the biggest change on kibbutz today is not the differential salaries, but rather that

> people who are not all members are living in the same place. That's a huge change, because if you can have the same quality of life, you can have the same apartment, but if you don't put your salaries in the box, this is not a kibbutz anymore. I was for this kind of change because my neighbor is my partner . . . my daughter can work here but not be a member.

"Now, there is an economic elite, and it is also a social elite," laments Binnie.

> When you have a few people who are heads of very large institutions that are providing the most for the people of the community, they receive a kind of prestige. If those people are also interested in governing the social life of the community, they have a huge advantage—people are afraid to go against them. You have a set of people who are controlling the life of the community, and then you have a set of hired people. At the meeting, you are like a stockholder; at work you are a worker. You can be fired.
> I didn't come here to be a worker. I teach at a teachers' college in Tel Aviv and work in multimedia educational material as a consultant. I have better security than the people in the kibbutz. How could that be? That's because of the changes.
> The people who wanted the changes kept going for a vote,

then another vote and another vote. Sometimes we would joke and say what difference is it how we vote, we're going to vote again next weekend. And there were people who were just stunned [by the designated salaries]. Suddenly, in a community where people work all of their lives, you decide to stop the merry-go-round and say this is who you are. . . . I think people feel it wasn't fair. The model we picked is not a model that is easily implemented emotionally, because it doesn't take into consideration the path for people who gave their lives for others. I thought we could set up a point system that would include the kinds of contributions you make in the community, which would effect your salary because people are still making very important contributions to the community.

Now, we're rich. We make a lot more money than we ever made before, but I feel uncomfortable that there are other people here who in the years when we worked shoulder to shoulder didn't contribute any less than I did. The wheel stopped in a good place for me. I'm outside working in private companies making a lot of money. That isn't what I intended to do—because if I intended to be rich, I could be a lot richer.

As they talk Neva, their daughter, enters the house, and without skipping a beat exclaims: "It's totally different from whatever they are saying."
Her father smiles and continues:

Young people don't stay on kibbutz today due to ideological reasons, not because of salary but because their self-image is different today and personal career is very important. I remember that in the youth movement to have a career was something disgusting; you were supposed to be fighting for the fate of the people, the fate of the state.

There are some aspects of the change that Jonathan and Binnie Zerach think were done quite well at Hatzor—for instance, the dining room. Binnie thinks that the change there was "done with considerable thought." And she approved of "the changing of the education system from a closed system to an open system."

It was losing money, and by opening it to the community it became a business that supported our education. The children's
houses were finished because we had a war [the 1991 Gulf War];
there was no way that the people in charge of education—I was
in charge at the time—would be responsible for these children.
So we sent them home, and that was it, nobody wanted to come
back. I think the kibbutz met that challenge well.

But our discussion kept returning to differential salaries. In addition to their dislike of the differential, they had doubts about whether
the progressive taxation would survive. This suspicion is probably
justified, in that several people admitted they have no idea whether
the progressive taxation and strong social safety net will survive the
next generation.

Binnie Zerach raises some of the same issues that Chava Tal raised
about the level of payment for work that Binnie once considered part
of her contribution to the community.

I'm a teacher, and I gave English lessons for free because the kids
needed English lessons. One day, a woman came to me and she
said, "You can get forty shekels for extra hours," and I said, "Oh,
thank god, I don't have to do it anymore." For forty shekels, I'm
not going to sit there for two hours when I can earn two hundred shekels somewhere else. I can't explain it, but when you
are doing things for money versus when you are doing things because you live here, because they are our children and you care
about them. . . . I think part of kibbutz life was about giving—
now, that's taken away."

Jonathan said:

There is a disappointment. We thought we were living in a society of the future, showing how people can live together in a
way that the human being is not a product of society where you
have to put somebody down so that you are up. People outside
the kibbutz are fighting all the time for something like this.
Even in high-tech they are fighting hard to stay human, not to
let the system get them. And we thought the kibbutz was the

way, and suddenly we have this kind of reaction that people want to be more like outside, and we are disappointed. In this system, the smart people protected the weak and the idiots. Now, I'm not sure. . . . I can't fight on behalf of other people because how can I be owner and worker?

Binnie and Jonathan Zerach end their interview because they have a date with their young grandchild who lives on the kibbutz. But as they leave, Binnie smiles and says, thinking about the younger generation, "The kibbutz raised radical individualists."

Neva yells after her, "We are not radical, Mom. We are not radical, we just married people from outside who do not like this kind of life. My brother is a radical, but my sister and I are not. I'm not going to stay here if I'm not going to get a better house." And her parents are out the door.

The housing issue is of great importance for Neva Zerach, as is the chance to fulfill her potential. These are more important for her than the issue of differential salaries. But mostly she is engaged in thinking about the changes because of her parents.

If it wasn't for my parents, I couldn't care less. I don't want to be a member of this community if it stays the same community. But if you put the change into an old community it will be a disaster, and it *will* be a disaster. I wouldn't stay on the old kibbutz. I would like to stay in the kibbutz but with a better standard of life—not quality, but standard.

I would really like to stay here for the rest of my life, and I would really like to raise my children here, but I can't, because I know what I want and I can't meet my potential here. It's not only financial. I'm not sure what I want to be. I'm starting in communications management at a college in Tel Aviv. I have many things to choose from, but I'm sure that I won't want to work inside the kibbutz. I would rather work outside—it comes from my character.

I don't think differential salaries are bad. I'm much more attached to the outside world than my parents are, and I feel it all the time with my friends, my fiancé—he is from Ashkelon. My boyfriend's issues are very different from mine, he is very aware of the need for money, much more than I am, so we have very different ideas about that. It's very hard for him to live here.

My problem with the kibbutz is not whether I will have money or not. It's the community. It's very suffocating. That is why I wouldn't want to be a member even if there is a real change, because a real change in an old society will create an ugly society, because you can't avoid it that the person you grew up with has a better car than you have, you can't avoid it. If you go to live in Tel Aviv, you know that's the world, that's how things go, but here it's not right. I feel that if someone wants a bigger house, build a neighborhood—why not? It's your children. But I know that people will feel that there will be second-class citizens.

I have to choose in the next few years where I am going to spend my life, if we are going to buy a house. I have to choose if I am going to be a teacher or a businesswoman, and the kibbutz doesn't give me an alternative that tempts me. It doesn't take much because I could be very happy doing something that isn't a big career and still be happy knowing that my children are growing up here. I am fully aware of the advantages of this place. It's the only place where I feel at home in a public place. My friends and I feel at home at the same place because when we go to the swimming pool, it's our swimming pool. I couldn't feel better in a different place.

Neva Zerach has thought a lot about what Hatzor could do to keep her.

It's very practical. We're thinking of getting married in six months. [They got married in June 2002.] In maybe a year, a year and a half, I'll become pregnant. The thing is if I'm not a member, I can't get a house bigger than my sister who lives here [as a nonmember]. If I become a member, that can happen only after I finish my degree; I have to wait another six or seven years to get a big house. If you're not a member, you can't rent a better house—there is a hierarchy among the members. My sister's apartment . . . she has two kids, and it's not even as big as [that of] a couple with one kid.

But, what if the kibbutz were to build a separate neighborhood that didn't include kibbutz membership? "We would stay definitely, and not just us." She wouldn't mind paying a percentage of her income to join the community in some fashion.

> I would think about it as preserving a part of this ideology that I think is right. If not, I can buy a house somewhere else—it's not just that it's five minutes from my mother and my father. It's the feeling that it's the only place—and I'm willing to give up some of my assets to preserve it. And even more, I would be willing to volunteer in something, and I do, I do now. I participate and I organize. People ask me because they know I'll do it, and I like to do it.
>
> I feel that the children's attitude toward money is different today, and that's because they have their own room [as opposed to the old system of collective child rearing], and a lot of reason that people are concerned about having more money is to be comfortable in their family. Here at home, to be able to buy their children the new video game that they want or a better bicycle— the things other people around the world think about and worry about.

Neva never saw herself as deprived when she was growing up:

> I didn't know. But today I look back and I think, "Oh my God, it's poverty!" I got to buy pants and shirts once a year for the holiday. I wouldn't want to go back. I wasn't a poor child in school. Everybody had the same thing. I think it's TV and the MTV generation. It goes one way and you can't go back. It's not just the kibbutz.
>
> I was in Hashomer Hatzair, but we were the last. We weren't as ideological as the people who went before, and even less after us. We were very, very into what was going on with us, not what was going on with Israel, not with what was going on with the kibbutz, not with Hashomer, nothing. We wanted a car because it was fun and we got to drive and meet boys.
>
> We have a plan—you finish high school, you go to army, you finish army, you go abroad, you come back, you go to university,

you finish university, you get married. Not many break it. Because you have so many friends, a structure, you feel easy in it. The army is very long, and you come out confused all over the place, and the thing to do to not get lost is start studying. So that's what we do, but then you don't explore, you don't go to build a new kibbutz in the Negev—and they used to do that.

I don't feel the kibbutz has a mission for the country, but I never did—I'm not talking about history. There isn't a feeling in the Israeli public that the kibbutz is contributing to Israel in any way. And I was very surprised to see that in the army. I'm not talking about ignorant people—I would hear people say, this, this and this, and I would think, nobody told me that, and this wasn't in my history class. I think my issues are much more global today. I feel that I'm responsible for human rights—I would fight for these things—and that's why I would give the money if I lived here because I think that people gave to this state and we should give back, but not because it's a way of life.

Neva Zerach raised a critical issue during the interview, that of the role of the young people on the kibbutz. For a society that is so dependent on the loyalty of the next generation, the kibbutz—as an institution—does little to involve those in their teens and twenties in the decision making. This is a perennial kibbutz problem and probably accounts for some of the lack of loyalty—or, to use an American word, "ownership"—that the current generation feels toward the kibbutz.

I think we all feel like the kibbutz is not involving young people in issues, and that is very problematic. Sometimes we have conversations about the kibbutz, and it's very frustrating because I don't have the right to vote until I'm a member. But they have to accept me for membership just after I finish my degree, when I'm what, twenty-seven? But by twenty-seven, often you're married with a child, so you have to make a choice before. I feel that the kibbutz isn't interested in our ideas because, you know, you are the first person to ask me as a representative of anything of what I think about the kibbutz. The kibbutz never did. The only encounter young people ever have with the kibbutz is to fix things, to change our status from this way to that. It's always meetings about little things that I don't go to any more.

I see that my father is a fighter, but it's very costly and I don't want to pay that cost. I would be willing to fight for something, I think, but I know that I would have the short stick because if I would go and say, "How about this?" they would say, "Listen it's not relevant to our problems because our problems have to do with the members." They are not concerned with us yet. And I think that's too bad, because I feel that we could be a very good next generation on this kibbutz. I wouldn't go live on another kibbutz, but on this kibbutz. There is very good energy, very strong, smart people. We feel like a group. I have many friends who love to come here on summer break. We love it here. I feel like it's a great country club, and I appreciate it, but the thing is that nobody realizes it—they call the young people to tell us about the drug problem, or whatever. People here work in a way that I don't relate to. These are little things, but eventually they cut down your energy to fight for something.

They don't nourish me, and I feel that I should be nourished. People younger than me are even more frustrated than I am—and their status on the kibbutz is like they are hired help. I can only hope that Hatzor, ten years from now—because things are moving in different directions—will open the possibility for there to be a different status than a member and still keep a membership for people who don't want the money—for my parents, my father. I don't think it will be abused; you have to sign a contract and everything. Because if not, I will definitely leave. I would live a much better way of life outside. But I choose not to because I am still on a vacation from life.

It's difficult to predict, but at Hatzor it appears that Neva Zerach's desires could be met. The kibbutz has made it through the change process, so far, perhaps not with everyone happy but with few terribly unhappy. And the community has a strong desire to keep their young people.

Uri Eshel puts the problem of kibbutz membership this way:

The fact is that you can live in Hatzor now. In some of the kibbutzim you can't live now because people don't like each other. In five years, we will all be residents, because this is the way the younger generation likes it to be. The difference between the kibbutz members and the nonmembers is that we have shares of the business and some assets that they don't have. I think that when they realize that the value of the shares is high, and when they have a chance to buy the shares for a low price, or they have a way to get shares in the future, they will have more interest in belonging to the kibbutz.

In the summer of 2001, Uri Eshel was anticipating the Knesset decision on whether or not a kibbutz could transfer ownership of an apartment or home from the collective to the individual. Some kibbutz members, certain that the outcome would be in their favor, were already beginning to build additions to their homes. And, Hatzor's economic council, which includes the directors of the different kibbutz businesses and communal representatives, had been forewarned that additional investment will be required to complete new housing construction, some of which was actually begun three years ago.

By the end of August 2001, an agreement was worked out between the Kibbutz Movement's representatives and the Registrar of Cooperative Associations that allows houses to be privatized and the kibbutzim to retain their status as cooperative associations.[19] In the beginning of 2002, the agreement was still waiting approval by the social affairs minister, who was Shas Party member Shlomo Benizri.[20]

No less important, the beginning of 2002 found Hatzor embroiled in the next phase of the change discussions: allocation of private parcels of land around members' homes. Among the questions of principle were: What are veterans' property rights versus those of the members of working age? Proponents advocating that veterans be compensated financially but that land distribution be carried out among the younger generations are once again faced with having to find a middle ground between guaranteeing the future of the kibbutz and providing basic rights for all its members.

# GAN SHMUEL

## The Classic Kibbutz in a Time of Change

> Everything that is being done in Gan Shmuel, in the name of the kibbutz, for the kibbutz, or by the kibbutz, is an expression of our loyalty, as individuals and as a collective, in the spirit of Gan Shmuel.
>
> —"The Spirit of Gan Shmuel," August 2000

Kibbutz Gan Shmuel with five hundred members and several hundred nonmembers is big enough to feel like a small town. It's surrounded by industry, several of the nation's earliest kibbutzim, Arab villages, the medium-size city of Hadera, the resort town of Caesarea, and an increasing number of suburban-style housing developments. The kibbutz is off of Highway 65, just past the Gan Shmuel Shopping Center (the kibbutz owns 51 percent of the center; the other 49 percent is owned by Eliezer Fishman, one of Israel's foremost entrepreneurs). The cornerstone of the shopping center is a modern supermarket, owned solely by Gan Shmuel, that grew from the kibbutz's *duchan* (or roadside fruit stand). Other tenants include Tower Records, McDonald's, and an outdoor café where you can sit with your iced double latte. There's a graveyard for old farm machinery just past the kibbutz entrance, across the road from Gan Shmuel Foods, a multi-million-dollar citrus processing plant. The factory, which earns about $80 million a year in exports, began during World War II when the kibbutz, unable to export its oranges, began producing orange concentrate. The kibbutz annual income is approximately NIS 1.52 billion, plus they have their real estate assets.[1]

At the time when all kibbutzim were agriculturally based, Gan Shmuel went against movement doctrine by investing in industry. Although the hyperinflation of the 1980s hurt the kibbutzim, the fact that Gan Shmuel already had a successful export-based industry helped save it from financial crisis.

Beyond the factory, the original kibbutz entrance is preserved near the parking lot, and off to the right is a state-of-the-art swimming pool and sports center that serves as a community center for the regional council. On the other side of the parking lot are the original water tower and the large communal dining room. Unlike Gesher Haziv (and like Hatzor), Gan Shmuel's grounds are populated at almost all times of the day.

Sela Ronen, a twenty-something son of Gan Shmuel, who we interviewed in the summer of 2000, laughingly made this comment while standing outside of the dining room near a cluster of parked bikes: "You can know what status you have on the kibbutz according to how many wheels you have. The two wheels are lower; the three wheels are for the elders—they are higher status. I am on foot, I am the lowest."[2]

Gan Shmuel is one of Israel's richest kibbutzim—both in financial capital and human resources—although historically the kibbutz philosophy was distinctly spartan when it came to the standard of living for individuals. Today, rising expectations have contributed to an undercurrent of discontent in Gan Shmuel.

Many of the community's members have contributed much in the nation's cultural and political spheres. This kibbutz is known for its fierce ideological commitment to the founding socialist ideals of the Kibbutz Artzi Federation and to the ethos of Zionist service to the state that is inculcated in its young people. Gan Shmuel members proudly tell the story about a kibbutz son, Uri Eilan, a paratrooper who was killed in captivity by the Syrians during the October 1973 War. When his body was eventually returned, a handwritten note was found in Eilan's shoe which read, "I was not a traitor." The story of Uri Eilan is taught in Israel's schools and in the army as a symbol of heroism and devotion to the country. Today, Gan Shmuel's young

Agriculture at Gan Shmuel has been secondary to industry since World War II. Pictured in the background is the factory owned by the regional kibbutzim. (Photo by Esteban Alterman.)

people still serve in large numbers in elite military units, but just as in other—and less well-off—kibbutzim, less than 40 percent of young people are choosing to stay at Gan Shmuel.

Founded in 1897 as a farm by a Russian immigrant named Shmuel, Gan Shmuel (*gan* means garden in Hebrew) was started with contributions from farmers in nearby Hadera, when Hadera was no more than a farming village. In 1921 it became a kibbutz, when the first group of Hashomer Hatzair from Poland settled at Gan Shmuel. Groups from Austria and elsewhere in Europe later joined them. The Haganah had an outpost at Gan Shmuel where they made ammunition.

From 1927 to the end of the twentieth century, the kibbutz housed the regional high school where Jewish teenagers from all over the world were accepted, including a significant number of Holocaust survivors. In the 1950s, Gan Shmuel took in a large number of Jewish teenagers from Arab countries, who had immigrated to Israel without their families.

Though Gan Shmuel is considered one of the most conservative kibbutzim (conservative in the sense that it is resistant to change), it was also the first kibbutz whose factory went public, trading on the Tel Aviv Stock Exchange. In order to prepare proper financial reports and forecasts, Gan Shmuel was the first to separate the kehillah from the economic enterprises. In 1993, Gan Shmuel Foods was established as a corporation. There was a big debate on the kibbutz about whether or not to go public, but at that point another guiding principle of this cautious kibbutz took over—the unwillingness to go into debt. Gan Shmuel needed to generate more capital to expand the factory, and going public was one way to do so.

They instituted differential salaries as part of the preparations for the public offering. However, these salaries are unknown to the members working there. They aren't reflected in the member's allowance. The management reports to a board of directors in the same way as any well-run business. Some directors even come from outside the kibbutz, although the managers are all kibbutz members.

Everything in the kibbutz is cost accounted. Even buildings have a cost attached to them. If there is a certain building that the supermarket uses for storage, the supermarket pays for the storage. Similarly, kibbutz plumbers and carpenters "sell their services" to the kitchen when they come to make repairs or to the classroom to put in new window frames.

Introducing such a system to kibbutzim was often as painful a process as differential salaries. Typically, it touched upon the weakest links in the community, the middle-aged members working in service branches, who had no sense whatsoever of the workings of market economies. For years they worked hard at their jobs until one day an economist came to tell them they were a drain on the community. They were measured against plumbers and carpenters and electricians outside the kibbutz rather than their peers.

In most kibbutzim, for rules to change two-thirds must vote in favor. But at Gan Shmuel, the rules are much harder to change. According to the kibbutzim's Articles of Association, in order to approve structural changes in the kibbutz, three-quarters of the members must vote, and of that three-quarters, two-thirds must vote in favor of change. In the past few decades, some individual kibbutzim have won approval to liberalize this draconian provision, so that now two-thirds of the voting members can implement such changes. Recently, even Gan Shmuel voted to alter its by-laws to override the Articles of Association in order to make future change feasible.

In the last several years, the one-third resisting change have been able to keep things on a relatively slow track. But, as we found in talking to people at Gan Shmuel (not unlike other kibbutzim), rules are made to be broken. If the two-thirds can't garner the extra votes needed to bring about a desired change, members take it upon themselves to find ways to create a situation so that changes are implemented de facto. These are not criminal acts, but they certainly represent a normative deviation.

There's a saying in the kibbutz movement that sometimes a kibbutz owns a factory and sometimes a factory owns a kibbutz. At Gan Shmuel, the latter isn't quite the case, but it's not completely wrong either. The kibbutz members are much more involved in community social and cultural life than at Gesher Haziv. But we were surprised to find out how much of the decision making (the decisions that have the most impact on the daily life of the kibbutz) is actually controlled by a small informal group of leaders, several of whom are clustered around the factory and the kibbutz economic sectors.

The kehillah and the economy are separate, so that one of the economic heads of the kibbutz, the gizbar, does not even take part in the economic leadership of the factory. The factory stands alone in its governance. That's how precious its vitality is to the life of this community. The paradox of Gan Shmuel lies in the importance of its capitalist enterprises to the economic well-being of the traditional socialist community.

The formal leadership in the kehillah sector has little control today over the path of change for Gan Shmuel. Unlike Hatzor, where a group of leaders clustered around Solbar—the kibbutz's main source of income—led the change but was also integrated into the formal leadership structure of the entire kibbutz, at Gan Shmuel the factory managers appear to have little involvement in the kibbutz itself.

We originally went to Gan Shmuel for several reasons. It is one of the best-known and wealthiest kibbutzim in Israel. We thought it had decided—as a collective—to remain pretty much within the classic kibbutz structure. We also thought it would be the antithesis of Gesher Haziv on a change module. And we expected Gan Shmuel to resist the kind of privatization (especially differential wages) that Hatzor had settled upon. In late 1999, Gan Shmuel decided to ask one of Israel's foremost philosophers, Tel Aviv University professor Asa Kasher, to develop a socialist ethical code of conduct for the kibbutz as it wrestled with questions relating to the market and privatization. We anticipated that the "Kasher process" would serve as an informative contrast to the more utilitarian approaches toward change we found at Gesher Haziv and Hatzor.

Kasher, winner of the famed Israel Prize, had developed an ethical code for the Israel Defense Forces. He is a socialist in the Old World–Israeli style. We investigated the Asa Kasher process when we visited Gan Shmuel in the summer of 2000. But the process had been abruptly halted by the time we returned in the summer of 2001.

By then, we found a community in turmoil. The relative well-being of the kibbutz kept tempers under wraps, but, despite the well-manicured grounds, tension was palpable. There was an icy politeness among the members that dissolved behind the closed doors of our interview room. For those who had put their hopes in an *amana* (covenant) written by Asa Kasher for the kibbutz to adhere to, there was profound disappointment and bitterness toward those who had stopped the process. For those who either opposed the Kasher process or felt shut out by the group that instigated it, there was anger and resignation toward the kibbutz.

The two key advocates of the Asa Kasher process are Rafi Ashkenazi and Omri Kenan. They began the process while they were in the leadership of the mazkirut. When a new mazkira was elected they tried to keep up the spirit of the process from the sidelines. Ashkenazi, a rotund, ideologically committed sixty-year-old—the kind of person who will quote Isaiah Berlin's thinking on complex equality to justify the traditional kibbutz lifestyle—came to the kibbutz from Egypt without his parents to attend the high school. He became a Gan Shmuel member after returning from the army.

Kenan, born on the kibbutz in 1951, has served in a variety of leadership positions. His parents came to Israel from Central Europe. He received all of his education from kindergarten through high school at Gan Shmuel. His wife was also born in Gan Shmuel. They have four children—a twenty-one-year-old son in the army, and daughters ages sixteen, twelve, and five. Kenan has held a number of positions within the kibbutz kehillah and the Hashomer Hatzair youth movement at home and in the United States. With a degree from Haifa University, he has taught high school and has held several jobs at Gan Shmuel Foods, where today he is responsible for one of the laboratories. His wife teaches in the regional elementary school.

Kenan experienced a typical kibbutz childhood of a certain time period, one that could never be replicated on today's global stage. As he recalls, "On the Hanukah vacation, the kibbutz organized one truck—we didn't have a bus then—and took the kids out with the parents, so even when we went out of Gan Shmuel, we had almost no connection with kids out of Gan Shmuel. And we were happy, because anyone out of Gan Shmuel was considered an enemy."

Today, with fewer young people on the kibbutz, Gan Shmuel has shut down its high school. Its youngsters attend the regional high school ten kilometers away. Old rivalries between Gan Shmuel and another large KAF kibbutz, Ein Shemer, still linger to such an extent that Gan Shmuel decided to throw ideology to the wind and send their kids to the regional school rather than to the kibbutz high school at

Ein Shemer, which is attended by young people from several area kibbutzim.

Even with all the turmoil, kibbutz education is still considered to be very good. The proof of this is that many moshav and city parents want to send their children to the kibbutz schools instead of a school closer to home. But there just aren't enough youth on any single kibbutz to run a high school. Today, only a few kibbutzim maintain their own elementary or high schools, and when they do, they are clustered together to accommodate a group of kibbutzim as regional schools. Merging regional high schools is more cost effective.

Harkening back to his younger days, Kenan says, "I got a different perspective after I finished high school and went for a year of national service in Hashomer Hatzair near Haifa."[3]

Kenan takes us through Gan Shmuel's evolution as a kibbutz. He explains that private TV came into people's homes in the early 1980s. Telephones appeared around the same time, but at first there was no outside connection. You could only call internally on the kibbutz.[4] He says:

> Young people didn't know any place outside of Gan Shmuel. We got our information from the newspaper, but of course we only read *Al Hamishmar*,[5] which the kibbutz would buy in bulk. We only had television after the Six-Day War, after 1968. We only had the radio—and I don't know if you've heard the stories, but for many years in Gan Shmuel, we had only one radio in the dining room and one person was in charge of the radio.[6] In 1968, we had one TV in the moadon—with one channel. In the moadon we got one copy of *Ha'aretz*, which was considered the enemy paper.[7]
>
> The big change came for me during the Yom Kippur War. I was of the generation of soldiers who were on the front line—I was in the air force—who realized that we couldn't trust the leadership of Israel anymore. To me, that extended to the kibbutz leadership.
>
> After the 1977 election, we had the feeling that we had nothing to look for in Israel, that it was all lost. But, in spite of Gan Shmuel's conservative attitude to the rules in the kibbutz, in

Duchan, the Gan Shmuel supermarket. (Photo by Esteban Alterman.)

economic activities we were pioneers. We had a very small supermarket, a duchan, which in the 1970s we turned into one of
the first kibbutz supermarkets.[8]

The kibbutz's conservatism didn't extend to keeping open the communal dining room if it wasn't cost effective. Unlike at Hatzor, today
Gan Shmuel's dining room is closed for dinner except for the Friday
night Shabbat dinner. It's open seven days a week for breakfast and
lunch. "We had to deal with the fact that people didn't come; the only
people in the dining room were the *toshavim* [temporary residents,
nonkibbutz members]," Kenan told us.

But, as is characteristic of Gan Shmuel, they didn't make a formal
decision to close the dining room for dinner until attendance had lost
critical mass. So, too, with the children's houses. They only officially

Above the Duchan entrance is a mural telling the story of Gan Shmuel. (Photo by Esteban Alterman.)

closed them after most of the parents had already taken it upon themselves to move their kids into the parents' tiny homes. As Kenan put it, "The members make decisions counter to kibbutz rules, and then the kibbutz changes the rules to match the facts, which were created by the members." This practice is characteristic not only of Gan Shmuel but of kibbutzim generally.

For Kenan and his colleagues, the problem right now is that Gan Shmuel's current structure doesn't provide the kind of individual freedom desired by the members. He, too, wants more freedom, but he wants a freedom that is, to his mind, true to the founding kibbutz values.

> I believe—and it looks like I'm one of the few who believe—that the kibbutz could be an example for a better and more just society. I thought that the Asa Kasher process could strengthen this by having a new, distinguished mission statement of what the kibbutz is for. I didn't know what type of answers they would give. But Asa Kasher saw almost two hundred members, and he got the impression that the kibbutz members wanted a society based on equality, solidarity, and that the totality of the kibbutz should belong to the kibbutz, to the society—not to the members themselves. This doesn't mean it will be the same as in the 1940s. He also got the impression that the members want to strengthen the family and give the members more control over their own allowances, but it doesn't mean that the members don't want the kibbutz. So, we have to do the change that is necessary, but the basic ideals, the values of the kibbutz, people want to keep. I have the feeling that the new leadership doesn't understand the necessity of dealing with values.
>
> I would like to take as much responsibility for my life as I can, to have as much freedom as I can to choose what's good for me. But I still have a dream that it will be done in a way to keep those who have less skills with a good level of life. I'm afraid that some of those who really want to break the old system don't realize that they will be in a much worse condition.
>
> The total budget of the kibbutz can give us very good freedom. You know, no one has total freedom. But today, the percentage of the budget that is the kibbutz member's responsibility doesn't allow him to deal with basic needs. I would like to be in a situ-

ation where at least half of the budget is under the responsibility of the member—and I think the majority of the kibbutz agrees with me.[9]

Omri Kenan fears that if the kibbutz doesn't satisfy the desires and needs of the members within a certain framework, members will continue to break rules and ultimately destroy the system itself. While he wants more flexibility, he also wants to preserve the basic framework of kibbutz. He predicts: "I would like to keep a certain standard of life. If the kibbutz will not find the way to give me tools in an equal manner, then I will have no other way but to look for a salary for myself so that I can manage for my family."

Even though Gan Shmuel lives according to a conservative dictum, it's obvious that one of the rules that gets broken is that some members have more money than others, which means that some form of outside income or inheritance isn't being reported or pooled collectively. Kenan said:

I went for a two-week vacation with my family in Europe this summer—first vacation in five years. I believe that if anyone on the kibbutz is doing this more often, they use outside money. It's okay to use outside money, but I don't want to live a lower level of life because I don't have it.

But, he doesn't support individual salaries. "I believe that any connection between the salary and the allowance is the end of the kibbutz, because what is unique is that the members of the kibbutz want to live equally in spite of the fact that many members know they can live better."

Still, although Omri Kenan occasionally participates in the Zerem Shitufi group, which disdains the introduction of individual salaries, he isn't condemning of those kibbutzim that do have them, like some of the other Zerem participants are.

I'm actually encouraged by a kibbutz like Hatzor, which was in a very difficult situation, to take all the necessary steps to be better. The fact that I believe—not only me, all the leaders of those twenty-seven kibbutzim [that are part of Zerem Shitufi] believe—that any connection between your job, work, and your allowance will end the kibbutzim. Okay, so I think it, but if it will strengthen the situation of Hatzor, then I am very happy about it. We are not in the situation where the Kibbutz Movement is in a position to help the kibbutzim. We don't have that luxury anymore. I was at Hatzor a month ago and spoke with my friends, and they told me that it's unbelievable to see how many of those who were in conditions that they couldn't work are now looking for a job. For me, that's good for the community and for the members.

What Omri Kenan is addressing is analogous to the debate about welfare reform in the United States. For decades, the kibbutz supported a member, whether they worked or not. Today, at Hatzor and other kibbutzim that have instituted salaries, a member must work unless they are seriously disabled. Even Gesher Haziv, as we noted, has a pool of money available—a solidarity fund—for those who are unable to work. Hatzor does too. But the emphasis has shifted toward a member doing productive work that will help "pay" for their membership in the community if they are to receive the benefits of the community.

Kenan's hope is that if the member's autonomy within equal allowances guarantees enough individual choice and a higher standard of living, then the move to something more radical like private salaries and less equality can be avoided.

We have to attack the question now. We have to deal with the question—not what we have to change but what is important to keep. For me, it's important to keep the budget of gardening under the responsibility of the kibbutz. I don't have much more. That's it—and maybe catastrophic health care. I don't care if education is under a member's allowance. In ten years, we will be close to what Hatzor is now.

In fact, Hatzor has not privatized education or its health coverage. Professor Asa Kasher, whom we interviewed in his office at Tel Aviv University in the summer of 2000, was hopeful that his efforts could keep the classic kibbutz intact. He possessed an impassioned and romantic notion of the kibbutz, as reflected in the document that he helped craft for Gan Shmuel. Kasher faithfully fulfilled the mandate given to him by Rafi Ashkenazi and Omri Kenan by designing a covenant laden with pronounced values and obligations. But these pronouncements evaded the everyday concerns of the kibbutz members. Kasher failed to account for the social and economic realities of today's Israel, along with the realities of contemporary Gan Shmuel. In opting for romance over reality, the Asa Kasher process inevitably became a nonstarter.

"The Spirit of Gan Shmuel" document written by Kasher in consultation with several Gan Shmuel members opens with a simple declaration of loyalty:[10]

> We, the members of Gan Shmuel, as individuals and as a collective, take upon ourselves the "spirit of Gan Shmuel" as an expression of the values and the principles that constitute kibbutz life, and to which we are obligated.
>
> Everything that is being done in Gan Shmuel, in the name of the kibbutz, for the kibbutz, or by the kibbutz, is an expression of our loyalty, as individuals and as a collective, in the spirit of Gan Shmuel.

"The Spirit of Gan Shmuel" continues by listing a series of fundamental concepts, including the meaning of kibbutz within a traditional framework—equality for all people, pure democracy, and collective responsibility.

Kibbutz is defined as "a unique moral way of life" that "expresses values in its everyday existence." According to Kasher's document, because these values are essentially "collectivist" and "humanist," they create the foundations for a "meaningful life" for the individual.

But for him, the meaning of life in Gan Shmuel goes beyond the individual, reaching back to the kibbutzim's national mission by including a reference to the "independence of the Jewish people in its homeland, underlying the foundations of the State of Israel [while] striving for peace among nations."

The next section of the document defines equality:

> As a kibbutz, Gan Shmuel articulates the equality of humankind in its organization and lifestyle.

As a kibbutz, Gan Shmuel upholds equality in all aspects of its collectivity.

As a kibbutz, Gan Shmuel upholds equality as the foundation for individual lives.

As a kibbutz, Gan Shmuel allows for inequality only where there is a recognized need for special assistance.

As a kibbutz, Gan Shmuel views devotion to the equality of humankind as a superior expression to creating economic inequality.

Among the moral precepts outlined in "The Spirit of Gan Shmuel" this definition of equality most epitomizes the differences between the diverse approaches of the three kibbutzim under discussion. Those engaged with this process were trying to achieve, through the Kasher process, a firm commitment to the historic kibbutz values as defined in the 1923 Articles of Association, rearticulated by the kibbutz movement in the early 1970s, which stress a form of pure communism. "Equality of humankind" renounces ambitious achievers as being antithetical to kibbutz values. Our interviews led us to conclude that advocates for change in the kibbutz realized this contradiction, along with the heavy price they paid over the last few decades. But, for the Kasher devotees, there can be no other equality than absolute and universal equality. The only exceptions to the rule are those incapacitated for one reason or another who rightly deserve their due above and beyond the general means of distribution.

This is an ironic paradox of kibbutz norms—the exalted generosity lavished on the weak or maimed, while the gifted and physically strong are left to shift for themselves. This was something noted even by the young people at Gan Shmuel, who felt frustrated by the lack of incentives for exceptional performance. Indeed, the failure of kibbutzim to hold on to their most talented children can be attributed to this principle of one-dimensional equality.

Kasher is one of the most renowned intellectuals in Israel. He has been able to achieve his unique place in the hierarchy of the Israeli intelligentsia. Yet in this document, he placed the categorical notion of equality as his highest value, with no reference whatsoever to the roles of excellence and achievement when considering the future of kibbutz life.

Kasher's document rightly defines democracy in terms of both freedom and responsibility:

> As a kibbutz . . . Gan Shmuel constitutes and cultivates personal freedom and personal responsibility . . . as part of [its] charter of rights and duties. Gan Shmuel makes decisions collectively through fair processes, with a preference for . . . broad and fair agreement rather than majority rule. Gan Shmuel manages its collective lifestyle by elected institutions that act with fairness, maximum transparency, and mutual trust.

The section on democracy concludes with a traditional socialist refrain: "Gan Shmuel maintains common and equal ownership by all its members over the means of production, infrastructure, and incomes." Collective ownership precedes "collective responsibility of all its members for the existence of appropriate [economic] branches." The latter rightly refers to the need to evaluate each branch of the kibbutz for its true economic contribution to the community. But the only reference in the covenant to economic rationality is immediately couched in terms of "the equality of people, leaving aside one's ability to create economic inequality and unfairness."

Under "responsibility" Kasher includes education and welfare that together contribute to "creating meaningful lives, all in the framework of life at Gan Shmuel." In a holistic fashion, "Gan Shmuel considers itself responsible, through cooperation by all its members, for maintaining cultural aspects of communal and personal lives . . . cultivating its kibbutz culture . . . [and] contributing to Israeli society as expressed by its values."

The collective temperament is vital: "As a kibbutz, Gan Shmuel considers it a moral obligation to cultivate the quality of human relations among members and fellow human beings . . . as an expression of human dignity [and] brotherhood." Gan Shmuel also recognizes the importance of the family, alongside that of the individual.

"The Spirit of Gan Shmuel" is an attempt to reaffirm the foundations of the kibbutz in the twenty-first century. It concludes with definitions of continuity and change in the context of Gan Shmuel's "unique moral way of life . . . by preserving the vitality that is essential when facing new conditions and promising possibilities."

Kasher's covenant claims to respect the traditional values instituted by the founders of the kibbutz while agreeing to "appropriate changes." In fact, continuity is the central theme of "The Spirit of Gan Shmuel." It arose as the result of a giant tidal wave of economic and social crises in kibbutzim throughout Israel, but it sidesteps the crisis by reiterating universal values and dictates:

> As a kibbutz, Gan Shmuel expresses its respect for the way of life of generations of forefathers and mothers, symbolically and practically, without undermining the vitality that enables the appropriate changes.
>
> As a kibbutz, Gan Shmuel respects the desire to seriously evaluate propositions for changes in the kibbutz way of life, without undermining the continuity of its traditional values.

Kasher wrote about the "vitality" of the kibbutz. But we found that most members of Gan Shmuel are much more concerned about the *viability* of their kibbutz, framed by the context of what is happening in the rest of Israel and even in the global economy.

As an ethical code intended to be formally endorsed by its members, the Kasher document and the accompanying process was a failure, essentially irrelevant to the members it addressed. It presumed that universal values could be dictated to a less than homogeneous population, while ignoring the members' expressed needs and aspirations.

Those who led the effort, for reasons unclear to us, appear to have excluded key people from the deliberations. This was reflected in our interviews, and not really refuted by either Rafi Ashkenazi or Omri Kenan.

Some of the language, using words like *loyalty*, for instance, reflects a kind of dogmatism from an earlier era. While we certainly don't disapprove of framing the kibbutz as "a moral way of life," we did not find this to be of utmost concern when we talked to Gan Shmuel members. We did, however, discover a group of individuals who care for one another, and in this context hope to improve their lives. Rather than a declaration of ideological principles, Gan Shmuel members expressed their desire to guarantee the future of their community—their home—while maintaining basic moral values together with the general welfare of all the members.

When we met with Rafi Ashkenazi in July 2001, there was no person on the kibbutz more disappointed by the collapse of the Asa Kasher process. A year before, he and Omri Kenan sat with us in the kibbutz dining room and offered an animated explanation for the notion of the entire community coalescing around a document expressing socialist values. He, along with his friend Omri Kenan, felt secure in the notion that they had provided for the vatikim so that the pensioners and founding generation would have no need to worry if the entire kibbutz project collapsed. And, along with Kenan, he felt certain that they were beginning the process of coming together as a community around a set of shared values at a time when they still had that luxury. As Omri Kenan told us in July 2000: "I believe that only the kibbutz that is not in a crisis situation can speak about values, because otherwise we can't speak of values when we are speaking of survival. Maybe we are still far from that point."

In 2000 Rafi Ashkenazi described their thought process in bringing Kasher to Gan Shmuel:

> The first subject was ownership of the land, the guarantee to the vatikim so that—if you compare it to the Soviet Union, those who gave to the country had nothing left when the Soviet Union collapsed—we are taking care of those who founded the kibbutz and built it. They are cared for in case of crisis. Social welfare is taken care of. This gives us the freedom to go through the process we are going through because the security net exists for older members.

For Ashkenazi, the kibbutz exists like a perfect square. If one corner collapses, there goes the whole kibbutz: "There are four conditions that determine whether the kibbutz is a kibbutz. If one of them falls, then there is no more kibbutz. If we cross the redline, we are in postkibbutz." He is a rarity in today's Israel (at least on the left), someone who would rather live on values than income.

Ashkenazi lamented that his friends who still consider themselves leftists now only focus on peace issues and not economic and social issues. In addition to his commitment to traditional socialist values, he also has more of a willingness to live a classic kibbutz life (rotating jobs, working in agriculture, living most of his life within the confines of the kibbutz) than the overwhelming majority of people on kibbutz today. "Most of my friends are left wing, but they are not living a left-wing lifestyle. We live our reality; for them it's only theoretical," he says, proudly. "I remember when I was a shaliach in France, Trotskyists told me I'm not a real leftist because I kill Arabs, and I told them that every morning at half past four when I have to wake up to milk the cows, I have to deal with a socialist life and experience."

Omri Kenan, a generation younger than Rafi Ashkenazi, is clear about what he wants in the definition of kibbutz for Gan Shmuel: "I would like this paper to be an understanding of the kibbutz so that my father will feel okay. We have to keep the main tradition of Gan Shmuel, but we must be aware that we must change."

While we sat with them in the dining room, with people finishing their breakfast around us, Kenan and Ashkenazi digressed into a side conversation about the amount of money the kibbutz spends annually on the Egged bus line. Historically, kibbutz members traveled for "free" on Egged buses throughout Israel; the Egged bus company was previously owned by the all-encompassing trade union movement to which the kibbutzim also belonged as part of the old-fashioned labor economy. In fact, the tickets were never "free," but the kibbutzim would purchase a block of tickets for their members at a discount. (This notion of "free" things is typical of the traditional kibbutznik. Because money never passed hands, there was a presumption that everything from bus tickets to electricity in a member's home to food in the collective dining room was "free," when, of course, the collective was paying the bills.) Today, Egged is privatized, with the former trade union leaders now wealthy shareholders, and few kibbutz members travel on the buses now that private cars—or at least large fleets of communally owned cars—proliferate on the kibbutzim. At Gan Shmuel, too, there are few people who still use buses, yet because the kibbutz can afford to purchase a block of tickets, it does, spending thousands of shekels a year on bus tickets that go largely unused. But, Rafi Ashkenazi still takes the bus twice a month to visit his daughter and grandchildren on another kibbutz. "I will give you a private bus, Rafi . . . it will cost the kibbutz much less," quips Omri Kenan.

The bus tickets, a relatively small expenditure in the overall scheme of things, are a good example of how form does not follow function at Gan Shmuel. Socialist tradition is allowed to remain because the kibbutz can afford it, but it doesn't make economic sense. When there is a financial crunch, and decisions are forced, the exercise of searching for shared values will probably seem moot. For instance, Kenan told us that he doesn't feel a need for a private car because the kibbutz fleet of public cars is sufficient. If, in the future, the kibbutz finds a need to cut back on the number of cars in the communal fleet, this luxury of a car—a necessity in contemporary Israel for someone who is not a kibbutznik—could force decisions unforeseen when the kibbutz is relatively flush.

Still, like Kenan, Ashkenazi holds tight to the belief that the ultimate breaking point is private salaries. In fact, he is more ideological than Kenan on this and other points. He says, "To speak about private salaries is to be condemned to death. For most of the members, that is the redline, and for us."

The duo arranged for a range of people on the kibbutz to meet with Kasher. Still, there was a strong feeling among some that the outcome of the Kasher process was predetermined. According to Omri Kenan and Rafi Ashkenazi, they gave out 550 questionnaires and received back 120, but several people whom we interviewed complained that they were left out of the process.

"A good kibbutznik means commitment, communal life, and equality," Rafi Ashkenazi told us when we saw him in July 2001. "Why are people upset at Gan Shmuel? Because the situation in the country is depressing. We brought in Asa Kasher because people were confused. We thought we could use him as an instrument to help people out of the confusion."

Ashkenazi's daughter, Rotem, is one of the postarmy young people who are taking advantage of Gan Shmuel's special "young people track," set up, as her father explained, to tempt the children of the kibbutz to remain. Postarmy, in exchange for work, the young people get 5,000 shekels per month for six months of work and free time to travel before going to university, which is also paid for by the kibbutz.

They have seven to ten years to decide whether or not to join the kibbutz. At Gan Shmuel, out of twenty-five young people in Rotem's *kvutza* (or age group), only five still live on kibbutz, and not as members (although Rotem has become a member so that she can begin to accumulate years, just in case she does stay).

Rafi Ashkenazi is rightly proud of his daughter, a parachutist in the army, who rose to the rank of corporal. When we interviewed her in July 2001, she was twenty-six and a student of social work at Haifa University. Rotem is beautiful in the way people think of Israeli sabra women, with long dark hair, deep-set intense eyes, and tanned skin. She came to the interview with her hair wet and an oversize T-shirt over her bathing suit—she was in charge of the elementary-age children in the kibbutz summer camp. She told us:

> One of the best gifts that any child can get is being brought up on the kibbutz. Until two years ago, I felt part of the kibbutz. In the last two years, I have more thoughts about the current social situation and the future of the kibbutz. I believe in the partnership and equality of the kibbutz. Most of the young people don't believe in it. If it's not kibbutz with traditional values, I'm not interested. I don't know whether I will live outside or not. My university training will make a difference. My boyfriend is from Kibbutz Tsora. He's in the air force now. Where he ends up will make a difference.
>
> Differential salary makes a kibbutz not a kibbutz. You met my father. It's very important to him and to me and to my mother. It's hard to see them struggle. My parents feel the change of the kibbutz as personal pain. They feel every decision personally. They are part of the conservative feelings of the kibbutz. I argued with them because I'm worried about my father getting a heart attack. It's hard for my parents to see the collapse of the kibbutz, what they thought and believed in all their lives. I have the mobility to leave, but they can't. It's a conflict between me and me.
>
> I see the hypocrisy of people taking the food to their rooms when I work at the dining room on Friday nights.[11] As an idea, I'm not in favor of change, but for the kibbutz, I understand it. I'm not going to vote in the election to privatize the food bud-

get. [The kibbutz did vote to privatize the food budget in the fall of 2001.] It doesn't feel fair to influence the kibbutz decision if I'm not sure that I'm going to stay. I do believe that privatizing the budget will influence members' social activity. If the members decide to look out just for themselves, then there is no reason to live with people I don't like to see every morning.[12]

I believe that the kibbutz allows members to develop high potential, but they don't take it. Instead, they take their kids to kindergarten, go to lunch, and take a nap. I wouldn't have a problem with paying mutual support. I am proud to be a kibbutznik, but because of the situation at Gan Shmuel, I'm uncomfortable.

Rotem Ashkenazi is reflecting a sentiment shared by other young people at Gan Shmuel and Hatzor. They feel that the kibbutz has fostered mediocrity and sameness. These young people want to excel, and they want to exploit their individuality. They resent their neighbors on the kibbutz who they think aren't pulling their own weight. They don't want to work to support those who could support themselves—but they are very willing to work to support those who can't fend for themselves.

When we met with him in the summer of 2001, Uzi Levi was the kibbutz gizbar. A friend of Rafi Ashkenazi, he is a bit less ideological. He wants to maintain the traditional ways but realizes that is becoming increasingly difficult. Levi explained to us that the young people who work on the kibbutz between army and college are especially helpful in October, the busy season for the canning factory, but they aren't enough: "The factory can't rely on the kibbutz providing young people for the assembly line."

This compromise seems to work for the kibbutz and for the youth, for now. The kibbutz factory gets cheap labor for their factory. The young people get pocket money for their travels. Meanwhile, the kibbutz continues to make calculations on the amount of jobs needed, cost, pricing, and spending—all with the system they have devised of virtual salaries. Levi told us:

There is an impression of stability here. We do the changes slower, but there is a difference between what people say they want and how they act. We gave each member a dividend of NIS

5,000 in 1999 and NIS 1,000 in 2000. Members were going
abroad because it became cheaper and more accessible. People
saved less, and they had less money in their own allowances. I
have had to to talk to people who are [living beyond their means]
and it became almost impossible—around seventy families are
on overdraft. Twenty-five percent of those who are working are
on overdraft. So, people vote for stability, but they are making
overdraft on the one hand and refusing to make changes on the
other hand. It's immoral. Usually what happens on a kibbutz is
that the leadership comes to the members and says the economic situation is very bad, and they limit the allowance. But
not here.[13]

Each member has a credit card on the kibbutz account. Last
year, we spent sixty million shekels on housing, partly because
of the changes for the children's house. Now, we have a delay
with the young people's housing.

I was very much in favor of bringing Asa Kasher. The process
itself was important, to sit and talk, review opinions. I was
naïve, but I believed that we could sign the amana. I was hoping
that we could come to an agreement to do changes, but slowly.

When we asked him why he thinks the Asa Kasher process ultimately stopped, we get a window into the harsh feelings among some
on the kibbutz. Uzi Levi is Old World, frankly chauvinistic. "Excuse
me," he says, pointing to Jo-Ann. "You can't have two women on the
kibbutz as general secretaries.[14] When you come to a job, you have to
respect what went before you," he tells us, implying that they didn't
respect the Kasher process or, more likely, the efforts of Kenan and
Ashkenazi, put in place by the previous regime. "They came and they
had no experience, and they didn't believe in it personally. Dinah is a
very nice woman, but we're still arguing because most of the secretariat supports going on with the process. It's very difficult because
you call for the members to come and talk, and just a few people come
together, the same people to talk," he confesses, perhaps unwittingly
putting his finger on something that others later tell us—there was a
small group of people on the kibbutz intensely attached to the Kasher
process, but that attachment didn't extend to the majority or even
near majority of people on the kibbutz.

There is no doubt that there is an element of chauvinism in the way many of Dinah Gavish Vergilese's male neighbors describe her and relate to her in a leadership position. Additionally, however, the system of job rotation—a traditional system that has ended at many kibbutzim (but not at Gan Shmuel)—makes it difficult to find people with managerial experience to serve in the role of managers. Additionally, the rotation system makes it difficult to continue with something like the Kasher process, unless the entire kibbutz is truly committed to it and involved. Otherwise, when there is a leadership change, the commitment disappears.

Indeed, we had heard such disparaging remarks about Dinah Gavish Vergilese that we didn't know what to expect. However, when we met her, we were pleasantly surprised to meet a woman who is genuinely frustrated, concerned, and impassioned about the kibbutz and its future. It's not easy being the mazkira of such a large kibbutz. It's like being a small-town mayor with little administrative backup, having to live next door to the constituents about whose lives you are making decisions.

Dinah Gavish Vergilese was born on Gan Shmuel fifty years ago. A registered nurse, she is married to a pediatrician who was born in Nahariya. When we interviewed her, her husband was studying at Sha'are Zedek Hospital in Jerusalem to obtain a specialty in lung disease, so he came home to the kibbutz twice a week, while Dina Gavish Vergilese worked at her job as mazkira and cared for the couple's three children. She and her family left the kibbutz during most of the 1980s but came back because it's a "good place to raise children—it's home."

For all the complaining about Gavish Vergilese's leadership, she may even serve a second two-year term because no one else wants the job. She agreed to try the co-maskira setup because of the large size of the kibbutz, but the other woman quit. So now, she works twelve hours a day, seven days a week. Before she became mazkira, she ran the kibbutz clinic for seven years. She thought being mazkira would offer a desired change in her life, and there was pressure among kibbutz members for her to take the position.

Dinah Gavish Vergilese has short curly hair. She is soft-spoken and thoughtful in choosing her words. Not surprisingly, she has a different take on the Asa Kasher process than those who are wedded to it.

She told us:

> There was no beginning or end to the process. There was no schedule for the process, and not enough people were involved. We should have had someone more professionally experienced in process issues—like a facilitator. Kasher is an expert on the subject, not an expert on process.
>
> He never met in a systematic way with the elected bodies of the kibbutz, and not everyone who wanted to meet with him met with him. On the kibbutz, if you're not invited, you don't come. There were instructions on who he should meet with. Some members complained that it was a done deal to vote for a certain set of values. That's my opinion. So, we wanted to bring in an outside consultant, but it was impossible to bring someone else from outside. The personal feeling is that at Gan Shmuel people are afraid to bring in outsiders; that's one of the problems.
>
> We have a divided population. There's fear. Everybody is afraid the result will lead to differential salaries. People are suspicious. The economic leadership in the kibbutz is very strong. And it doesn't allow the social community to grow up. Two years as mazkira is not long enough to make the necessary changes. We need to create cooperation between the informal social leadership and the economic leadership. The perception is that the economic leaders see themselves and Gan Shmuel as one and the same. They are so identified with the kibbutz, not because they have bad intentions, but the leadership is clustered around the factory and farm.

Gavish Vergilese's comments offer a window into the frustrating situation at Gan Shmuel today. The kibbutz, with its strongly held ideas and proud history, is struggling with its own internal change in the midst of a transformed Israel, and the strain is showing in human relations on the kibbutz.

> Rafi won't speak to me because I stopped the Asa Kasher process. This is a problem of kibbutz—when people don't speak. If one reason to live together is the quality of togetherness, then

this raises questions about living here. Gan Shmuel people are not tolerant of a true exchange of ideas. Most of the economic leadership is men. Being a woman is certainly part of it for me. One of the most important things that must be preserved here is that people are autonomous beings and not soldiers receiving orders. We are in a global village, whereas before we were goal oriented and things were clear. There was a clear line of authority. Now, we have to have individual initiative.

Gavish Vergilese is struggling with how and with what to supplant the failed Kasher process.

Our plan is to start a process for issues important to the members, with internal moderators. I have started it. I invited Rafi to a group of twelve people. He said no. It's very difficult to be at a crossroads where I have to get the people opposed to me to talk to me.

Maybe the change will happen itself, if the financial situation gets so bad. If I see that I can't go forward with this and it's a waste of time, I'll go on chofesh, in my own direction, withdraw.[15]

Members don't know enough about what's going on in the kibbutz economically. A member doesn't know what he costs or what he earns. They need to be educated. If they knew, they could make choices. For so many years, they've been able to run the kibbutz without knowing. And it has worked. There are three people holding up the whole thing, with another five or six around them, all around the same age.

It's around 7 P.M., and Dina Gavish Vergilese has to rush off, as she has more kibbutz work to do.

Someone who agrees with Dinah Gavish Vergilese's assessment is Motti Gazit, who was general manager of Gan Shmuel Foods from 1989 to 1999. But, he also thinks that Gavish Vergilese has failed to tackle the problems of Gan Shmuel, "not because she read the map wrong, but because she did not have the political experience and didn't know how to build coalitions for change." Gazit is blunt in his assessment of kibbutz society—he thinks it is "stuck."

Since 2000 he has worked outside the kibbutz as manager of Zohar Dalia, a factory at Kibbutz Dalia. For a decade, he successfully managed Gan Shmuel Foods before turning it over to a new generation. Gazit was born in Argentina in 1943 and made aliyah with his parents to Gan Shmuel in 1954. He and his wife Rivka have three children. Their oldest son studied at the Technion and left kibbutz. The second son, recently finishing the army, has embarked on the world trip typical of many Israeli young people. Their daughter is in her last year of high school.

"I don't care if my children return to the kibbutz," he says. "They should live where they can achieve excellence. I do care that they continue to live in Israel." The notion that young people are flocking back to Gan Shmuel, put forward by several of those we interviewed, "is a bluff," according to Gazit. "It is all connected to special arrangements, to the money given to them."

Motti Gazit wasn't involved in the Asa Kasher process. He doesn't mince words when discussing it. He thinks that the initiators

> apparently did not want to see me among the participants. In my opinion, this was an attempt to turn the wheel back and not allow the process of rethinking for change to take place. It was a Stalinist approach. There is no real democratic dialogue in Gan Shmuel. Asa Kasher was an attempt to block any dialogue. Asa Kasher was their tool. Those who pushed Asa Kasher and the vote to join Zerem Shitufi are not prepared for a real dialogue.

While the supporters of Zerem Shitufi told us that the decision for Gan Shmuel to join this group was made at a sicha kibbutz, with input from the whole kibbutz, Motti Gazit recalls it differently:

> The vote to join the Zerem was very strange. I don't believe that members invested too much thought in the decision. It was more indicative of the sociology of Gan Shmuel and its informal leadership than anything else. I don't believe that most members, 90 percent, even understood what was being discussed. A real dialogue would consider some connection between income and the responsibility of the individual member.

He echoes a sentiment often heard at Gan Shmuel—that he and others who work hard are carrying those who aren't. He says:

> Now there are reverse differential salaries; the less you do, the more you get. I cannot accept that these parasites receive an income. The kibbutz society in general is not productive. In the real world, 1.4 individuals support the family. In kibbutz, 0.6 or 0.7 individuals support the family. The result is each one according to the abilities of the kibbutz and everyone according to his/her own desires.
>
> The social fiber of the society is coming apart, principle after principle. Today, there is almost no social contract within Gan Shmuel. There are people with principles, but no social contract.

Motti Gazit believes that Gan Shmuel Foods, the mega factory that sits at the entrance to the kibbutz, is keeping the kibbutz from ruin. "The factory is guaranteeing that the walls don't fall down. The factory managers don't agree to rotten compromises."

Our impression from the discussion with Gazit and others from Gan Shmuel is that the factory managers are not active in the social aspects of Gan Shmuel, in the kehillah. Nor are they proponents of change. Their voices are heard, however, on matters of fair distribution of the wealth of the kibbutz.

Gazit's prescription for change includes an agreement for mutual, collective guarantees such as social security and a certain degree of communality. He doesn't want to privatize health, but he does want to privatize homes after the kibbutz equalizes living conditions. And he thinks that the service branches should be privatized after balancing their books and conducting a thorough cost accounting of the kehillah, including the true cost of labor in different social services.

"Right now, we are in good shape," Motti Gazit concludes. "If Gan Shmuel would face ten years of financial crisis [like that faced by Gesher Haziv], it would fall apart too. The day one or two of the key financial people in the kibbutz give up and decide to leave Gan Shmuel, the kibbutz will begin to fall apart."

Reuven Shapira shares Motti Gazit's grim assessment. A sixty-one-

year-old son of Gan Shmuel, his parents came to the kibbutz from
Poland. (His ninety-three-year-old mother still lives on the kibbutz.)
He began working in Gan Shmuel Foods after high school. Today,
Reuven is a sociologist with a Ph.D. from Tel Aviv University. He
writes about the kibbutzim's regional enterprises.[16] Having worked
at the Institute for Research of the Kibbutz at Haifa University, he
now teaches sociology, anthropology, and social movements at Western Galilee College. His wife (a daughter of Kibbutz Hatzor) is a bio-
chemist who manages the factory microbiology lab where she is
responsible for instituting a process of quality controls to meet international standards and certification. Shapira said:

> I think Gan Shmuel is living on our past, completely living *in*
> the present but *on* our past. We are trying to be steadfast re-
> garding what was successful in the past and change as little as
> possible because Gan Shmuel sees the kibbutzim that are
> changing getting into trouble with their changes. So, Gan
> Shmuel members prefer to change as little as possible.
>
> Gan Shmuel didn't really decide what to become. We leaned
> toward Zerem Shitufi, but there was no formal ratification. As
> I remember, it was brought to the general assembly and not de-
> cided. [Kenan and Ashkenazi recall that the general assembly
> gave its approval.] When we decided to join, Gadish came to talk
> to us, and ten or twenty members were present. They went to
> ballot. But people didn't know what they were voting for. Al-
> most no one at Gan Shmuel is interested in Zerem Shitufi, be-
> cause the ideology of collectivism is gone. There is a waning
> ideology of egalitarianism. The general assembly really is a joke;
> it mostly includes twenty, thirty members in their sixties. It
> meets on odd days, sometimes Thursday, sometimes Sunday.[17]
>
> Four or five years ago, when it met on Saturdays, fifty, sixty
> members were coming. In 1960, it was typical to have one hun-
> dred and fifty members in attendance.[18]
>
> Gan Shmuel is in a kind of inertia. The malaise is not in-
> evitable. In order to change, people have to have agreement on
> what needs to change. Asa Kasher is a very intelligent man, and
> few question his grasp, but he didn't help Gan Shmuel. I wasn't
> asked to talk to him.

What happens next? Gan Shmuel will roll on with this inertia, but changes will happen because of the system. It is not
communal, and each has his personal interests. It will come to
a major conflict. The standard of living is low. The kibbutz is
functioning. People are not without meals. But the differences
are growing into an animosity between the haves and the have-
nots.

We are waiting to see how other kibbutzim are coping with
these problems. After seeing, we might imitate one way or another. *Most* young people are leaving. But, unlike other kibbutzim, 30 to 40 percent are joining. That's one reason the
kibbutz isn't worried about its future.

It's built now on much hired labor—everywhere in the factory, including professionals, in agriculture, in all the branches.
But from 1970 to 1980, the kibbutz could supply workers, and
we were profitable, one of the most profitable in the country. We
were almost all dependent on export. Our cotton was not dependent on the government price of water. Cotton was irrigated
by water pumped in winter from Nahal Hadera and conserved
in our fishponds, so we got two for the price of one [that is, fish
and irrigation water].[19] Our factory was 95 percent export. At
that time, the kibbutz had leaders, and they recognized good
work. For me, to be production manager was prestigious. At that
time, it was clear that someone working for export was as important as someone working for high tech for the country. But,
no more.

Shaul Knaz is also distressed about the situation on the kibbutz. An
editorial cartoonist, he looks the part—intense and sardonic with
grayish-white hair and a beard. His wife, Hannah, looks like an American hippie in the best sense—free and open, wearing her gray, curly
hair in a sort of Afro.

Shaul is sixty. Hannah is fifty-six. He was born on Gan Shmuel, second generation with parents from Poland. Hannah's parents also came
from Poland, but she was brought up in Pittsburgh. She came to Israel
in the early 1960s when her father was in residence at the Weizmann
Institute of Science. She met her first husband and came to Gan
Shmuel to be with him. "It wasn't Zionism, it was personal," she con-

fesses. Eventually, that marriage split apart, as did Shaul's marriage, and they married each other. A nurse by profession, Hannah worked in her profession on the kibbutz for nineteen years. When we interviewed the couple in July 2001, Hannah was working in the customer service department at the Gan Shmuel supermarket. Throughout our conversation, she wistfully talked about leaving Israel because of the lack of a peaceful solution to the Israeli-Palestinian problem, perhaps moving to New Mexico, a part of the United States that she thought Shaul would like.

Today, Shaul is a graphic illustrator at *Ha'aretz*. His curriculum vitae includes newspapers from the left, all long gone—*Davar*, the former Labor Party and trade union daily, and *Al Hamishmar*, the newspaper of Mapam and the Kibbutz Artzi. Hannah describes her husband thus: "He's an artist, writer, and prophet of doom on the kibbutz. People look up to him here—he won't say this, but I will say it."

Shaul Knaz, himself, says:

I'm a little bit of a troublemaker here. I try to convince the people on the kibbutz to go a different way. Gan Shmuel is not in a good economic situation. It's in a good financial situation—there is a difference.

The whole community is paralyzed. There's no culture of meeting together, being together. Asa Kashar couldn't continue because of the goal he placed for himself. There's no point in finding mutual goals between somebody who is eighteen years old and going into the army and someone who is eighty.

A community needs conflict, not common denominators at all times. The thing is that people do want this kind of life, they want to continue living as a kibbutz, but they can't find the way of living; they can't find the *how*, and therefore they are too easily ready to give up the *what*.

What Asa Kasher tried to find was the ideological common denominator, and that isn't important. Automatically, if someone is on kibbutz, they have that. But he tried to give it his own interpretation—Asa Kasher said he wants to find an ethical code for life in the kibbutz. I say, the problem is not that we don't have an ethical code. The problem is that we *do* have it—all kib-

butzim have it—centralistic control; they have to control everything that happens in the kibbutz economy and the culture, and
this doesn't let Gan Shmuel develop in any way, because we are
still holding on to this ethical code that everybody has to agree
to. [Shaul Knaz was not invited to meet with Kasher.]

We're stuck because we're looking for the wrong thing. The
people who led the Kasher process were looking for ideological
agreement. I want to be with the same people, but each one will
live his own life, and they'll agree on the basic ideas of kibbutz.

Salaries, they're not important. I like money like everybody
else, but it's not really important. People are afraid to talk about
things that really bother them—social security, togetherness—
because they can't talk about these things for all sorts of reasons.
They talk about things that can be translated into money—it's
much easier. But they are not really dreaming about having
enough money to have a secondhand car. That's not their real
concern. They're lost because they haven't found a way to live.
We should privatize the society, not the money.

Hannah Knaz suggests:

Have the group of young people decide among themselves who
is going to study whatever—have each group make their own
decision. I'm not against privatization of food and things like
this, but it won't make people happy. Gan Shmuel, we still have
a chance, maybe. At Gesher Haziv or Hatzor, they have a pic-
ture already—they don't have a chance—but we can still decide
which way we want to go. And, we're trying so hard not to find
the strength to find a different model—we're trying so hard not
to find a new road. We need our own Gan Shmuel way.

Shaul Knaz interjects:

Yes, we are a small Polish village. Meaning, everyone around us
is trying to screw us. Gan Shmuel never worked in cooperation
with any other kibbutz. Not in education, not in anything. I'm
joking, but, on the other hand, I think in the subconscious it's

the philosophy of centralism—the kibbutz is very ideological, very strong. We are a strong kibbutz because we don't waste money on the members, only on the kibbutz.

Hannah laments:

There is no ideology left after three generations, except for the religious kibbutzim. I think this is a natural sort of deterioration, and I realize kibbutz days are doomed.

People don't know how to discuss things here. You have your opinion, and if someone doesn't agree, you knock 'em down and that's it. What they said about the woman secretary is terrible, but on the other hand there is such a macho, materialistic way of thinking here that it's very difficult.[20] I felt the same thing when I was holding a position of responsibility. You're knocked down wherever you go. You can't just say, "Wait a minute, let's just talk about this, you don't know everything." We need to talk about what we want, if we want. Young people are not here. Those who are coming back are those who can't make it outside.

Shaul Knaz agrees:

The decision of the young people who came back here is a strategic decision. It's a good deal for a certain time; they get all the money they need for studies. We're corrupting our youth. They need some responsibility; they need to take responsibility for their life. In the end, they have to leave the kibbutz. They get to age thirty, and they get everything that is coming to them from kibbutz, and they leave.

Hannah Knaz says that in the end Gan Shmuel will turn out like Gesher Haziv. "Of course it will. It will take a longer time because we have more money."

Shaul Knaz thinks it's obvious that the younger generation will leave at age thirty, "because they are coming from parents who are frustrated. They gave everything for their children; they feel they have missed something in life."

Still, Shaul Knaz knows what is good about kibbutz. When we ask him, he doesn't even flinch, but answers right away:

Even if all the kibbutzim go in the end, the need for people to live a worthwhile life with equality for all people that has existed since biblical times will exist. Even if we don't find the way of doing this, the need will continue. I leave with the feeling that Gan Shmuel has really missed something. We have the possibility of building a new model of how to live this kind of life.

We want to know if he is optimistic, but his wife exclaims, before he can answer: "He's never optimistic."
And, Shaul Knaz says emphatically:

No. All the time we need to protect the kibbutz from its members. Nothing is left here from this Polish code we started with. This is like the last days of the Soviet Union, to protect the government from the people. We have to find the model for a maximum amount of freedom, responsibility, and democracy. If there's something good in the people, it will come out. All the models, at Hatzor and elsewhere, they always talk about the bad side of the members.

Hannah Knaz expresses regret:

The kibbutzim can't sell themselves anymore, they don't believe in themselves anymore. The kibbutz was something very special within the country. We are something very special. There are people who still believe that people can live in a communal framework and care about each other and work to keep this framework going. I wish it would continue, but people don't want it anymore. Especially with everything that's going on around us nowadays. People don't give a damn, except what's going on in their own little stomach, and we haven't been able to keep up the beauty of what we've tried to do.

Shaul Knaz describes a key problem of the classic kibbutz:

Different age groups can't live on the same allowance and still take part in life. Older people can't live like they're twenty-five. It's not fair. Kibbutz is a society young people decided on. Young people invented the kibbutz, and they forgot they are going to be old. As they got older, they were afraid that the young people would leave and they stopped taking care of themselves. A society that wants to live forever has to have ways of life for all the different ages.

This is the one important sentence: I think that the society can't be better than the potential that the people have in it. The kibbutz, in a very strong way, is much less successful than the individual potential that the people have, and that is because of the structure, the organizational structure, which doesn't allow the personal potential of the individuals within the society and, therefore, doesn't realize the society as a whole. This is all because of the fear to open up a more democratic society and understand that we won't lose anything. We can't protect the kibbutz against the members. The kibbutz can only gain.

Shaul Knaz predicts, in true Marxian fashion, that the only thing that will create radical change at his kibbutz is an economic crisis: "I hope there will be one very bad year in the stock market, and people will have to start thinking about what we are going to do and how we will change."

Meanwhile, if they stay, Hannah Knaz worries about her old age: "The pension is very, very symbolic. I don't know if I can stay in the country much longer. I don't know if I can take it, the political situation. For my children, what I give, I give; what I can't give, I can't give. They received education, worked their way through, and they'll be okay. Right now, I don't know how we are going to grow old and who is going to help us."

Even within the storm of uncertainty raging on the kibbutz, conversations with the children born on Gan Shmuel reveal a generation of young people who are thoughtful and committed to the ideals of a just society. In July 2000 Jo-Ann Mort interviewed Hovav Lapidot, Sela Ronen, and Daphna Yasur, all twenty-somethings between army and college. They expressed their love for the kibbutz, even as they questioned whether they could remain in their home.[21]

None of them said that they wanted to leave to make more money, but each of them did stress that they wanted more independence. (This was a theme expressed by young people at Hatzor also. At Gesher Haziv, we couldn't find any young people to talk to.)

"I think that life on the kibbutz is really a high quality of life, but there are some difficulties for the members in the lack of independence and in economic life. You cannot save here and spend more there. It's not your own decision," Hovav Lapidot complained. He wants to decide how to spend the percentage of money used by the kibbutz on his entertainment.

Independence is more important than money. I can't save money. If I don't go to the swimming pool or I won't go to the movies we have every Friday here, I should be able to say that I can save that money, but it won't happen. I think this causes some frustration for the young people.

People want to develop in their own profession. For me, that's very important. Maybe I can do that on the kibbutz, but not everybody can, because not everything you study at university can be efficient here. Things like art, photography, cinema—not everything that might be very interesting for some young person can be a profession here. So, not everyone can find his own niche here. I think this is another factor that will force a decision for some. It's more important than the economic factors.

Daphna Yasur, a young woman with short dark hair and a wide smile, declares:

It's very comfortable when you live in a community that decides how to live and where to work; but there is also something very annoying. You can be dissatisfied all of your life and you can complain all the time, but it's very comfortable when you have economic security and education and health for you and your children and it's quiet and calm. Okay, it's very mediocre. Kibbutz is against human nature, and with the young people you will often hear the word "money," but it's not just the money. We say "money" maybe because we have lack of it; we can choose many things with money, but it doesn't mean anything if we don't have choice. I feel that it's not reality sometimes, but it is very nice—the grass, the quiet, the swimming pool. I like most of the people. I really don't know what I will do when I finish my degree, but I don't know how life here will be for me and if we are going to be like any other place in the world—what is the meaning of kibbutz?

In July 2000 Daphna Yasur was working in the kibbutz kindergarten in order to earn money before she starts studying social work at Haifa University. She served in the military police in the army. Her mother was born on Gan Shmuel, and her father, a Holocaust survivor, was born in Poland. Her parents are in their sixties. Her older brother lives in Paris. She has a sister in Binyamina, a town near the kibbutz, and another sister living on the kibbutz.

Sela Ronen, twenty-six years old, also doesn't know if he'll return to the kibbutz after university. His parents are separated, and his mother lives outside the kibbutz and "has lots of money," according to her son.

I think that if I succeed in my studies [he wants to be an engineer] it would be much better for me to find someplace to live somewhere and develop myself. That is the major factor.

When I look back [on growing up on the kibbutz] it was very nice. But it is really very anachronistic today, because the kibbutz is a form of life that belongs to the past more than the future. It was made for a certain need.

When he's asked if the cooperative aspect is also anachronistic, Sela Ronen answers:

It depends on how you define equality. It depends how much space you give to the individual to develop himself in the community. It depends how you see work and cooperation. Is it for the collective itself, or is it to be a contribution of the individual? I think it's very important for everyone to have education and health care. There is no deciding factor but rather lots of them—to whom I will be married, and how many kids I will have, a lot of things, not just money.

Twenty-seven-year-old Hovav Lapidot, also born at Gan Shmuel, was about to start university a few months after our interview. His parents and grandmother were on the kibbutz with him. He served nine years in the air force as a pilot, something about which the kibbutz is quite proud. He said:

I don't know if I will come back to the kibbutz after university. I think there are only a few young people on the kibbutz that can tell, because generally young people don't know about their future. If you grow up in the city, you don't think about leaving the kibbutz. But here we have the option, so it's more confusing. We look outside and we see what is going on outside the kibbutz in Israel and abroad. We keep ourselves updated. There are professions like high tech, and the quality of life that everyone can have outside.

I think that life on the kibbutz is really a high quality of life, but this form, I think, is going to change in the next ten years, and there are some difficulties of the members like lack of independence and in economic life. You cannot save here and spend more there—it's not your own decision.

The members have everything here. But, there is lots of frustration, and members think that if they live in Tel Aviv and work so hard they could have more money and a car. So there is something attractive about going outside. People want to develop in their own profession. For me, that's very important. Maybe I can do that on the kibbutz, but not everybody can. Not everybody can find his own niche here. In the past people worked harder and they did what they had to do. You go to work in the factory here and that's it. But now people care more about their career.

Daphna Yasur, who, during her interview was struggling with a computer-type gadget that translated her words from Hebrew to English, chimed in: "If we will work, we share the same things, we live the same, but it's hypocritical. In the rest of the world, if you work harder you can live better. Here, if you work less, you live better. It's not normal. It's a lie."

Yasur's comments were among the most striking in our interviews.

All the young people nodded their heads in agreement when she said it. While all of these impressive twenty-somethings seemed to honestly believe they were committed to the social welfare of their neighbors, they resented what they saw in growing up on the kibbutz—that some members worked harder than others and all lived relatively equally. This resentment came partially from the young people's awareness of the possibilities available to them in the broader Israeli society. Once a new generation has that awareness, the kibbutz either has to satisfy it or risk losing the next generation. Indeed, even if the kibbutz changes in such a way as to satisfy the yearning for career accomplishment and independence desired by this new generation, it may still lose the children of the kibbutz. But without the change it's a certain loss.

Hovav Lapidot articulates it this way:

> When the kibbutz was founded, the idea of equality was essential to life. It was a group of people who lived in conditions back then who had to join their efforts and their income to survive. Now, it's not essential. People know that there will be no attacks from outside, and the economic condition is stabilized. So people start to ask questions like, "Is it necessary?" Back then, nobody asked any questions, and no importance [was given] to individual needs or desires. But now, when this idea is not necessary for work, people ask themselves why are we doing it? can we do it better? The individual is more important now. And it's not just the young people asking questions. They didn't invent it. We hear it around us, and young people are confused.
>
> Even my grandmother thinks that we need change. I don't think she wants differential salaries, but she wants to give members a differential, individual allowance. You divide the main budget equally but more to the members' needs. They will have to pay for some services that are free, but they can control their economic life.[22] My parents think there should be differential salaries. As for my living on the kibbutz after university, they won't try to talk me into staying here.

Sela Ronen's family situation is different, because his mother doesn't live on the kibbutz. His father is still at Gan Shmuel:

My father likes the old-fashioned way. He would like to make small, but not crucial, changes. He is sixty. I think people his age have a lot of problems, a dilemma regarding change here, because obviously they can't leave the kibbutz because at the age of sixty to find a profession is quite hard. So people like our parents' age, they will stay on kibbutz because they know that the rest of their life is on the kibbutz, and it's very important to them how the kibbutz will look in a few years—not a matter of life and death, maybe, but important. For us, it's not as important, we don't have the problems of the other generation.

Daphna Yasur admits:

I'm not sure my parents want me to stay here. I can live better than them because I am young and have the power and energy to change things and to live like I believe I need to. My father is sixty-eight and my mother is sixty-four. They are in the age group for which change is very difficult. They aren't afraid for the actual change but for how it might be—will they have enough money. People who work here all their lives, they still work and see outside people who are in their forties with three children who live more comfortably. They live better than my parents, than people who live here all their lives and they earned nothing.

When it is suggested to them that, albeit not in a traditional manner, their parents did earn to send these young people and their siblings to university and to give them health care and education before university, by working on the kibbutz and maintaining the kibbutz economy, the young people answer, "Yes, but . . . "

"If I stay on the kibbutz, yes," Daphna Yasur responds, "but if I go outside, they can give me nothing.[23] My parents are afraid for *hafrata* [privatization] because they don't know how things will be."

These young people have compassion for the founding generation. As Yasur put it, "The people who worked here all their lives should get something more than a member who is newer. It's normal when you are older you get more rights, privilege, money, things, a pension." It's the third time that she has used the word "normal" in our conversation. For their grandparents' generation "normal" was the norm they created by building a new life on the kibbutz, but for the grandchildren "normal" is the life outside the kibbutz.

"Gan Shmuel is a very conservative kibbutz," Yasur insists. She confides:

> My parents, it's very hard for them. They have the ideal of kib-
> butz, and my father is a Holocaust survivor. It's very important
> for him to be safe and secure in one kind of lifestyle. But for me
> and people in their thirties and forties, they have other interests.
> They have aspirations, needs, and dreams. We have many, many
> old people here, and we are a more conservative kibbutz. But,
> also, processes are never, never done well, and one of the rea-
> sons is that if people won't talk about things they think they
> won't happen. That's ridiculous.

Whether or not these young people stay at Gan Shmuel is partly in their own hands and partly up to the adults making the decisions. Everyone thinks change of some sort is inevitable, no matter where they line up in the debate. "I think something will happen in the future, because of the general direction of other kibbutzim," Rafi Ashkenazi concedes. "Some people think there could be a war at Gan Shmuel. There is no direction. Things are not good. We created the young people's track so that they would stay. But you can't bribe them. They have to choose the kibbutz."

# END OF KIBBUTZ OR A NEW BEGINNING?

It took the economic crisis of the 1980s to demonstrate to the kibbutzim that their way of life was really in danger. The 1989 agreement dealing with the debt showed us that the kibbutz movement and the kibbutzim themselves are changed forever. It was the final proof that the old unwritten treaty between the State of Israel, the Jewish people, and the kibbutzim was over—it was broken, and no one was going to respect it anymore.

—Micha Drori

Sderot is located south of Ashkelon and east of the Gaza Strip. It is known for its pop stars and its poverty. Some of Israel's top new rock bands hail from there. It's been called Israel's "Seattle" because of the proliferation of new grunge-style, Moroccan-influenced rock bands that took off in the 1990s. However, unlike Seattle, the rock stars who grow up in Sderot leave instead of settling there. Amir Peretz, the town's former mayor and head of the Histadrut trade union federation, is another Sderot luminary.

One of Israel's development towns, Sderot was created to settle the wave of new immigrants in the 1950s and to populate the southern periphery. Sderot was incorporated as a city in 1996. Today, 45 percent of the population is from the former Soviet Union, mostly from the Caucasus region, and the remainder is of North African descent, Mizarachi Jews, many of whom are first- and second-generation Israelis. While some of the Moroccan Jews have risen to a relatively higher living standard, the newer immigrants from the former Soviet Union have brought with them a multitude of social and cultural problems. With its high unemployment and school dropout rates, Sderot is far from being an integrated and thriving society.

Sderot has few jobs and almost no cultural venues. The first movie theater—an art cinema—opened in 2001. It's expected to serve the population from the surrounding kibbutzim as much as people from Sderot. Whenever possible, parents in Sderot send their children to the surrounding regional schools with the kibbutz children. The alternative is the Shas religious schools and other Shas social services.

Sderot is located less than five kilometers from Israel's border with Gaza. During the Second Intifada (2000 to 2003) Sderot was shelled from Gaza, and once, fields immediately bordering Sderot were hit with mortars. Several fell five hundred meters from a new neighborhood, where upwardly mobile immigrants from the 1950s had moved to build relatively large, ornate villas with yards and wide driveways. In this part of town, the surrounding public lawns are green and tall palm trees line the streets.

This is the same neighborhood where a new-style, urban kibbutz has taken hold. It's called Migvan, which in Hebrew means "diverse." In July 2000, a mixed bag of fifty young people (nine families, twenty children, and two singles) had just moved into their new homes, away from the rougher part of town.

Before building the new neighborhood, they lived in an apartment complex for thirteen years, in a block of twenty apartments with two of them combined for public space, including a communal kitchen. Other residents were mostly new immigrants, including a number of Albanian refugees from the Balkans and Chechnyans fleeing their war-torn nation. The housing project is as stark and rough as anything in the inner cities of the United States. The neighborhood is rife with drugs and violence. Only desert sand and garbage surrounded the buildings. The Migvan folks planted trees and grass around the housing blocks. Eventually, they began a small nursery business. They provided such a significant, stable part of the local minimart's business that the kibbutz has agreed to come back to the old neighborhood to buy groceries.

Naomi Tzion is cofounder of Migvan and also its oldest member.[1] She was twenty-seven at its founding. By the time she got her own house, she was forty, and one of the few members of the kibbutz who was single.

It's intriguing to imagine what Naomi Tzion's grandfather would think of his granddaughter's attempt to re-create the kibbutz in the context of a new Israel. Yaakov Hazan, her maternal grandfather, together with his longtime colleague, Meir Ya'ari, was the founder of the Kibbutz Artzi Federation's Hashomer Hatzair youth movement. As left-wing ideologues they ran their Kibbutz Artzi Federation, to which Gan Shmuel and Hatzor belong, with an iron fist. Naomi Tzion is devoting a large chunk of her life to keeping her grandfather's vision alive, but in a manner of which he might not have approved.

In addition to Migvan, Naomi Tzion is active in a group sponsored by the Kibbutz Artzi to encourage the cooperative impulse among the young. In addition, she heads up a small think tank devoted to economic justice in Israeli society named in memory of Hazan and located at the Van Leer Jerusalem Institute.

Naomi Tzion grew up on Kibbutz Reshefim (in the Beit Sha'an Valley), where her mother, a retired journalist, still lives. Her father, prior to his death, was for many years the managing director of the avante-garde theater and cultural center for the Israeli left, Tzavta, in Tel Aviv, which is sponsored by the Kibbutz Artzi Federation. Naomi Tzion has studied film, and with her bohemian looks and attitude would fit in perfectly in New York's East Village.

It took Migvan five years to build its new neighborhood on the other side of Sderot. The members' houses, which look like Mediterranean-style suburban split levels with front and back yards, patios, decks, and driveways, are all on one long landscaped street. An architect from Jerusalem designed the kibbutz, after winning a Migvan-sponsored competition.

Naomi Tzion explains:

We learned from the old way of kibbutz and decided everyone would have their own home. I pay a mortgage. I also pay for the neighborhood and own a share in the public house. Once in the middle of the week and every Friday night everyone eats together. These are the two official meals. The dining room is the heart of the kibbutz. All is voluntary, and it works. Everything is collective but the private houses. The group must approve selling or renting. We built an additional five houses and sold them for income to families. We know the families. They are friends of ours. If they want to join us to eat or to play with our children, that's okay.

The nursery started by Migvan expanded to serving the surrounding development towns of Netivot and Ofakim and was eventually sold to an Ethiopian Jewish businessman. For seven years, Migvan ran a progressive kindergarten in the city, open to all. They closed it because it wasn't economical, and now their children go to other kibbutzim's schools located near Sderot.

Today, Migvan has two main sources of income. One is a high-tech company that develops advanced Internet applications for commercial and educational clients. The second is a community-based organization that runs forty social projects for the people of Sderot, employing ten kibbutz members and fifty people from Sderot proper. Their community-based work brings in a decent amount of foundation support. The remaining kibbutz members work outside the collective arrangement, in high tech, or as lawyers, social workers, and in other professions. Several are still students. Tzion works outside the kibbutz, writing educational software programs via the Internet for another kibbutz company and also continues with her political work. Migvan has a joint bank account where all paychecks are deposited. People often deposit their personal money there too. Each member has a symbolic budget, which is approximately 470 NIS a month.

Migvan is also carrying a lot of collective debt, because of the new houses. The houses all have the same design. The kibbutz owns four cars, shared by all. This was purely an economic, not an ideological, decision. Parents of one of the members, former kibbutzniks who now live in Los Angeles, donated $20,000 so that Migvan could purchase a washer and dryer for every two families.

It's no accident that Migvan was founded in Sderot. Tzion said:

> We wanted to be more involved. We felt to do that we needed to build a new model of life. We wanted to build a bridge between the two populations [Ashkenazi and Mizrachi Jews]. We realized we would have to break the wall and create a new dialogue and live in the heart of a different society. I feel that [in the past] we translated socialism in the wrong way. If we believed in a communal life, we should live our life in a different territory. We had to build our lives with people who lived differently than us.

This is an important distinction, especially in the Israel of the twenty-first century. The rift between Ashkenazim Israelis from Eastern Europe and Mizrachi Israelis from North Africa and the Middle East is one of the tangled threads in contemporary Israel's frayed social fabric. Whether actual or perceived, the kibbutz is a symbol of an Ashkenazi, privileged lifestyle. As we have shown, aside from a handful of wealthy kibbutzim, this is more perception than reality.

But perception can sometimes snuff out reality, and in Israel today, no matter how dire an individual kibbutz's situation may be there lingers a sense of the kibbutzim as a privileged caste.

While Migvan's practices reflect the earliest days of the kibbutzim, there are fundamental differences. First, of course, Migvan is urban, rather than rural. Second, it is organized specifically to engage with the outside world, including places of work. Ignoring the experience of the historic kibbutz movements, Migvan is intent upon remaining quite small. The people of Migvan actually want to limit the kibbutz to another ten families. Finally, and importantly, they have instituted private property from the beginning.

Migvan members cherish their individualism and pay heavily— even willingly taking on more debt as a community—to indulge people's interests in careers, culture, travel, and more. Tzion observes:

> The orientation of the kibbutz is to invest a lot of money in the individual, which is very different from the [traditional] kibbutzim. If you want to study, you study—up to Ph.D., whatever you want. We don't, like the [traditional] kibbutz, build up branches and then have to maintain the branches. When someone comes from university, people sit with him and help him figure out what he wants to do. That's how we build up new jobs—everyone feels that the sky is the limit and that is the important feeling.

We would like to report that Migvan and the handful of other urban kibbutzim scattered in Israel's smaller cities herald a new era for the kibbutz movement, perhaps providing a fourth case study for our narrative. But, that is not the case.

We don't believe that the urban kibbutz phenomenon is the harbinger of a new beginning for the kibbutzim. Nor will they have the impact on the larger society that the earlier generations of kibbutzim did. They do, however, capture a yearning among at least some young Israelis to cultivate the socialist ideal. They represent the best impulse of young Israelis to live in a collective fashion while attempting to better integrate the disparate constituencies that make up today's Israel. Because of that, we think this experiment is worth mentioning.

The Migvan experiment appears to be closer to the communes found in many Western societies than to the original Israeli kibbutz that was central to the establishment of the nation. The unique nature of the kibbutz lies in its penetration into almost every facet of Israeli social, political, and economic life.

It is the kibbutz's lack of relevance to Israeli society today that lies at the root of the contemporary crisis.

No doubt, the people of Sderot and the people of Migvan are already the better for Migvan. However, the urban kibbutz doesn't—on its own—signify the continuance of the kibbutz movement. What Migvan does teach us is that a handful from the younger generation considers the term *kibbutz* relevant to their being, and worthy of recreating according to their own vision.

Kibbutz, as a general idea, is in flux. The doctrinaire Hazan would most certainly have disapproved of the revisionist interpretations of kibbutz—whether at Migvan, Gesher Haziv, or Hatzor—although we are inclined to believe that the social experiment initiated by his own granddaughter would have warmed his heart just a little.

A common denominator linking privatized Gesher Haziv, third-way Hatzor, the classic Gan Shmuel, and the urbanized Migvan is the desire for private property. Gesher Haziv was one of the first kibbutzim to initiate a process of parceling homes to its members and creating an adjacent neighborhood for its real estate value. Hatzor is currently debating the parceling of homes. Hatzor's younger generation of sons and daughters are awaiting a kibbutz decision to approve a new track of membership—called "economic independence"—which will allow young couples to become members of the collective association (holding shares in the kibbutz enterprises) while building their own homes and sharing in the rural community life (by paying taxes well above current Israeli standards).

Following an old Hebrew expression, *"L'olam lo hosen"* ("not forever powerful"), or immune from the imminent changes, even Gan

Shmuel has created a "virtual process" of parceling assets to secure members' property rights in the event of fundamental changes in the future. Another kibbutz that is a pillar of tradition and economic achievement—Ma'agan Michael—has done the same. These are "sleeper" resolutions, which can be aroused in the event of economic crises or renewed social pressures.

The transition from "collective ownership of all property and assets" to the goal of having "my own home," private pension, and the possibility of inheritance is now part of the kibbutz movement's consensus. Even the Zerem Shitufi is beginning to acknowledge some of these basic desires.

Nearly a century ago, private property was as far from the minds of the founding members as exiling themselves from the Land of Israel. (Stories are told of kibbutznikim who could not bear the hard pioneering life and left Palestine altogether rather than admit their "failure" by moving to Tel Aviv or one of the other urban centers.) But eighty years after the establishment of the first kibbutz, property, in the guise of private housing and venture real estate, is shaping up to be the next defining moment in the saga of the kibbutzim. On one hand, this is a clear reflection of the shifting sands in Israel, where personal desires often take the place of public good. On the other, what is driving the advocates of change is not in the least bit egocentric. They face a serious dilemma (and an equally demanding challenge) by trying to secure a future for an aging population in an era where the welfare system in Israel is near collapse. The tragedy of this kibbutz crisis is compounded by the unwillingness of the state to offer any further financial support.

In September 2001, the Kibbutz Movement published the pamphlet "Madrich Leshiuch Dirot" or "Guide for Privatizing Homes."[2] *Shiuch* is a tricky word to translate. It refers to the attempt of the kibbutz to ascribe private property and homes to the members. This is the first time in their lives that the right of ownership has been accorded them. The "Guide for Privatizing Homes" is really a plan for privatization of the apartments and houses together with one to two dunam of land. The guide, authored by a team of experts, was a first attempt at addressing the different ways of parceling homes and land from the kibbutz collective to the individual member.

The loose-leaf guide has four sections. According to the first section, "Privatizing apartments to members is a development that in the end transfers the rights over a home and the land surrounding it from the kibbutz to the kibbutz member."[3] Tzafrir Ben-Or, part of the team who wrote the guide, explains in depth the issues that need to be addressed by the kibbutz making such a decision. These include social organizational issues such as the following: Where does the individual kibbutz stand in relation to other changes, including differential salaries and privatization? What are the demographics of the individual kibbutz? What about physical-planning issues involving the buildings, infrastructure, geographical plan of the kibbutz, statutory status of the plan, and quality of the construction? How should land and property issues be handled, especially the rental agreements and decisions of the Israel Land Authority concerning each individual kibbutz? What about financial and accounting issues—for instance, what is the standing of the individual kibbutz in relation to the kibbutzim settlement arrangement?

In a multigenerational kibbutz, can an agreement be reached for fixing the date for privatizing homes and adjacent lands? And what are the rights—if any—of people who left the kibbutz or heirs of people who died before the date when the privatization becomes effective?

It will take years before all the above issues are resolved. Many of the older generation may die before a principled decision is made. What rights do older folks have now? What about inheritance? Is there a difference when it comes to inheriting a kibbutz home if a son or daughter is still living on the kibbutz or if they have left? Should there be cash remuneration rather than physical inheritance of the home if the heir is not a kibbutz member? For example, in 1989 the second generation of Kibbutz Hatzor dedicated itself to full economic recovery, a process that took more than a decade. At the stage of property allocations, should those who left the kibbutz long ago have property rights identical to those who remained and who also guaranteed the welfare of the older generation (including the parents of those who left the kibbutz)? These are just a few of the issues facing the kibbutzim today.

As we explained, some kibbutzim, which did not take the route of differential salaries, did introduce a sleeper clause for dividing property in case the kibbutz changes one day. Like Gan Shmuel and Ma'agan

Michael, they have established a system of guidelines that state that if the kibbutz is dismantled, property will be divided among kibbutz members according to shares determined by seniority up to a maximum of thirty years seniority. In this manner, a thirty-five-year-old member with ten years seniority will receive only one third the assets of a fifty-five-year-old member with thirty years seniority. On this, Ariel Halperin, the administrator of the kibbutz settlement arrangement, commented, "They believe that a divorce contract strengthens communal life, just like it strengthens a marriage. Why? Because each member knows his rights if the divorce actually occurs."[4]

Gan Shmuel has begun a virtual process of parceling out assets to ensure security for the members in case something happens in the future. That means that when and if the dissolution of the collective comes, each member will have a bundle of property and money. But none of that financial package is available to any member today; just like their differential salaries, it exists in name only.

Gesher Haziv took advantage of its location on the periphery of Israel to get government approval to parcel part of its lands for a real estate venture designed to help erase the kibbutz debt. As reported by the Israeli daily *Yediot Aharonot* in early 2002, the tract of land called Ziv Estates will include two hundred private homes on land parcels of one-half dunam (approximately 500 square meters), and sixty lots had already been sold.[5] The price of a house and a plot of land varies from $215,000 to 270,000.

Shai Grossman, the Gesher Haziv member responsible for marketing the project, said:

> We were surprised at the high response. Most of the new tenants are coming from Nahariya, Akko, and the Krayot [suburbs of Haifa]. From the center of Israel we've received only a few inquiries, because it is difficult to find work here, and with the current economic situation in Israel, people are not inclined to leave their jobs. We've offered buyers seven styles of homes. They will enjoy, of course, the benefits given [by the government] to residents in the periphery, first and foremost tax benefits. Moreover, we have on the kibbutz two very good schools, which the children of the new tenants will attend.[6]

One new tenant, interviewed in *Yediot Aharonot*, explained why he was moving from Nahariya to Ziv Estates:

> Among our considerations for moving to the kibbutz was the desire that our children will be educated here, where the schools are better than in the city. . . . Other than that, there are the broad lawns and the serene atmosphere. The kibbutz is not far from the city, and the price is relatively cheap. We purchased a lot 650 square meters at a price of $230,000. An approval committee interviewed us before the purchase was confirmed, but they didn't make any special limits or demands.[7]

Urban dwellers, seeing the advantages of rural living and kibbutz-style education (for moral values and less competition) find living adjacent to a kibbutz an attractive proposition.

Historically, most of the land in Israel was publicly owned and administered by the government or extragovernmental agencies, especially the Jewish National Fund. The kibbutzim formed before 1948 were established primarily on JNF land. In 1960, the Israel Land Authority was formed, comprising the government and the JNF administrations for overall control and management of public land.

Micha Drori, chief legal director for the Kibbutz Movement, and a member of Kibbutz Ga'ash,[8] explained the situation of the kibbutzim in terms of both property rights and pension funds. As a lawyer for the Kibbutz Movement, he is clearly an interested party in an ongoing legal battle. However, while others may offer a different scenario of the way the conflict will play out in the courts and the political landscape, Drori's assessment of the situation at the dawn of the new century helps to summarize the dilemmas and challenges facing the kibbutzim today:

> Of the 22 million dunam of public land, 4 million dunam [approximately 4,000 square kilometers] were distributed mainly to kibbutzim and moshavim [upon Israel's founding and in the Yishuv prior to the state]. This was considered the proper way to settle the land, because the main principle was that you have to work the land yourself and you have to live there, too.
>
> Historically, the JNF always gave long-term leases—forty-

nine years plus an option for another forty-nine—to kibbutzim. After 1948, because of the whole process of resettling the many new immigrants in kibbutzim and moshavim, they started to work in short-term contracts of one to three years—with the assumption that the long-term contract would come later. These were called "renewing short-term contracts."

Fifty years went by, and people were still being told that "we're drafting the long-term contract." But the main factor was that no one even considered dealing with this problem, because it was not crucial, so unimportant. It was like a little formality that would be taken care of sometime.

One thing to remember is that at most times the agricultural community—kibbutzim and moshavim—actually controlled the Land Authority. The Ministry of Agriculture is in charge of the Land Authority, and most of the members of the council came from kibbutzim and moshavim. In the early years, agricultural land was sacred. Nobody could touch it. If you wanted to establish a new town, you first took free public land, next from private landholders. Later on, as the country became more and more populated, the Land Authority began to pass decisions to persuade those with public agricultural land to change it for urban land for building purposes. During the 1970s, this took place only on land where there wasn't a kibbutz or a moshav. Nevertheless, the decisions were a public record. We could have turned our lands into urban settlements, if we wanted to. But in the 1970s, who dared thinking about it? So, the land was changing, but we weren't in the process. We weren't needed. They could get along without us. . . .

I can say bluntly that in the past—and this is mainly true for the "younger" kibbutzim and moshavim, which were settled in the 1950s, right after the War of Independence—when you joined a kibbutz it was like going into the military. You were young and you were on a mission. You were supposed to go where they sent you. . . .

All these questions about what do I live from, should planned agriculture fail or cease to exist? what about my social security? my salary?—all these were not important really.

What really happened in the 1980s was that Israel was changing rapidly from socialism to capitalism. Suddenly we were not getting ammunition, we were not getting credit, and we were not getting the supplies we needed. We were out there in a capitalist world with no formal social rights or property. They told us that each kibbutz should take care of itself; and the kibbutzim, in turn, told the members that they should take care of themselves. The movement didn't have the resources and was not allowed to do so. For instance, money through the government and the banks was always issued as a loan to the kibbutzim through the movements, and the flow of cash now stopped.

When you were sent to Gesher Haziv, for example, nobody asked, "How the hell are we going to support ourselves?" Is agriculture enough? Is tourism a real prospect? The important thing—for the whole nation and for you—was that you were going to settle the land, the nikudah. And suddenly you are told at the age of sixty, this is *your* problem. Your mission is not your mission anymore. Only the younger people of the kibbutz could take care of themselves, but they also had to take care of the older ones.

There is no state pension plan in Israel; there are private pensions, which is why it was such a catastrophe when the kibbutzim had to either use up their pension funds to pay off debts or didn't have pension funds at all. The state workers have a pension. And, as Drori pointed out to us, so do "the bureaucrats from the Jewish Agency and the JNF, the ones who sent us out there. They took care of themselves with a budgetary pension plan, meaning the budget of the state or the budget of the Jewish Agency or the JNF would guarantee their pension plan." Drori is making an important point here. Many of these "bureaucrats" came from a labor-oriented background. They were all part of the same project, with the kibbutzim, of a socialist-Zionist Israel. While one brother might move to a kibbutz to be a farmer, another might have joined the Histadrut trade union movement to become an officer of Egged, the cooperative bus company. When the once-socialist agencies and institutions reorganized as profit-making enterprises, they left the kibbutzim to fend for themselves. Drori continued:

The kibbutzim had cooperative wealth, but no assets—the rules said that you aren't supposed to accumulate wealth. When they said the rules have changed, we were left out there like dinosaurs. The kibbutz took care of its members, and the kibbutzim took care of one another via the movements. We even cosigned loans through the movements.

When all of this collapsed, the government and the banks said, okay we'll consolidate your debts and decide how much you owe. It was supposed to be realistic, but it wasn't. We actually took part in camouflaging the disaster with this first agreement [1989] because we were ashamed of how bad the situation was. We didn't realize that this debt settlement was not enough to solve the problem—that the kibbutz as it was structured couldn't solve the problem alone.

In 1992, [Yitzhak] Rabin came to power, and the leaders of the kibbutz movements decided since our friend, the Labor Party, is back in power, let's try to amend the agreement and correct its inequities. We always had high regard for the land as land. You could use it for agriculture, building factories and more, but you could never give away or sell the land.

However, we learned from the Rabin government—*our* government—that land is about money. Land is real estate. That's when we lost our innocence. We were told by the government, "Look, now that you know what the land is really worth, you should give a chunk of your land to pay back your debts." So the second agreement, which was signed in 1996, said that the kibbutzim had to give some land to settle the debt that couldn't get settled from the 1980s.

This is when the turmoil started—when we really discovered what this is all about. If our land is good for paying debts, it could also be used to create the missing pension and property needed to survive in this brave new world.

Prior to the early 1990s, we lived in a different world. Although legally this is not true, at least conceptually it is. We started seeing the world differently. We realized that our situation with the land was different, and so we wanted to formalize the contract. We had allowed ourselves to live without writing down and formalizing the rights we had, because, at the time, doing so was not important to us. We were so sure that our rights were widely recognized. During the years 1990 to 1995 we tried to improve our situation with the Land Authority, but they fought against us. Now, they are telling us that what's not in writing doesn't exist. They had a need for the land, and so we reached a kind of compromise. By the end of 1995, three major decisions were reached: regulations 717, 727, and 737.[9]

These decisions pertain to the rights of the kibbutzim to use their lands for purposes other than agriculture. They are all quite complicated. A fourth law—751—relates to "changes in the organizational structure and allocations of land in the kibbutzim." In the jargon of the kibbutzim, this law refers to the assignment of homes and land to the kibbutz members, giving them property rights. Law 751 was passed in February 1996. It formally separated the agricultural land from the housing property, allowing for expansion and parceling of the latter. As we stated earlier, implementing 751 requires principled decisions by the kibbutz as well as professional teams to address the issues as they are defined in the "Guide for Privatizing Homes." As of this writing, none of the kibbutzim have successfully implemented 751. All are at different stages in the process, with Gesher Haziv being closer to implementation than most.

The legal case regarding land ownership has been in the Israeli courts largely through the initiative of Keshet Mizrachi.[10] Translated as Mizrachi Rainbow Coalition, Keshet Mizrachi is a group of Mizrachi intellectuals, artists, and media personalities who promote ideas of social and economic justice in Israel. Their legal briefs argued that the kibbutzim were lent the land by the state for agricultural purposes, not as real estate. The tensions that have evolved over the decades and still exist in contemporary Israeli society between the kibbutzim (with their mostly Ashkenazi population) and the development towns (mostly populated by Mizrachim) are played out in this court battle. Many in the kibbutz movement blame the Labor Party for turning its back on the kibbutzim at a particularly tenuous time.

After years of litigation and speculation, a decision at the end of August 2002 by Israel's High Court of Justice dramatically voided the land decisions 717, 727, and 737 that were all adopted in 1995 as part of the kibbutzim debt arrangement. This court decision was a result of lawsuits brought by the Keshet Mizrachi and the Society for the

Protection of Nature in Israel against the kibbutzim and moshavim (they are one legal entitity for the sake of agricultural land law in Israel) after the 1995 land pact. Rejecting the kibbutzim's historic reading of the law, the judges decided that the previous decisions ignored important societal interests such as preserving open space.[11] Although this struggle is still not over, with appeals looming and perhaps several more years of litigation (and, most likely, each kibbutz and moshav trying to cut its own deal, rather than depend on a collective agreement), the message is clear: The kibbutzim are no longer considered central to the overall mission of Israel. This 2002 legal rendering makes the need for change even more critical for each kibbutz and for the kibbutz enterprise as a whole.

When we began our research, we wondered to what extent the kibbutzim's troubles were the product of the political shift from the hegemony of the labor movement to the Likud in 1977 and how much of it was the result of the inherent structural crises. We believe the political shift is a crucial part of the story. It released other forces of change that moved a somewhat state-directed economy—with a strong welfare program and a Zionist commitment to absorbing millions of new immigrants—to a society guided by the unpredictable tensions of the free market. But, essentially, the entire Israeli political map moved away from socialism or social democracy to a free-market mentality. Today, the left in Israel is defined as the peace camp that advocates an independent Palestinian state, not a movement with progressive social and economic policies. The left desperately needs a social and economic agenda, one that mirrors the best of the kibbutz vision of social democracy.

The crises of the kibbutzim in the 1980s and 1990s may have occurred regardless of the political transformation of the country, as Daniel Rosolio claims. But it was the overall political earthquake that removed the outer circles of support, analyzed by Ariel Halperin, that left the kibbutzim to fend for themselves. This is the real story of the kibbutz in today's Israel. What we find most fascinating about the process that is taking place in the kibbutzim today is not the unbending resistance by what remains of the founding generation and the Zerem Shitufi but the ability of most to adapt to the new norm in contemporary Israel.

Within a polyglot of laws (and lack of them), the kibbutzim are trying to sort out how best to make use of the most lucrative asset they have—the land on which they settled and made a home for several generations. Additionally, they are trying to accommodate the middle and new generations' yearnings to own homes of their own and to have the right of inheritance.

By February 2003, Gesher Haziv could be confident that the Israeli government would soon finalize an agreement to transfer ownership of homes to the members themselves. Privatization was completed. At that time Hatzor was continuing with the process of exploring how to allow its members to own their own homes. If trends in Israel continue as they are—and there is every indication that they will—it is likely that debate over private ownership of homes at Gan Shmuel will intensify—if not for the present kibbutz members, then for their heirs to be able to inherit a piece of the dream.

The fact that the kibbutzim thought they would exist forever and that their social and political support would exist forever has, as we've noted, left many of the kibbutz members with serious financial concerns for their future. Today, every kibbutz, even the most conservative, understands that it must fend for itself and its members. This is a seismic shift in the history of the kibbutzim.

As we said at the onset, we chose to look at three kibbutzim in three different stages of change. All three kibbutzim are now in relatively secure financial shape. And, for now, all three remain in different stages of economic and social change.

Gesher Haziv has strengthened itself by privatizing everything as quickly and as efficiently as possible, while maintaining a tiny safety net for the founding generation and for those who can't provide for themselves.

Hatzor is attempting a third way and, we believe, will hold on to the social democratic, social welfare model for as long as possible. Because of the economic changes it instituted, Hatzor is in good economic standing today. In fact, according to Dun & Bradstreet's 2002 rating of the 150 leading Israeli companies, Hatzor's Solbar factory was number 137.[12] It had a 43.4 percent growth in sales in 2001, as it had for the previous five years. (Of the twelve kibbutz industries listed in the D & B 150 rating, six have established committees for change.)

Gan Shmuel, sheltered by its strong economy (its factory was number 107 in the D & B rating), is determined to fend off change.

We found much to admire in everyone we interviewed. Gesher

Haziv has made difficult decisions that were dictated by their circumstances. We don't see how they could have chosen a different path. Our hearts are mostly with the Hatzor model, where Gary Brenner lives. Yet, as we said, whether this social democratic model will survive long term is still an open question.

Regarding Gan Shmuel, we believe that the majority of people at that kibbutz want to be on a faster trajectory of change than the group around Asa Kasher is willing to acknowledge. We even found a fair amount of support for differential salaries in Gan Shmuel. We don't believe that the members of that kibbutz will be willing to survive with such limited personal budgets for much longer.

Indeed, the economy may aid the future of Gan Shmuel in an unexpected manner. Motti Gazit, the former factory official at Gan Shmuel, thinks that the balloon bursting in Israel's high-tech sector could keep more young people on the kibbutz. Kibbutz young people, like their peers in Israeli society, were dreaming of becoming young millionaires. With that option less viable now, and the Israeli economy generally worsening, more of them may stay on the kibbutz. However, Gazit predicts that if the young people remain, they will be the ones to bring about structural change, not based on values but on following the rest of Israeli society.

We can't say with certainty that the three models will remain as they are. As we mentioned, today, each time a kibbutz changes, learning from the new models, it skips some of the steps that other kibbutzim have gone through and moves further away from the original socialist vision. However, while we don't claim to predict the future, we do think that there must be room in Israel for a social democratic vision that includes the best instincts and successes exemplified by the kibbutzim.

We have no poetic conclusion to the story of the kibbutzim. Although the vast majority of them are engaged in a process of change, it is not clear how many will survive as coherent and defined communities. The kibbutzim portrayed in this book are each engaged in a continuing process. As communities they are rethinking an ideology and a way of life in ways that could not be imagined even twenty years ago, let alone by their pioneering founders. While the starting points for entering the process are quite different, similar models for change are taking shape.

Until relatively recently, the Kibbutz Movement was more an obstacle for change than a catalyst. If the movement had the financial resources to support the kibbutzim in the process, things might be very different. But those days are long gone. The Kibbutz Movement can be no more than a moral voice of support, a consultant on financial and legal issues, and a platform for sharing new ideas, as the individual kibbutzim learn by trial and error. We conclude from our interviews that if there was a failure, it was rooted in a kind of naïveté. The people of the kibbutzim believed in the old Zionist values well after the state and the rest of society—including what remains of the Israeli Zionist labor left—went forward with other agendas.

On the surface, today's kibbutz is a utilitarian community with some idealist trappings. Changes are rooted not in ideology and the virtues of creating a better human being but in costs and benefits and—most importantly—in the interest of individuals' survival. It's clear that the center of gravity is no longer the communal moadon but the family home. Kibbutz members—two and three generations after the founding—are no longer revolutionaries serving their country. They are normal human beings, who are sticking together in order to re-create or reengineer or simply defend a society in the throes of economic and social disorder. While they still hold values reflecting an impulse toward social solidarity, their own survival and quality of life take precedence over principles and ideals formulated by earlier generations.

But in examining these lives, we found a commitment to collective responsibility for health, education, and welfare still very much alive. Even where they fail to uphold the classic kibbutz model, they still largely share a desire to make the world better. Riffi Schlossberg, the Gesher Haziv leader for change, yearns for the Habonim youth movement to use her kibbutz as an educational enclave. A Hatzor enterprise takes care of autistic children. And the questioning socialists of Gan Shmuel postpone fundamental change in order to establish an ethical community, first and foremost. Perhaps kibbutznikim—educated to be skeptics—would do better to be a little less self-critical and embrace and applaud some of their innermost beliefs. We have checked the pulse of these people. After penetrating the layers of frustration and personal disappointment, we have found that the heart is still beating—at a pace that many in other societies would envy.

# NOTES

## Chapter 1: Setting the Stage

1. In our usage of the word "Palestine" for Israel before its official modern founding in 1948, we are following the style of Zionist scholar David Vital. We thought it worth clarifying, because the names "Israel" and "Palestine" have a different meaning in today's context. "There remains the question of the name of the Land. One or two critics have questioned my use of the term 'Erez-Israel' (literally: 'Land of Israel') to denote a country that a great many people do indeed think of as 'Palestine.' The difficulty is that for centuries, until the British took it over at the end of the Great War, it was an exceedingly loose geographical expression at best; and no political or administrative unit of that name, or covering that territory even approximately, existed. The Jews . . . tended to think of it in their own traditional terms, one of which was 'Erez-Israel.' They most certainly did so in the particular context of the modern Jewish revival and of thoughts about a Return, although 'Palestine' did creep in to speech and writing, especially when not conducted in their own languages and in discourse with non-Jews. On the other hand, few non-Jews used the term except, perhaps, in flights of Biblical fancy. I have therefore thought it right to use the term 'Palestine' when the context or the documents required it and 'Erez-Israel' when it seemed the more appropriate." David Vital, *Zionism: The Crucial Phase* (Oxford: Clarendon Press, 1987), xiii.

2. Amos Elon, *The Israelis: Founders and Sons* (New York: Bantam, 1972), 172.

3. These statistics are based on the official numbers from the Takam and Kibbutz Artzi federations.

4. This is known as *shanat chofesh*. Kibbutz members have been taking shanat chofesh to make a decision regarding whether or not to remain on the kibbutz, either because of frustration with the pace of change, lack of change, or desire to see if they can make it on the outside.

5. Anita Shapira, *Berl: The Biography of a Socialist Zionist* (Cambridge: Cambridge University Press, 1984), 28.

6. Aaron David Gordon, "People and Labor," in *The Zionist Idea*, ed. Arthur Hertzberg (New York: Atheneum, 1981), 374.

7. For more on the youth movements see the glossary.

8. Development towns were set up by the state of Israel in the 1950s to improve the economic and social situation of new immigrants. Over the years they were neglected by the various Labor governments and formed a significant part of the opposition to Labor and the left, eventually voting as a bloc for either the Likud or the Shas Party.

## Chapter 2: From One Century to the Next

1. "Articles of Association of the Kibbutz," quoted in Daniel Rosolio, *System and Crisis: Crises, Adjustments, and Changes in the Kibbutz Movement* (Tel Aviv: Am Oved Publishers, 1999), 26.

2. Rosolio, *System*, 26.

3. Kibbutz Gvulot, located just west of the Gaza Strip within Israel's 1967 Green Line borders.

4. Authors' interview with Micha Drori, Tel Aviv, 2001.

5. Rosolio, *System*, 13. Rosolio served as a Member of Knesset from 1977 to 1983. From 1983 to 1990, he was secretary general of Chevrat Ovdim. Prior to 1983, he served as secretary general of Takam. Since 1990 he has been a researcher at the Institute for Research of the Kibbutz and the Cooperative Idea at the University of Haifa and a lecturer at the University of Haifa and Regional College of the Western Galilee.

6. Israel's political parties have been fluid since before the founding of the state, and they continue to be fluid today, with parties splitting and new parties forming during each election cycle. "Workers' parties were dominant in the prestate Zionist movement and in the political leadership of the Yishuv (the Jewish community in Palestine) in the mid-1930s. This situation continued after the establishment of statehood in 1948 through 1977. Among these parties, which may all be defined as social-democratic, Mapai, the party of David Ben-Gurion and the largest among them, was the most pragmatic and moderate. Mapam was the most Marxist and remained pro-Soviet until after the death of Stalin. Ahdut Ha'avoda was most nationalist and activist in terms of Israel's territorial

demands and the Arab-Israeli conflict (after the Six-Day War some of its leaders joined the right). The mixed Jewish-Arab Communist Party was non-Zionist, at times anti-Zionist, and never played a central role. . . . The Labor Party was founded in 1968, when Mapai, Ahdut Ha'avoda, and Rafi (a party formed by Ben-Gurion in 1965) united. . . . As of the mid-1960s various smaller, more radical left-wing parties—some of which were more human-rights than socialist-oriented—emerged and disappeared. Mapam, which from 1969 to 1984 was part of the Labor Alignment, eventually united with the liberal-socialist Ratz and the liberal Shinui, to form Meretz in 1992. . . . From 1977 to 1984 it [Labor Alignment] was in opposition, and from 1984 to 1990 the Alignment, without Mapam, participated in national unity governments with the Likud. Labor, together with Meretz and for a short period Shas, ran the government from 1992 to 1996." From "Jpost Special—Elections 2003: Israel Decides," *Jerusalem Post*, www.jpost.com.

7. Amos Elon, *The Israelis: Founders and Sons* (New York: Bantam Books, 1972), 172.

8. Anecdote familiar to Gary Brenner.

9. Volumes have been written on the Yom Kippur War and the Israeli government being trapped in a particular concept of regional politics that did not permit political leaders to see that Egypt's president Anwar el-Sadat may have been prepared to make peace before 1973. Criticism of military leaders lies in their sense of infallibility following the 1967 victory, as they built a seemingly impenetrable "Maginot Line" (called the Bar-Lev Line) along the Suez Canal. The tragedy of the war, like most, was that it could have been prevented, and not just in hindsight.

10. In the Jewish religion, the initial mourning period, the shivah, lasts for seven days; the second stage of mourning is the *shloshim*, lasting thirty days.

11. Later, Mapam left the alignment with Labor and along with several smaller parties formed Meretz, where there is still an active Kibbutz Artzi presence both in the party and in the Knesset delegation. The KAF supplied early and continued funding for Peace Now, and the KAF and the Kibbutz Movement provide many of the activists for the peace movement.

12. Daniel Rosolio, "The Kibbutz Movement and the Way It Functions as a Cause of the Kibbutz Crisis: A Study in Political Economy," *Journal of Rural Cooperation* 22, nos. 1–2 (1994): 70. This article was a precursor to Rosolio's book, *System*. On the economic crisis of the 1980s, Rosolio refers to M. Heth, *Introduction to Economics: An Israeli Version* (Jerusalem: Bialik Institute, 1989) (in Hebrew), and Michael Bruno, "Israel's Crisis and Economic Reform in Historical Perspective," *Economic Quarterly* 40, no. 141 (1989).

13. Rosolio, *System*, 70, 71.

14. Stanley Maron, "Recent Developments in the Kibbutz: An Overview," *Journal of Rural Cooperation* 22, nos. 1–2 (1994): 5–6.

15. Ariel Halperin was born on Kibbutz Yifat in the Jezreel Valley. As an officer in the Israeli Defense Forces, he was severely wounded in service. He left the kibbutz to study economics and received his Ph.D. at Hebrew University and did postdoctoral study at Massachusetts Institute of Technology. We quote Halperin from three sources: an interview we did with him (July 2000), a videotaped lecture he supplied us from Kibbutz Saad (July 1997), and two annual reports of the government's Administration for Implementing the Arrangement for the Kibbutzim (1996 and 1998), also supplied by him, all documentation in Hebrew.

16. Rosolio is our "primary source." But, in many instances, he is referring to primary sources for his own theoretical work.

17. Rosolio, *System*, 13.

18. Janos Kornai puts soft constraints this way: "The firm can go beyond the budget constraint without any grave consequences. If it suffers financial losses because of uncovered expenses, the state will sooner or later cover these." From Janos Kornai in "The Dilemmas of a Socialist Economy: The Hungarian Experience," *Cambridge Journal of Economics* 4, no. 2 (June 1980): 147–57.

19. Rosolio, *System*, 54–55.

20. Rosolio, *System*, 23.

21. Avishai Grossman is a second-generation member of Kibbutz Ein Shemer and a key contemporary thinker and writer from the Kibbutz Artzi Federation. Grossman was one of the editors of *The Seventh Day: Soldiers Talk about the Six-Day War* (New York: Scribner's, 1970), a compilation of interviews with Israeli soldiers who were kibbutz members following the 1967 Six-Day War, which demonstrated their commitment to peace and distaste for war.

22. Rosolio, "The Kibbutz Movement," 67.

23. Task Plan, April 1982, Takam convention resolution.

24. Rosolio, "The Kibbutz Movement."

25. Rosolio, "The Kibbutz Movement," quoting Krol, 71.


## Chapter 3: The Crisis and the Search for Solutions

1. Ariel Halperin, *Annual Report of the Administration for the Implemention of the Kibbutz Arrangement* (Israel, 1996), 6; submitted to the Government of Israel, the kibbutz movements, and seven banks involved in the settlement arrangement.

2. Quoted from Vered Levy-Barzilai, "A Vision of Poverty," *Ha'aretz*, September 15, 2000.

3. Authors' interview with Ariel Halperin, Tel Aviv, July 25, 2000.

4. Halperin, "Toward a New Conception," excerpts from a videotaped lecture to the general assembly of Kibbutz Saad, translated by Gary Brenner (Israel, September 25, 1997).

5. Jo-Ann Mort interview in Gadish's office at Kvutzat Yavne, July 2000.

6. Authors' interview with Ariel Halperin, Tel Aviv, July 25, 2000.

7. Menachem Rosner, "A 'Third Way' to Save the Kibbutz?" *Dissent* (fall 2000): 91.

8. This is a standing joke at Kibbutz Hatzor, first told by a factory manager who has since left the kibbutz.

9. Authors' interview with Shlomo Getz, Haifa University, July 2001. Getz has been a member of Kibbutz Gadot since 1971 and is a graduate of Tel Aviv University. He served as *mazkir*, or general secretary (feminine, *mazkira*), of the kibbutz, and worked in citrus orchards and as a high school teacher before joining the Institute for Research of the Kibbutz in 1986.

10. The narrative is synopsized by Gary Brenner from conversations with Haim and Tzippi Amitai. The Amitais are an example of members who fulfilled the expectations of the kibbutz society in all areas, what we might describe as good kibbutznikim devoted to the community.

11. Israeli men serve reserve duty until they are forty-five years old, usually for one month a year.

12. Halperin, *Annual Report*, 51.

13. Halperin, *Toward a New Conception*.

14. Authors' interviews with Yisrael Tsufim, Givat Haviva, July 2000 and July 2001.

15. *Kibbutz* (December 20, 2001): 12–13.

16. Documents from Yaakov Gadish, Zerem Shitufi leader, given to authors.

17. Jo-Ann Mort interviews with Yaakov Gadish, Kvutzat Yavne, July 2000 and 2001.

18. An exception is the small, relatively new kibbutz, Lotan, founded by a majority of Americans, members of the Reform stream of Judaism. This kibbutz, located in the Negev, near Eilat, is highly ideological along the classic kibbutz lines. The median age at the kibbutz in 2000, when Jo-Ann Mort spent time there interviewing members, was thirty-two years old, and in that year the kibbutz was experiencing its first birth. There were no older members on the kibbutz.

19. Jo-Ann Mort interview with Gavri Bar Gil, Tel Aviv, July 2000.

Chapter 4: Gesher Haziv

1. "Son of the kibbutz" denotes the communal concept of child rearing. When children were raised in the children's houses, they were considered literally to be either "sons" or "daughters" of the kibbutz. The entire community cared for them, economically and socially, taking part in all their life-cycle events.

2. German Jews were considered by others to hold elitist attitudes (because they mostly came from the upper middle class of German society). They had a more difficult time than most adjusting to the hardships of pioneering Israel, including learning Hebrew.

3. Even though Peter Braun is a native English speaker, he pointedly uses the phrase "went out" when describing the five-minute trek from Gesher Haziv to Nahariya, the closest city. That's because, under the classic system, a kibbutz member's entire life was virtually contained within the kibbutz property. Rather than saying we "went" to Nahariya, the thinking was that you were going "outside" the kibbutz.

4. That is, the incorporated entity known as Gesher Haziv, which holds on to all remaining communal properties.

5. See chapter 7 for more on the land issue.

6. "Kibbutz of the Ghetto Fighters," founded by survivors of the Warsaw Ghetto Uprising, a wealthy kibbutz because of an industry, Tival, established in the late 1980s. Tival produces a famous line of vegetarian instant meals. Tival is now owned 49 percent by the kibbutz and 51 percent by Osem, a subsidiary of Nestlé, making Lochmei Hagetaot and Nestlé partners. But even with collective wealth, the kibbutz has almost no young people. This demographic exemplifies the social problem faced by most kibbutzim.

7. Shavei Zion is located across the street and a bit south down the road from Gesher Haziv. Because of its location right on the Mediterranean, it has incorporated within its grounds a villa neighborhood of private homes that is one of the most expensive in Israel.

8. It's now a regional school, situated on the kibbutz.

9. This number is based on Riffi Schlossberg quoting Natan Tal. The phrase "come back" means return to the kibbutz of their birth after they go into the army, which most Israeli kids do between high school and college.

10. Most kibbutzim used to celebrate holidays communally. During Passover, they would hold a secular ceremonial meal for everyone in the communal dining hall.

11. Yisrael Tsufim, the kibbutz consultant, worked with Gesher Haziv. He recommended that the authors study Gesher Haziv.

12. One of the ways in which kibbutzim behaved as their own countries was in foregoing individual pensions paid by the state.

13. In Israel, young people who serve in the army between high school and college receive money from the army for their university education. Also, there is a tradition in Israel of public universities. Only recently is there a new phenomenon of private colleges, similar to U.S. colleges.

14. Herzl is referring to 1977 when the Likud government took power.

## Chapter 5: Hatzor: A Third Way?

1. During the 1991 Gulf War, all ideological debates about how to rear the children were cast aside by parents who frantically snatched their children from the communal children's houses to take them to the safety of their own gas-proof sealed rooms. The kids never returned to the children's houses. This happened in many kibbutzim throughout Israel.

2. Jo-Ann Mort interviews with Gadish at Kvutzat Yavne, July 2000 and July 2001.

3. According to a survey by the Institute for Research of the Kibbutz, 2000.

4. Because Hatzor is Gary Brenner's home, Jo-Ann Mort conducted most of the interviews there, the idea being that people would speak more freely with her.

5. Here, Eshel is pointing out that the gizbar or treasurer—which, like all jobs in a classic kibbutz, was a floating appointment—used to oversee all kibbutz finances and readily intermixed the economic and living expenses. Today, at Hatzor and most kibbutzim, even those that still follow a classic model, expenses are separated between the economy, or business, part of the kibbutz and the living, or community, part of the kibbutz.

6. Reminiscent of Rawls's theory of justice in John Rawls, *A Theory of Justice* (Cambridge: Harvard University Press, 1971).

7. Reflected in Michael Walzer's response to Rawls, Michael Walzer, *Spheres of Justice* (New York: Basic Books, 1983).

8. This is an interesting observation, since Yaakov Gadish, the Tamid leader, remarked in an interview with the authors that the Amish are preserving a cooperative way of life, as if that offered hope for the classic faction within the kibbutz movement. However, Gadish, along with other Tamid leaders, is a successful businessman dealing in a global arena; therefore, it doesn't appear to be a comparison that makes much sense.

9. At Hatzor, historically, outside income from families in America was supposed to be pooled. In the founding decades, this rule was strictly

adhered to, in keeping with the hardcore Stalinist ideology for which Hatzor was known. People even had toys taken from their children if they were given by an outside relative, as much for economic equality as social equality. But as the decades progressed and the ideology lessened, so too did this practice. Before the differential salaries were instituted, people were keeping their outside income or taking advantage of families on the outside to provide vacations and also holding on to income earned in a black market atmosphere. For example, repair work on the kibbutz, or translating, or tutoring, were occasionally done by members who didn't hand over the rewards to the communal pool.

10. Tal, while lamenting the loss of the old nonmaterialistic kibbutz culture, is also complaining about the lack of choices. Often, the "Stalinist" approach to consumer goods was not purely ideological; it was also practical. In a scarcity society and in a nation that didn't have many consumer options, it was ideologically shrewd of the kibbutzim to limit choices. But once the overall culture became richer, it was more difficult to make the ideology stick.

11. Tal is referring to the system of mediation that the kibbutz put in place to negotiate the differential salaries.

12. Tal is referring to a system at Hatzor that rewards seniority with bigger homes, even though younger members have to accommodate their children at home. This is changing now that the members are going to own their homes instead of all housing belonging to the kibbutz—and they will be able to build on additions.

13. Of course, as stated earlier, in the old-style Hatzor, private money shouldn't be able to be used anyway. However, kibbutz members often used private money without declaring it. In Chava Tal's case, she was so diligent in her commitment to the collective that she didn't take extra money from her parents except when she was on vacation, and her family contributed generously to the kibbutz when the kibbutz made special accommodations for Tal's son.

14. Jo-Ann Mort interview with Sylvia and Yitzhak Kedem, July 2001.

15. Kochav Yair is a wealthy suburb near the Green Line in central Israel. It is a former moshav whose inhabitants—mostly high-ranking military personnel, including former prime minister Ehud Barak—took advantage of land laws that transferred high-end homes to military personnel for a fraction of their market value.

16. By young people, Yitzhak Kedem means the change group, who by 2001 are in their forties and fifties.

17. Yaakov Hazan was one of the founders of the Kibbutz Artzi Federation, a legendary figure who led the kibbutz movement with an iron hand, at a time when the kibbutzim fell in line behind their leaders.

18. Binnie Zerach is referring here to a trip to the United States and seems to also imply that her ticket was paid for with outside funds, perhaps from her family in the United States.

19. Historically, all the housing in a kibbutz belonged to the collective, and members could be moved around by dictate of the kibbutz. The next phase of the change, however, includes placing housing in members' names and allowing members to build improvements and additions in their homes. However, the national laws overseeing the housing are still based on the cooperative model. While many changes are already being made, it wasn't clear, at the time of this writing, what the final outcome would be.

20. Shas, a religious party with a base among the Jews of North Africa, many of whom live in development towns, is not considered an ally of the kibbutzim.

## Chapter 6: Gan Shmuel

1. Based on Gary Brenner's interview with Motti Gazit, former manager of Gan Shmuel Foods, August 2002.

2. Authors' interviews at Gan Shmuel, July 2000 and July 2001. They conducted some interviews together and some separately. Brenner conducted additional interviews from July 2001 to the end of 2001.

3. It is traditional, among kibbutz young people, to spend a year in the kibbutz youth movement doing national service before going into the army.

4. Up through the 1980s, even into the early 1990s, on many kibbutzim outside phone lines were limited, and in order to reach someone on the kibbutz, someone had to call the dining room when a meal was being served and hope that someone would pass a ringing public phone, answer it, and find the person requested. This was a typical kibbutz practice— something that was initially instituted out of scarcity, but with an overlay of ideology. It added to the kibbutz members' isolation and to the myth of the kibbutz. However, today, not only does each apartment have a phone, as do all the kibbutz offices, but they have Internet connection, and cell phones abound.

5. *Al Hamishmar* was the newspaper of Mapam, the left-wing political party with which KAF was affiliated. It went out of business in the early 1990s. The Takam kibbutzim, affiliated with the Labor Party, read *Davar*, which was the Histadrut (trade union) paper, and which also went out of business in the early 1990s.

6. Gan Shmuel was notorious for its Stalinistic tendencies in the 1950s

and early 1960s. These tendencies were famously played out by a radio "czar" who dogmatically controlled what station could be played in the dining room.

7. *Ha'aretz* is often called the *New York Times* of Israel. Its roots were in General Zionism, which was a political movement based on traditional free-market European-style liberal politics. Therefore, the socialist movements in Israel once considered it the enemy. Its economic beliefs are still free-market today, but with the demise of both ideological left-wing papers, *Ha'aretz* is the voice of the Israeli dovish intelligentsia today; but it is socially progressive, not economically progressive. There is no journalistic voice for a social democratic or Marxist type of politics after the demise of *Al Hamishmar* and *Davar*.

8. Today, the Gan Shmuel supermarket, Duchan, is one of the most modern supermarkets in Israel. It is comparable to any American suburban market.

9. However, a majority isn't enough to force change at Gan Shmuel. Two-thirds are needed to make a change.

10. Gary Brenner translated the document provided by Omri Kenan.

11. Rotem Ashkenazi is referring here to people taking food back to their rooms to create, in essence, a private stock of food. This was because they did not allow members to bring in outside food to their rooms.

12. This particular sentiment was voiced by most of the young people we interviewed. When a communal structure is in place, you are willing to put up with people you don't necessarily like, but when that structure disbands, the reason to live in a community with people not necessarily of your own choosing is not evident.

13. There is a concept in the kibbutz economy that says that the kibbutz members are wealthy but the kibbutz isn't, which means that the member's allowance is held in a common pool or internal bank managed by the gizbar. This is how the gizbar finances the collective budget, which includes health, education, and welfare. In the past, kibbutznikim led a relatively frugal existence, so there was more money for the gizbar to spend on health and welfare. But, as standards of living increase with expenses such as regularly traveling abroad (and as members in their forties and fifties need to put out more money for their children), this puts pressure on the gizbar.

14. When we conducted interviews in the summer of 2001, there was only one general secretary, Dinah Gavish Vergilese, but she had previously shared the position with another woman.

15. What Gavish Vergilese is referring to is the phenomenon of chofesh, which in literal translation means "freedom" and normally refers to vacation. However, in this case, unlike the "vacation" off the kibbutz taken by some members we interviewed at Gesher Haziv and Hatzor who

were awaiting change, she is referring to another kind of chofesh, also deployed by kibbutz members as a way of dealing with the lack of change they desire. Her use of "chofesh" describes a sort of internal vacation, where a kibbutz member still lives on the kibbutz but withdraws from communal life.

16. Shapira's most recent work is an unpublished manuscript, "The Misunderstood Kibbutz: Moral Leadership and Trust in the Blossoming and Decay of Communal Cultures," 2001, which he kindly shared with us.

17. Historically, each kibbutz would hold a general assembly on Saturday morning in the dining room.

18. Today, on almost all kibbutzim, the general assembly can be viewed on an internal cable system. Most people don't attend the general assemblies. At an earlier time, the majority of members participated in the general assembly, and the life of the kibbutz revolved around the assembly. However, Gan Shmuel still employs a form of pure democracy where there are no elected committees and each person votes on everything. Other kibbutzim have moved to a representative model that includes committees. It could be argued that the direct democracy system, considering the lack of participation in the general assembly, is less "democratic" than if the kibbutz were to elect committees. Presently, whoever shows up to vote makes the decisions for the kibbutz community or kehillah. The only thing that is shielded from this sort of decision making at Gan Shmuel is, as we noted, Gan Shmuel Foods, the financially successful factory.

19. The high cost of water to irrigate the cotton fields was one factor that drove many kibbutzim into financial trouble in the 1980s. Nahal Hadera is a reservoir near the kibbutz.

20. Hannah Knaz is referring to our telling her what a couple of her male neighbors said about Dinah Gavish Vergilese, that she couldn't handle the job of kibbutz general secretary because she is a woman.

21. They were selected by Rafi Ashkenazi.

22. The idea that things are "free" is one of the things that got the kibbutzim into heavy financial debt.

23. Daphna Yasur's response reflects one reason that kibbutzim are now grappling with the idea of inheritance.

## Chapter 7: End of Kibbutz or a New Beginning?

1. Jo-Ann Mort Migvan interviews, Sderot, July 2000; Naomi Tzion, Tel Aviv, July 2001, and follow-up via E-mail until February 2002.

2. "Madrich Leshiuch Dirot," translated as "Guide for Privatizing

Homes," Yaakov Setter, editor, sections by Tzafrir Ben Or (lawyer), Eldad Shaham (lawyer), Mira Yehudai and Danny Bar Kama (architects), Smedar Shavit (organizational consultant) (Tel Aviv: The Kibbutz Movement, September 2001).

3. Setter, "Guide," section 1, p. 5.

4. Ariel Halperin, lecture at Kibbutz Saad, September 25, 1997.

5. *Yediot Aharanot*, February 21, 2002. Translated by Gary Brenner.

6. Ofer Petersburg and Goel Nevo, "Surprise: Private Villas on the Kibbutz," *Yediot Aharanot*, February 21, 2002, "24 Hours" section. Translated by Gary Brenner.

7. "Surprise," *Yediot Aharanot*.

8. Authors' interview with Micha Drori, Tel Aviv, July 2001.

9. Interview with Micha Drori.

10. Mazal Mualem, "An 'Assertive' Group Flexes Its Mizrachi Muscles," *Ha'aretz*, September 5, 2002.

11. Moshe Reinfeld, Amiram Cohen, and Ziv Maor, "Court Overthrows Lucrative Rezoning Policy on Farm Land," *Ha'aretz*, August 30, 2002, front page, English edition.

12. *Hakibbutz* magazine, June 20, 2002.

# GLOSSARY

*Achdut Avodah Party*   Zionist Socialist Labor Party founded in Palestine in 1919. It joined with Hapoel Hatzair in 1930 to form the Mapai Party.

*Aliyah (pl., aliyot)*   Generic term for moving to Israel; literally means "ascending," as in ascending to heaven, to stress the hallowed position emigration to Israel plays for the Jewish people. The First Aliyah took place at the beginning of the Zionist movement in the late nineteenth century. It was followed by the socialist-Zionist aliyot of 1904–1913 (Second Aliyah) and 1918–1925 (Third Aliyah).

*Amana*   Covenant

*Articles of Association*   Kibbutz movement document comprising the laws of the communal settlements

*Asafa*   General assembly in those kibbutzim that were part of the Takam movement. (It is called *sicha kibbutz* in the Kibbutz Artzi movement.) Both harken back to the days when there was direct democracy in the kibbutz. Today, the general assembly is often held via cable hook-up, and voting is by ballot box.

*Ashkenazi (adj., Ashkenazic)*   Jews of European ancestry

*Atid*   Future. See also kibbutz atid.

*B'rashit*   "In the beginning God created"; from Genesis

*Ben/bat Kibbutz*   Son of or daughter of the kibbutz; children born on the kibbutz

*Bituach leumi*   Israeli social security system

*Ber Borochov, Dov*   Philosopher, writer, Yiddish linguist, and historian (1881–1917). He was active in Poalei Zion (Workers of Zion), one of the first socialist-Zionist political frameworks. Poalei Zion believed in a return to Zion where Jews would become the avant-garde of the international class struggle. This party, mostly under his leadership, dominated the social and political fabric of Zionism for decades and later became the Labor Party.

*Chalutzim*    Pioneers; early kibbutz members

*Chevra*    Friendship or a society of close friends, used in reference to a collectivist model like a kibbutz

*Chevrat Ovdim*    Collective welfare societies, once part of Histadrut

*Chibat Zion*    Love of Zion; a popular movement for the redemption and rebuilding of Israel that sprang up among the Jews in Russia and spread to other countries at the end of the nineteenth century.

*Communa*    A collective laundry on the kibbutz

*Conceptzia*    This word entered Israeli common usage after the fiasco of the 1973 Yom Kippur War. It reflected the hubris of the generals and politicians who were overconfident in their predictions regarding Egypt's and Syria's war plans. Today, the word means someone who is overconfident.

*Duchan*    Fruit stand; the name of the Gan Shmuel–owned supermarket

*Emet*    Truth

*Eretz Israel*    Refers to the biblical "Land of Israel"; using this phrase harkens back to the yearnings that Jews have had through the ages to return to Israel.

*Erev Shabbat*    Eve of Shabbat, which religious Jews celebrate by going to synagogue and with a meal at home; in Israel secular Jews create a communal setting that often includes a celebratory Friday evening meal with family and friends.

*Ezra Hadadit*    Collective responsibility for health, education, and welfare

*Galut*    In exile; diaspora Jews living outside of Israel

*Gan*    Garden; kindergarten

*Garin*    Age group formed to make aliyah to kibbutz from outside or within Israel

*Gizbar*    Kibbutz treasurer

*Gordon, Aaron David (A. D.)*    Born in 1856 in Podolia, Russia, he immigrated to Palestine at age forty-seven to begin a life of agricultural labor first in Petah Tikvah, later in Rishon Letzion, and finally in Degania, the first of the kvutsot (or collective settlements).

*Greater Israel*    Concept and movement formed after the 1967 Six-Day War for an enlarged Israel to include the biblical borders of Judea, Samaria, and also include Gaza.

*1967 Green Line borders*    Israel's borders before the Six-Day War

*Ha'am, Ahad*    Believed that the creation in the Land of Israel of a Jewish cultural focal point would reinforce Jewish life in the Diaspora. His hope was that in this center a new Jewish national identity based on Jewish ethics and values might resolve the crisis of Judaism. He joined the Chibat Zion movement but soon became a severe critic of its settlement activities, preferring instead cultural work for a Jewish regeneration.

*Habonim*    Youth movement affiliated with the Labor Party in Israel; it acted as a feeder to two kibbutz federations—Ichud and Meuchad—which joined in 1980 to become the Takam or United Kibbutz Movement

*Hachshara*    Training farms in the United States and Europe that prepared urban young people for kibbutz life. The U.S. Hashomer Hatzair hachshara was in Hightstown, New Jersey.

*Hafrata*    Privatization

*Haganah*    The Israeli army before Independence and throughout the 1948 war. After the war the army was organized into the Israel Defense Forces (IDF).

*Hanhala rachava*    Factory management or steering committee in the kibbutz industries

*Hashomer Hatzair*    Youth movement of the Kibbutz Artzi Federation kibbutzim, once affiliated with what became the Marxist Mapam Party. See also Kibbutz Artzi Federation.

*"Hatikvah"*    National anthem of Israel; the words were written by Naftali Herz Imber around 1870. The melody is based on a folk song known in many European countries in various forms.

*Hatzran*    Caretaker; the overall handyman on the kibbutz who is every member's helper, setting up for weddings and funerals, bringing clothes to and from the laundry, and so forth. A kibbutz institution: no kibbutz manager would become a hatzran, but no kibbutz would be the same without one.

*Herut Party*    Founded by Menachem Begin in 1948, with roots in the revisionist Zionism of Zev Jabotinsky and in opposition to the organized labor movement. In 1965 a coalition (Likud) was created from Herut, Gahal, and other right-center parties. However, in 2003, a right-wing, breakaway faction still maintains the name Herut Party.

*Histadrut*    Israeli trade union federation

*Jabotinsky, Vladimir "Zev"*    Established the revisionist Zionists in 1925 and advocated for an aggressive nonsocialist approach to formulating the modern state of Israel on both sides of the Jordan River (in all the territories later occupied by Israel after the Six-Day War). His successors in Israeli politics are the leaders of the Likud Party.

*Jewish Agency*    See World Zionist Organization.

*Jewish National Fund*    See World Zionist Organization.

*Katznelson, Berl*    A leader of the Zionist labor movement and a central figure of the Second Aliyah (1944–1988). Founder of the Histadrut and many of the Labor-Zionist institutions, Katznelson also helped found the consumer cooperatives for the sale of food, known as Hamashbir. He helped initiate Kupat Holim, the Sick Fund or workers' national health insurance system.

*Keshet Mizrachi*   "Eastern rainbow"; an advocacy group with a social democratic-dovish orientation organized to support Jews of Mizrachi background

*Kibbutz (pl., kibbutzim)*   Communal settlement

*Kibbutz Artzi Federation (KAF)*   Left-wing kibbutz federation founded by the Hashomer Hatzair youth movement and affiliated with the Mapam and later, Meretz Parties and the Labor Alignment. Hashomer Hatzair, the first Zionist youth movement, was founded in Eastern Europe just before World War I. Early on, it was influenced by Lord Baden-Powell's Boy Scout movement and the German Wandervögel (hikers) movement. It promoted scouting as a way to teach Jewish urban and shtetl (village) youth self-reliance and independence. It eventually embraced Zionist and socialist ideologies and stressed the need for the Jewish people to change from being merchants and professionals to chalutzim or workers and farmers in the Land of Israel. The first members went to settle in Palestine in 1919.

*Kibbutz atid*   Proponents of fundamental changes in the kibbutzim

*Kibbutz federations*   Political federations of kibbutzim. Ichud and Meuchad merged in 1980 to form the Takam or United Kibbutz Movement. In 2000 the Takam and the Kibbutz Artzi Federation merged to form the Kibbutz Movement, bringing together all kibbutzim except for those in Kibbutz Hadati, the religious kibbutzim settled by Orthodox Jews and affiliated with the National Religious Party. One Orthodox kibbutz, Haefetz Chayim, is associated with Agudat Israel. See also Poalei Agudat Israel.

*Kibbutz Hadati Movement*   Religious kibbutzim affiliated with the National Religious Party

*Kibbutznik (pl., kibbutznikim)*   Kibbutz member

*Kibbutz Tamid*   Movement that aspires to some form of continuity (tamid means "always") and which arose as a reaction to an indigenous movement for change within the kibbutzim

*Knesset*   Israel's parliament

*Kupat Holim*   Collective health insurance, part of the Histadrut until the end of the twentieth century, when it became a public/private insurance organization

*Kvutza (pl., kvutsot)*   Age group; a handful of kibbutzim evolved with the name "kvutza."

*Liberal Party*   Also known as the General Zionists, a faction of the World Zionist Organization before the establishment of the Israeli state. The General Zionists included people of a center-right political persuasion who were not part of any other organized political group. Most Zionist activists in the early part of the movement were either self-defined leftists or supported a right-wing agenda. In 1965 the Liberal Party merged with the Herut Party to form the Gahal Party, which became part of the Likud Party in 1973.

*Likud Party*   In 1973, Herut, Gahal, and other right-center parties formed a coalition party (Likud or "union"). Since 1977, the Likud has either been the ruling party in the Knesset or the leading opposition party. In addition to its support for a Greater Israel, the Likud Party is hostile to the kibbutz movement and to all the vestiges of socialism in Israeli society.

*"L'olam lo hosen"*   "Not powerful forever" or "not immune from losing power"

*Machane*   Encampment; the heart of the kibbutz that includes the public buildings

*Mapai Party*   Israel's major labor party, Mifleget Poalei Eretz Israel or Land of Israel Workers' Party, affiliated with the Takam kibbutzim, was established in 1930 as a socialist-Zionist party and was the dominant political party in the prestate and early poststate years. The left-of-center Mapai led every coalition and was represented by the prime minister in every government from 1948 until 1977. In 1968, Mapai allied with the more leftwing Mapam, to form the Labor Alignment, which lasted until 1984.

*Mapam Party*   Socialist-Zionist, Marxist party affiliated with the Kibbutz Artzi Federation. Mapam (United Workers Party) was the second largest political party in the early years of the state. Mapam aligned with the labor party (Mapai) from 1968 until 1984, ran independently in 1988, and joined with the Ratz and Shinui Parties in 1992 to form Meretz. Meretz was part of a coalition government under Prime Minister Yitzhak Rabin in 1992 and Ehud Barak in 1999. Meretz opposed Labor's entry into the unity government after Ehud Barak lost in his 2001 reelection bid to Ariel Sharon. Meretz returned to the opposition.

*Mazkir/mazkira*   General secretary of the kibbutz (the "a" denotes feminine) who runs the communal part of the kibbutz

*Mazkirut*   General secretariat, equivalent of the central committee, that runs the communal part of the kibbutz

*Meretz Party*   Affiliated with the Kibbutz Artzi kibbutzim; it was founded in 1992 when the Mapam, Ratz, and Shinui Parties merged. (Not the same as the Shinui Party represented in the Knesset in 2003, which is not affiliated with Meretz. See Shinui Party.) Meretz is considered the home of the Israeli peace camp. It promotes social and economic justice, civil rights for all Israelis, and territorial compromise, which means a Jewish state in Israel alongside a Palestinian state. Since 2001, it has been in the Israeli opposition.

*Mercaz meshek*   Farm manager

*Merekez*   Work coordinator in the traditional kibbutz system

*Meshula*   Reengineering or radical restructuring of a kibbutz

*Metapelet*   Caretaker (traditionally a woman) who took care of the children in the communal children's houses

*Mizrachi*   Eastern; Jews from North Africa and other Arab countries as opposed to Europe or the Americas; now used more widely than the older term, "Sephardi"

*Moadon*   Kibbutz community center, used historically for general kibbutz meetings, socializing, and reading after dinner, as well as for weddings and the start of funeral processions

*Moatza*   Regional council, largely dominated by kibbutzim and moshavim, and functioning in a parallel manner to the urban municipalities

*Mosadot*   Governing institutions of the kibbutz

*Moshav (pl., moshavim)*   Cooperative farm where the land and other means of production were collectivized, like the kibbutz, but organized around the family unit, with private homes

*Moshav shitufi*   Moshavim that were historically closer in temperament and politics to the kibbutzim, with a more collectivized economy than other moshavim. The literal meaning of shitufi is "collective."

*Mossad hinuchi*   Kibbutz school, often a boarding school

*Nahal*   Farming or pioneering unit; a group of soldiers who form a settlement corps while serving within Israel's 1967 borders; often the nucleus of a new kibbutz

*Narodnik*   "Going to the people" in Russian (*narodniki* in Hebrew); the name for Russian revolutionaries of the 1860s and 1870s

*National Religious Party*   Mafdal in Hebrew. Established in 1956, the National Religious Party seeks to make Israeli law consistent with halacha (Talmudic law). When the Labor Party (Mapai) was the predominant political force in Israeli politics and there was a consensus for labor hegemony over Israeli social and economic structures, the NRP was also in coalition with the Labor-dominated governments. After 1967, as the socialist-Zionist project began to wane and with the capture of the territories in the West Bank and the rise of the Gush Emunim (Bloc of the Faithful) within the NRP, the NRP made a profound shift to the right. Its settlement policy became focused on the occupied territories, and its religious bent became more messianic. Today, only a few in the older generation on the handful of religious kibbutzim represent the original coalition of the Labor Party and the kibbutzim. The NRP's primary focus now is to support the settlers in the occupied territories.

*Nikudah*   Plot of land

*Nir Shitufi*   Cooperative association that held formal title to all kibbutz properties on behalf of the kibbutz movements

*Olim*   Those who make aliyah to Israel

*Oppenheimer, Franz*   Leader of the General Zionists who proposed Jewish collective settlement at the 1903 Zionist Congress

*Palmach*   Prestate Israeli elite military formation, largely led by and composed of kibbutz members but reporting to the Haganah

*Peace Now*   Movement founded in 1978 by 348 reserve officers of the Israel Defense Forces who believed that only a negotiated end to the conflict in the Middle East could bring true security to Israel. Peace Now, which has grown into a mass extraparliamentary movement, favors trading land for peace and a two-state solution. The kibbutzim support Peace Now with financial and human resources.

*Pesach*   Passover; commemorates the Exodus of the Jews from Egypt and is celebrated with the seder meal. Most kibbutzim used to celebrate holidays communally with a secular ceremonial meal.

*Pilug*   Split; refers to the split in many kibbutzim in the 1950s over support for Stalin and whether the Soviet Union conformed to their socialist ideals

*Pinsker, Leon (Judah Leib)*   Born in Russian Poland in 1821, a doctor and a founder and leader of the Chibat Zion movement. Author of "Autoemancipation," a pamphlet written in 1882 as a plea to the Jewish people to accept the nationalist or Zionist solution in Eretz Israel.

*Poalei Agudat Israel*   Ultra-Orthodox youth movement founded in Poland before World War II that encouraged aliyah to Israel and to kibbutz. Today, it comprises two kibbutzim, affiliated with the Agudat Israel Party, an ultra-Orthodox party primarily of Jews from Poland and elsewhere in Europe. It is insignificant in the kibbutz movement itself.

*Rasham*   Israeli government official who oversees all collective associations including the kibbutz

*Renta*   Reparations money paid by the German government to survivors of the Holocaust

*Reshet bitachon*   Social safety net; one model of change on the kibbutz

*Ruppin, Arthur*   Sociologist and Zionist settlement leader (1876–1943). He became an advocate of pragmatic Zionism, believing that the most immediate need was to amass land and, through a variety of urban and rural communities, systematically settle the country and thus build a state.

*Sephardi (adj., Sephardic)*   Jews from Arab countries of the Middle East and North Africa, Salonika (Greece), and Spain (from which they were expelled in 1492)

*Shabbat*   Sabbath

*Shaliach*   Emissary; those who represent the kibbutz movement in Jewish communities abroad. Historically, Zionist youth movements sent emissaries to Europe, the Americas, and South Africa to encourage young people to emigrate to the kibbutzim. Today, these emissaries are staff people of Jewish organizations with ties to Israel.

*Shanat chofesh*    Vacation year or sabbatical from the kibbutz

*Shas Party*    Mizrachi protest party with a religious, social, and economic base that emerged toward the end of the twentieth century

*Shavuot*    Jewish holiday that marks God's deliverance of the Ten Commandments to Moses. The holiday, which falls in late spring, also marks the time for the spring harvest.

*Shinui*    Change; refers to the economic and structural changes on the kibbutzim; unrelated to the Shinui Party.

*Shinui Party*    Anticlerical, center-right party whose leader in the 2003 Knesset was journalist Joseph "Tommy" Lapid. Although the party shares the same name as an earlier Shinui Party that merged into the Meretz Party, it is a new formation with no connection to the earlier party.

*Shiuch*    Assigning or allocating public property as private on a kibbutz

*Shivah*    First seven days of mourning

*Shloshim*    End of the thirty-day mourning period

*Sicha kibbutz*    General assembly for kibbutzim of the Kibbutz Artzi Federation. (Takam kibbutzim call it *asafa*.)

*Syrkin, Nachman*    Leader of the socialist Zionists at the First Zionist Congress; Syrkin was also an early proponent of the Jewish National Fund and submitted a resolution suporting its creation at the Second Zionist Congress in 1898.

*Tabenkin, Yitzhak*    One of the principal thinkers and main voices of the kibbutz movement. He was a founding member of Kibbutz Ein Harod in 1921, which later formed the center of the Kibbutz Meuchad movement. He supported the idea of large kibbutzim or collective settlements open to large membership.

*Tafkid*    Position of responsibility; a task, duty, or function

*Takam*    United Kibbutz Movement, the association made up of the merger of two kibbutz movements, Ichud and Meuchad, in the 1980s

*Taksiv*    Budget or allowance

*Tamid*    Always; also continuity

*"Tamid pekuda anachnu"*    "We are always at the command of . . . "; kibbutz saying to express kibbutz members' belief that their first priority was service to the state or to their ideology (which used to be one and the same)

*Toshavim*    Residents or renters on kibbutz

*Ulpan*    Intensive Hebrew study course for foreigners that was frequently hosted by kibbutzim and often led to recruitment of new kibbutz members

*United Kibbutz Movement*   See Takam.

*Vatikim*   Founding generation, or veterans, of the kibbutzim

*World Zionist Organization*   Organization founded by Theodore Herzl as the Zionist Organization at the First Zionist Congress in Basel, Switzerland, in 1897; it was renamed the World Zionist Organization in 1960. Its goals were "to establish a home for the Jewish people in Palestine, secured under public law." It created institutions to carry out its policies, including the Jewish National Fund. The Mandate for Palestine, which the League of Nations gave to Great Britain, called for the formation of a Jewish Agency to represent the Jewish people and to cooperate with the Mandate in establishing a national home. The Zionist Organization became the Jewish Agency. In 1929, an expanded agency was established that also included non-Zionist, public Jewish groups with Dr. Chaim Weizmann at the head. The Jewish Agency was a tool for the involvement of the entire Jewish people in the building of the land. Eventually, the executive body of the Jewish Agency became identical with that of the Zionist Organization.

*Yishuv*   Pre-1948 Israel

*Yishuv kehillati*   Cooperative neighborhood, similar to an American planned suburban development or even a small town where taxes pay for such combined services as parks, trash collection, and education

*Youth movements*   Founded in Europe before World War II and spreading to North and South America, they preached aliyah—immigration to Israel—specifically to kibbutz. Hashomer Hatzair is a youth movement once affiliated with what became the Marxist Mapam Party and with the Kibbutz Artzi Federation kibbutzim. Habonim is a youth movement that was affiliated with what became Israel's Labor Party, and acted as a feeder into two kibbutz federations—Ichud and Meuchad—which joined to become the Takam federation. (Kibbutz Artzi and Takam are now merged in the Kibbutz Movement.) These youth movements sent emissaries throughout Europe, North and South America, South Africa, Tunisia, and elsewhere, recruiting young people to make aliyah to kibbutz. In Israel, they helped solidify the kibbutz mission among young people. They are still in existence, though weak reminders of what once was.

*Zerem Shitufi*   Collective stream; connotes traditional kibbutzim; name of a movement opposed to the changes on the kibbutzim; also called Kibbutz Tamid

*Zionist Organization*   See World Zionist Organization.

# INDEX

Achdut Avodah Party, 2
Agudat Israel Party, xi, 16
Ahdut Ha'avoda Party, 184n. 6
Aliyah, 60, 78, 108
    First, 5–6
    Second, 6–11
    Third, 8–11
    Youth, 6
Amana, 129–30. *See also* "Spirit of
    Gan Shmuel"
Amish, 189n. 8
Amitai, Batya and Uri, 68–71
Amitai, Haim and Tzippi, 40–42
Archer Daniels Midland (ADM), 87–
    88
Articles of Association, 16–17, 128,
    138
Ashkenazi, Rafi, 130, 137, 140–43,
    164
Ashkenazi, Rotem, 143–45
Ashkenazi Jews, 165–66, 168–69, 178
Automobiles, 59, 120, 143, 155, 168
Autonomy, 118–20, 159–61

Bankruptcy, 36, 67, 79, 105
Barak, Ehud, 23, 61–63
Bar Gil, Gavri, 48–49
Bar-Lev Line, 185n. 9
Begin, Menachem, 11, 25–26
Benedikt, Eddie, 97–100

Ben-Gurion, David, 2, 14, 25
Benizri, Shlomo, 123
Ben-Or, Tzafrir, 172
Berlin, Isaiah, 130
Bituach leumi. *See* Social security
Black markets, 58, 190n. 9
Borochov, Dov Ber, 7
Braun, Peter, 59–62, 66–68
Brenner, Gary, 36–37, 84, 94, 96
Brenner, Jonathan, 96
Brenner, Joseph Hayim, 7, 9
Brenner, Tamar, 84
Brinker, Menachem, 3, 8–9
Bus transportation, 142–43, 176

Chevrat Ovdim, 7, 22
Chibat Zion, 7
Children
    housing for, 11, 13, 19–20, 32, 58,
        103–4, 132-34, 146, 189n. 1
    rearing of, 2, 37, 40–41, 58, 106–7,
        117, 120, 188n. 1
    subsidies for, 100
    *See also* Education
Chofesh, 68, 149, 193n. 15
Clothing, 9–11
Cotton crop, 27, 30, 73, 153
Covenant, 129–30. *See also* "Spirit of
    Gan Shmuel"
Credit cards, 71

Debt, 34–36
  Histadrut trade unions and, 28–29
  restructuring of, 27–30, 177–79
  *See also specific kibbutzim*
Degania, 3
Development towns, 14, 25, 184n. 4,
  191n. 20
Dewey, John, 6
Dining, communal. *See* Food services
Dobkin, Herzl, 78–80
Drori, Micha, 19, 165, 174–78
Dunam, xii

Ecology, 178–79
Economic recovery principles, 93–96
Education, 40, 42
  military service and, 77, 189n. 13
  real estate development and, 174
  *See also specific kibbutzim*
Egged bus line, 142, 176
Eilan, Uri, 125
Elkon, Aliza, 13, 58
Elon, Amos, 4, 16, 22
Erez-Israel, 183n. 1
Eshel, Mira, 91, 106–7
Eshel, Uri, 90–92, 96–97, 122–23
Etzman, Yehuda, 68
Exchange rates, 26–27

Farhi, Jacob and Yehudit, 23–24
Fashion, 10–11
Fishman, Eliezer, 124
Food services, 9, 19, 41, 44, 54, 85. *See
  also specific kibbutzim*

Gadish, Yaakov, 37, 46–47, 89, 189n.
  8
Gavish, Yeshayahu, 46, 67–68
Gavish Vergilese, Dinah, 146–49
Gazit, Motti, 149–51, 181
Gazit, Rivka, 150
General Zionism, 9, 192n. 7
German Jews, 58
Getz, Shlomo, 39–40, 42, 57
Globalization, 16, 31, 121, 149
Gordon, Aaron David, 7–8
Greenfeld, Marcia, 75–78
Grossman, Avishai, 32, 173, 186n. 21
Gulf War (1991), 117, 189n. 1

Ha'am, Ahad, 7–8
Habonim, 11–13, 56–58, 60, 78

Haganah, 1–2, 127
Hagshama atzmit, 7–8
Halperin, Ariel, 28–29, 179, 186n. 15
  on kibbutz reform, 32–38, 46, 173
  on labor system, 42–43
Hanhala rachava, 39
Harari, Micha, 37, 94–95
Hashomer Hatzair, 11–12, 85, 91,
  107–8, 120, 131
"Hatikvah," 2
Hatzran, 102
Hazan, Yaakov, 112, 167, 170
Health care, 7, 55, 101, 103, 136. *See
  also* Social security
Herut Party, 25
Histadrut trade unions, 1, 7, 22, 101
  kibbutz debts and, 28–29
  Likud Party and, 26
  Solbar factory and, 86
Holocaust survivors, 3–6, 57
  renta for, 58, 75, 79
Housing, 27–28. *See also* Children;
  Privatization; *specific kibbutzim*

Inheritance, 39, 79, 172, 180
Institute for Research of the Kibbutz
  and the Cooperative Idea, 33, 38–
  39
"Internationale," 2
Israel Defense Forces (IDF), 2, 13
  ethical code of, 129
  Nahal of, 14
  reserve service of, 41
Israeli Communist Party, 185n. 6
Israel Land Authority (ILA), 16, 18, 62,
  174

Jewish National Fund (JNF), 17–18,
  174–76
Job rotation, 37–38, 147

KAF. *See* Kibbutz Artzi Federation
Kasher, Asa, 129–30, 134–43, 146–50,
  154–55, 180–81
Katznelson, Berl, 1, 9
Kedem, Sylvia and Yitzhak, 12–13,
  106–9
Kenan, Omri, 130–37, 140–43
Keshet Mizrachi, 178
Kibbutz Artzi Federation (KAF), xi, 5,
  11, 19, 47, 85, 125
  demographics of, 5

food service and, 90
founders of, 167
investments of, 32
Kibbutz atid, 47–48
Kibbutz Be'eri, 57, 62
Kibbutz Bet Ha'Arava, 57–58
Kibbutz Dalia, 150
Kibbutz Ein Shemer, 130–31
Kibbutz Evron, 78
Kibbutz Gadot, 39–40, 80
Kibbutz Gan Shmuel, 5, 18, 50, 124–64
  agriculture at, 126–27
  Articles of, 124, 128, 138
  debt of, 127
  education at, 77, 130–31, 136, 143, 155
  factory of, 124–30, 145–46, 151
  food service at, 44, 85, 131–32, 144–45
  housing at, 146, 180
  living standard at, 61, 135–36
  machane of, 20–21
  map of, 53
  pensions at, 158
  principles of, 93–94, 154–55
  salaries at, 127–28, 135–36, 143, 145–46, 155, 181
  supermarket of, 124, 132–33
  youth programs at, 143–46, 153, 155–56, 164
  Zerem Shitufi and, 47
  *See also* "Spirit of Gan Shmuel"
Kibbutz Gesher Haziv, 5, 18, 20, 49–83, 151
  debt of, 55–56, 59, 61–64, 70–71
  education at, 66, 68, 71–72, 77–79
  food service at, 44, 54
  founding of, 57
  housing at, 64
  living standard at, 61, 64–66, 69, 81
  map of, 53
  new members of, 63–65
  pensions at, 54–56, 67, 70–72, 80
  privatization at, 54–55, 180
  real estate development by, 61–65, 81–83, 173–74
  salaries at, 56, 60–61, 68, 74–76
Kibbutz Hadati Movement, 16
Kibbutz Harduf, 43
Kibbutz Harel, 19

Kibbutz Hatzor, 5, 17–18, 20, 49–50, 84–123
  disco of, 84–85, 88
  education at, 77, 90–91, 116–17, 136
  factories of, 61, 86–88, 92, 94, 96, 129
  food service at, 44, 85, 89–90
  Gan Shmuel and, 136
  housing at, 111–12, 118–20
  living standard at, 61, 118–19
  machane of, 111
  map of, 53
  private homes at, 180
  real estate development by, 119–20
  recovery principles of, 93–96
  salaries at, 89, 96–97, 100–105, 114–18
Kibbutzim
  affiliations of, 16
  Articles of Association for, 16–17, 128, 138
  definitions of, 16–17, 47–48, 89
  demographics of, 3, 5
  labor shortages on, 42–43
  laundries of, 9–10, 81
  legal status of, 16–18, 72–73, 178–80
  as military outposts, 18
  new members of, 63–65
  reform models for, 34–50, 93–96
Kibbutz Kabri, 57
Kibbutz Kvutzat Yavne, 58, 89
Kibbutz Lochmei Hagetaot, 63, 188 n. 6
Kibbutz Lotan, 187 n. 18
Kibbutz Ma'agan Michael, 47, 62, 171, 173
Kibbutz Migvan, 166–70
  child care at, 168
  communal dining at, 167
  debt of, 169
  education at, 168–69
  housing at, 167
  real estate development at, 167–68
Kibbutz Movement, xi, 16, 19, 48–49, 91, 123, 136, 174, 181–82, 185 n. 11, 194 n. 2
Kibbutz Ramot Menashe, 49
Kibbutz Tamid, 46–48, 89. *See also* Zerem Shitufi

Knaz, Hannah and Shaul, 153–58
Koor Industries, 86
Koren, Asher, 66–67, 81–82
Kornai, Janos, 29, 186 n. 18
Kraines, Menucha, 51
Kupat Holim, 7, 22

Labor Alignment Party, 185 n. 6
Labor Party, xi, 2, 177, 179
    founding of, 185 n. 6
    Six-Day War and, 24–26
Lapidot, Hovav, 158–59, 161–62
Lapidot, Zmira, 71–75
Laundries, communal, 9–10, 81
Lebanon War (1982), 26
Levi, Uzi, 145–46
Likud Party, 25–26, 30
Living standards, 35, 45. *See also specific kibbutzim*

Machane, 19–21, 52, 111
Malaria, 7, 11
Managers, 37–39, 91, 147, 151
Mapai Party, 2, 184 n. 6
Mapam Party, 184 n. 6, 191 n. 5
Maron, Stanley, 27
Marxism, 7–8, 98, 112, 158. *See also* Socialism
Mazkirut, 24–25, 37, 67
Merekez, 39
Meretz Party, xi, 185 n. 6
Meshulav model, 44–46, 49
Military service, 41, 120–21, 187 n. 11
    college benefits and, 77, 189 n. 13
    land law and, 189 n. 13
Mizrachi Jews, 6, 25–26, 165–66, 168–69, 178
Moadon, 19, 131
Moatza, 63
Mort, Jo-Ann, 110–11, 158
Mosadot, 37
Moshavim, 1, 30, 175, 179. *See also* Kibbutzim
Moshav shitufim, 63
Mourning periods, 24, 185 n. 10

Nachtomi, Moshe, 37
Nadil, Nitza and Atar, 106
Nahal, 14
Narodnik movement, 7
National Religious Party, xi, 25

Neoliberalism, 34. *See also* "Third way" economics
Nestlé, 188
Netanyahu, Benjamin, 25
New Israeli Shekels (NIS), xii
"New" Jews, 16
Newspapers, 131, 154, 191 n. 5, 192 n. 7
Nir Shitufi, 18
Nursing homes, 88

Omen Metal Works, 86, 104
Oppenheimer, Franz, 9
Overtime wages, 102

Palestine, 3–6, 183 n. 1, 184 n. 6
Palmach, 2
Passover celebrations, 69
Pensions, 36, 47, 189 n. 12. *See also specific kibbutzim*
Peres, Shimon, 23, 26–27
Pilug, 2
Pinsker, Leon, 7
Plasgod, 80
Poalei Agudat Israel, 16
Polyziv, 59, 61
Private funds, 56, 58, 75–76, 103, 106, 114–15, 135, 159–60, 190 n. 13
Privatization, 35, 44–45, 54–55, 122–23, 144–45, 155, 163
    of housing, 122-23, 167, 171–75, 178–80

Rabin, Yitzhak, 23, 177
Radios, 131
Rasham, 79
Ratz Party, 185 n. 6
Rawls, John, 189 n. 6
Real estate development, 38, 123, 171, 177–78
    education and, 174
    at Kochav Yair, 190 n. 15
    *See also specific kibbutzim*
Regba, 63
Renta, 58, 75, 79
Reshet bitachon model, 44–46, 49
Revisionist Zionism, 11
Ronen, Sela, 125, 158–60, 162–63
Rosner, Menachem, 38–39
Rosolio, Daniel, 22, 26–27, 29–30, 32, 179, 184 n. 5
Ruppin, Arthur, 9
Russian immigrants, 3–9, 51, 165–66

Sadat, Anwar, 26
Salaries
    overtime and, 102
    virtual, 145–46
    women's, 104
    *See also specific kibbutzim*
Scarcity, 30–31, 190n. 10
Schlossberg, Riffi, 56–57, 62–63, 67,
    82–83, 182
Schlossberg, Yehuda, 80–82
Sderot, 165–66
Sephardic Jews, 6, 25. *See also*
    Mizrachi Jews
Shamir, Yitzhak, 26–27
Shanat chofesh, 184n. 4
Shapira, Anita, 7
Shapira, Reuven, 151–53
Sharif, Aharon, 55
Sharon, Ariel, 25
Shas Party, 123, 166, 185n. 6
Shavei Zion, 63, 188n. 7
Shekels, xii
Shinui Party, 185n. 6
Shitufi model, 44, 46
Simon, Yohanan, 10
Six-Day War (1967), 24–26, 131
Socialism, 4–6, 22, 29, 55, 139–43
    constructive, 9
    Marxism and, 7–8, 98, 112, 158
    scarcity and, 30–31, 190n. 10
Socialist-Zionism, 1–3, 6–8, 22–23,
    176
Social security, 54–56, 73, 83, 100,
    151, 155. *See also* Health care
Society for the Protection of Nature,
    178–79
Solbar factory, 61, 86–88, 92, 94, 96,
    129, 180
Soviet Union, 6, 157. *See also* Russian
    immigrants
"Spirit of Gan Shmuel," 93–94, 124,
    129–30, 137–40, 154–55
Stalinism, 103, 112, 150
Steiner, Rudolf, 43
Student Nonviolent Coordinating
    Committee (SNCC), 112
Syrkin, Nahman, 7
Syrkin, Yaron, 96

Tabenkin, Yitzhak, 9
Takam kibbutzim, xi, 11, 16, 48
    advisors of, 67–68

demographics of, 5
    new members and, 64
    settlement plans of, 32
Tal, Chava, 103–6
Tal, Natan, 64
Taxes, 45–46, 52, 55, 75, 89, 100, 102,
    117
Telephones, 20–22, 110, 131, 191n. 4
"Third way" economics, 34, 88–89,
    180
Tival factory, 188n. 6
Tolstoy, Leo, 8, 105
Toshavim, 86, 132
Trade unions. *See specific types*
Tsufim, Yisrael, 43–45, 70, 188n. 11
Typhus, 11
Tzavta, 167
Tzion, Naomi, 166–69
Tzur, Noa, 90

Underground economy, 58, 190n. 9
Unemployment insurance, 56, 136
United Kibbutz Movement. *See*
    Takam kibbutzim
Utopianism, 4, 7–9, 22

Vacations, 22, 68, 105, 135, 145–46,
    192n. 15
Vital, David, 183n. 1

Weizman, Ezer, 25
Work ethic, 43, 68

Ya'ari, Meir, 167
Yasur, Daphna, 158–64
Yishuv, 3–6, 184n. 6
Yishuv kehillati model, 44–46, 55, 85,
    109
Yom Kippur War (1973), 24, 125, 131,
    185n. 9
Youth programs, 143–46, 153, 155–56,
    164

Zerach, Binnie and Jonathan, 111–18
Zerach, Neva, 110–11, 116, 118–22
Zerem Shitufi, 46–48, 89, 135–36,
    150, 152, 171
Zionism, 3–9, 17, 32, 125. *See also*
    *specific types*
Ziv Estates, 61–62, 65, 82–83, 173–74
Zohar Dalia, 150

Jo-Ann Mort has written about Israel, Jewish issues, the Middle East, and trade unions for various publications, including the *Jerusalem Report*, the *Chicago Tribune*, the *L.A. Weekly*, and the *Forward*, where she was a columnist. Her opinion pieces have been published in the *Los Angeles Times* Sunday opinion section and elsewhere. She is a member of the editorial board of *Dissent* magazine and editor of the book *Not Your Father's Union Movement: Inside the AFL–CIO*. She worked for thirteen years in the trade union movement as director of communications for UNITE and ACTWU. She has traveled extensively in Israel and other countries in the region. She lives in Brooklyn, New York.

Gary Brenner has lived on Kibbutz Hatzor since emigrating from the United States to Israel in 1971. He has served in a number of leadership positions in Hatzor and the Kibbutz Artzi Federation and is currently chairperson for the Givat Haviva Institute, a Kibbutz Artzi Federation education and research center promoting coexistence and tolerance. He is also marketing director for Solbar, one of the kibbutz industries. His wife, Tamar, was born on the kibbutz, as were their three sons, Yonatan, Yermi, and Yanai.